THE
CHRISTIAN
COMMONS

THE
CHRISTIAN
COMMONS

ENDING THE SPIRITUAL FAMINE
OF THE GLOBAL CHURCH

Tim Jore

distant shores|media

The Christian Commons
v. 1.0
by Tim Jore

Published by Distant Shores Media
ISBN 978-1-62666-001-4
ISBN 978-1-62666-000-7 (electronic)

© 2013 Distant Shores Media
PO Box 19229
Minneapolis, MN 55419-0229
http://distantshoresmedia.org

To James, Waks, Sivini, Ray, and Stephen

Contents

PART 2

PART 3

Illustration Index

Introduction

Hundreds of millions of Christians, in thousands of people groups all over the world, are theologically malnourished and in a severe spiritual famine. People who speak 92% of the languages in the world do not have a translated Bible in their own language.[1] Fewer still have adequate teaching materials and resources to help them grow in basic knowledge of the Bible and sound doctrine. Eighty-five percent of churches around the world are led by people who have no formal training in theology or ministry.[2] The growth of the global church—as high as 178,000 new converts daily—has far outpaced the number of leaders equipped to shepherd the rapidly growing flock.[3] The global church urgently needs discipleship re-

---

1   "Scripture Access Statistics 2012." *Wycliffe Global Alliance*, 2012. http://www.wycliffe.net/resources/scriptureaccessstatistics/tabid/99/Default.aspx.

2   Livermore, David A. *Serving with Eyes Wide Open*. Baker Books, 2006. 41.

3   Ibid, 33.

sources in their own languages to help foster their spiritual growth.

The technology of the 21st century provides unprecedented opportunities for ending the spiritual famine of the global church. We have the technology that could be used to help meet their need. We have the capacity of bringing spiritual famine relief to anyone, anywhere, efficiently, and at extremely low cost. What we do *not* have (yet) is adequate Bible translations and other discipleship resources that provide the legal freedom to take full advantage of these opportunities. In the legal context of "all rights reserved" the global church is unable to work together without restriction or hindrance to leverage Internet and mobile technology to the fullest for the purposes of God's Kingdom and the equipping of His Church.

There is an urgent need for discipleship resources that are made available under open licenses so that they can be translated and adapted to provide effective theological training and increased Biblical knowledge for Christians speaking all of the nearly 7,000 languages in the world. The global church cannot be expected to reinvent the wheel theologically for every people group and language. Instead, the process of equipping believers in every people group with adequate discipleship resources can be greatly accelerated by releasing some of the copyright restrictions on some existing discipleship resources. This gives the entire global church legal freedom to build on what has already been created by their brothers and sisters in Christ. Until that happens, however, the global church in thousands of languages is legally locked out—on the other side of a legal "wall" that hinders the much-needed spiritual famine relief.

The View from the Other Side

Many are not even aware that this legal wall exists. I was oblivious to it until a number of years ago when I accidentally ran into it from the other side. At the time, I was the advisor for a team of Papua New Guineans who were learning to translate the Bible into their own language, Uturuva. The team had completed the introductory Bible translation training course and were now ready to start using Bible translation software to facilitate the translation of the Bible into their language.

We ran into a snag during the installation of the software. Everything had been going fine until the software installer prompted us for a license key. We had no idea why anyone should need a license key to translate the Word of God, but since we did not have a license key, we could not proceed with the installation of the software.

This software was used every day by my missionary colleagues, but our Papua New Guinean brothers and sisters in Christ, whom we were there to serve, were not legally allowed to use the same software. The reason, I was told, was because the Bible translation software included many discipleship resources—exegetical helps, translations of the Bible, commentaries, etc.—that were the Intellectual Property (IP) of other entities, not our mission organization. The copyright restrictions on these resources prevented their free use and distribution. They could only be used with the express, written permission of the copyright holders. The organization with which I served was relatively large and had worked out a legal agreement with the copyright holders that apparently said something to the effect of: "members of the mission organization who are translators may be granted a free license key to use the software." But the legal agreement did not extend beyond that organization's translators.[4]

---

4   I have never seen the actual agreement that was in place; this is how the situation was explained to me at the time. In the years since this story happened, much has taken place in this language group and with their translation project. Reportedly, the terms of use that govern the use of the Bible translation software have also changed and the latest versions of the software do not require a license key for installation. The discipleship resources are available as separate add-ons, however, and still require a license key for access.

And that was the problem. The people on the Papua New Guinean translation team were not members of *any* organization. Like the rapidly growing multitude of believers in people groups all over the world, they were "just" people who sensed the call of God to translate His Word into their language. I was a member of the organization, but because I was not the translator (I was merely the advisor to the project), the legal agreement that was in place did not apply to me either. Copyright restrictions on discipleship resources prevented us from making the most of the technology that would have helped us translate the Bible into their language.

The Walled Garden

Imagine a lush garden full of fruit-bearing trees that can be freely enjoyed by anyone. Now imagine that the garden has a massive wall around it, permitting only a handful of people to enjoy the fruit within the walls. Many are on the outside of the garden in a perpetual famine. But the wall prevents them from coming into the garden to satisfy their hunger.

This is not hyperbole. It is illustrative of the real problem faced by hundreds of millions of the global church in thousands of people groups and speaking thousands of languages, all over the world. They have virtually no discipleship resources in their languages to satisfy their spiritual hunger. The discipleship resources that could meet their need are in other languages, and they are not legally permitted to translate them for effective use in their own languages.

There is something curious about this walled garden. Although the masses of people locked on the outside of the wall are in terrible need, few on the inside are even aware there is a problem. Fewer still attempt to meet the need. In this analogy, these attempts to provide for those on the outside are noble efforts, but they come nowhere near actually ending the spiritual famine. These efforts are either prohibitively costly (harvesting and shipping fruit outside the wall as a business venture) or illegal (tossing fruit over the wall without permission). There is a solution, but it does not involve either of these approaches.

The solution to the problem in this analogy is for owners of fruit trees who desire to meet the immense need of those on the outside to transplant their trees outside the wall, creating a Christian "commons" of legally-unrestricted discipleship resources. Instead of trying to meet the needs one at a time, moving the source of nourishment "outside the camp" enables the entire global church to work together in parallel to meet their own needs, legally.

That day in Papua New Guinea when the translation team could not have a license key was the first time I ran into this wall. I had never seen the wall before, much less experienced running into it. Up until then, I had only ever been on the "inside" and had never before seen the view from the vantage point of the rest of the global church. My view from the inside had led me to believe all was well and we just needed to work harder in world missions. The perspective from the inside had blinded me to the reality that all is very much *not* well on the other side.

This Book, in a Nutshell

The goal of this book is to paint the picture of a realistic and achievable means of ending the spiritual famine of the global church in every people group, through the openly collaborative building of a legally-unrestricted core of discipleship resources in every language—the Christian Commons. To arrive at this goal, I attempt to provide a detailed explanation of the missiological, technological, and legal factors necessary for understanding the immensity of the problem and the strategic significance of the proposed solution. It is my hope that, as more believers come to understand the need and how we can meet that need together, many who are the legal owners of Bible translations and other discipleship resources will willingly release some of their content under open licenses and into the Christian Commons—an unwalled garden—for the glory of God and for the good of His Church.

The Christian Commons contains ten chapters, divided into four parts, as illustrated here and explained in the sections that follow:

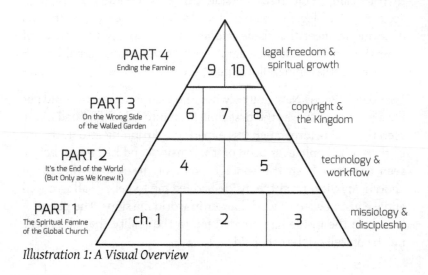

PART 4
Ending the Famine
9 10
legal freedom & spiritual growth

PART 3
On the Wrong Side of the Walled Garden
6 7 8
copyright & the Kingdom

PART 2
It's the End of the World (But Only as We Knew It)
4 5
technology & workflow

PART 1
The Spiritual Famine of the Global Church
ch. 1 2 3
missiology & discipleship

Illustration 1: A Visual Overview

Part 1: Missiology & Discipleship – The Spiritual Famine of the Global Church

This book is built on the foundation of the mandate Jesus has given to the Church: "Make disciples of all people groups" (Matthew 28:19). Evangelism and church-planting are necessary aspects of discipleship, but neither is the ultimate goal. In chapter 1 of *The Christian Commons*, we will see that accomplishing the goal of making disciples is dependent on the Word of God, translated into the languages of the world, made accessible to oral communicators, and forming the basis for other discipleship resources that explain the Word of God with clarity in that particular culture and context.

Making disciples of all people groups requires using their "heart languages" in order to teach them to "obey everything Jesus has commanded" (Matthew 28:20). The magnitude and complexity of this task is immense, and much remains to be accomplished. Merely "working harder" is an inadequate approach for accomplishing the Great Commission. Chapter 2 argues that equipping every people group with adequate discipleship resources in their own language requires a fundamental shift in our approach to world missions.

The global church in every people group needs adequate discipleship resources in their own languages. This is a daunting task, especially in light of the reality of language change. Bible translations and other discipleship resources are static works. Languages, however, change over time, and small languages often change rapidly. Apart from ongoing revision of a discipleship resource, language change will eventually result in the resource itself ceasing to be useful to the speakers of that language. Chapter 3 suggests that the global church needs to be equipped not only to translate and create discipleship resources, but to maintain them through time.

Part 2: Technology & Workflow – It's the End of the World (But Only as We Knew It)

Chapter 4 introduces one of the most significant opportunities for the advance of God's Kingdom in the 21st century: the mobile phone. The mobile phone has rapidly become the most widely used technology in the world. It is far more common than traditional computers, the Internet, and even traditional media like television and radio. Spanning cultures, countries, and socioeconomic classes, the mobile phone is uniquely positioned as a strategic tool in the task of making disciples of all people groups.

In the pre-digital, "paper" era, large, complex projects could only occur in industry (private production) or government (public production). With the advent of the digital era, where content is comprised of "bits" of digital data, a new means of accomplishing such projects has emerged. Social production, using computing devices (like mobile phones) connected via the Internet, enables a geographically-distributed team of self-selecting individuals to accomplish complex objectives by collaborating openly toward the common goal. Compared to traditional models, these objectives can often be achieved in less time, with better results, and at a marginal cost approaching zero. In chapter 5, open collaboration is put forward as a model that can go the distance and provide adequate discipleship resources in every language of the world.

Part 3: Copyright & the Kingdom – On the Wrong Side of the Walled Garden

Chapter 6 discusses the role and purpose of modern copyright law, explaining that it was invented to encourage the creation of content by granting exclusive rights to owners of creative works, restricting the distribution and use of the content by others. This creates an artificial scarcity of the content, which preserves a higher price for the content and maximizes the revenue stream from it. The exclusive right of distribution also preserves the revenue stream for resources that are given away free of charge, by providing the content owner with numbers and statistics that may be useful for procuring donations. Using copyright law in either of these ways is neither illegal nor unethical. Given that copyright law has as its objective the limiting of access to and reuse of content, it is not surprising that it has had only limited success in meeting the need for discipleship resources in the thousands of languages spoken by the global church.

The Bible is essential for spiritual growth and is the foundation on which every other discipleship resource is built. Chapter 7 explains how restrictive licenses governing translations of the Bible tend to hinder the global church from growing spiritually by creating a "single point of failure" for every discipleship resource in a given language that is built on it. Most languages that have any translated Scripture have only one translation in their language. Because of the way copyright law works, this translation is the legal property of an entity, with all rights to the translation owned by them. This hinders how freely and effectively the Word of God can be used and built on by others to create discipleship resources that foster the spiritual maturity of people who speak that language. In addition, Bible translations that are under copyright cannot legally be revised by speakers of that language without permission. Apart from ongoing revision, language change will result in the Bible translation itself eventually ceasing to be useful to the speakers of the language.

In chapter 8, we address ethics and copyright law. The eighth commandment is simple and direct: "Do not steal." In the physical world, this was unambiguous, because physical objects are intrinsically "rival"—they cannot exist in more than one place at the same time. In the digital world, however, content can effectively exist in any number of places at the same time. This ability to share content in a "non-rival" way opens up new opportunities for the advance of God's Kingdom, but it conflicts with the "all rights reserved" of copyright law. We must not adjust our ethical standards based on convenience or the likelihood of getting caught or prosecuted. Instead, we must strive for integrity and uphold the law even when it hurts. That said, it is crucial that adequate discipleship resources be made available under open licenses in order to provide an honest and legal means of meeting the urgent spiritual need of the global church from every people group.

Part 4: Legal Freedom & Spiritual Growth – Ending the Famine

Chapter 9 describes an open license that gives the global church the legal freedom they need to make discipleship resources effective for spiritual growth in any language. Licenses governing the use of discipleship resources tend to be very restrictive, focusing on everything that people are not allowed to do with the content. These licenses do not enable the global church to legally work together in the translation, adaptation, distribution, and use of discipleship resources in any language. By contrast, the Creative Commons Attribution-ShareAlike License grants anyone the freedom to use and build upon the content without restriction, subject to the two conditions of the license: attributing the original content to the original owner, and releasing what is created from the original content under the same license. This license is ideally suited to provide the freedom the global church needs to legally equip themselves to grow spiritually, while minimizing the likelihood of commercial exploitation of the content by others.

Chapter 10 introduces the Christian Commons as a core of discipleship resources released by their respective owners under open licenses, like the Attribution-ShareAlike License. These licenses permit the unrestricted translation, adaptation, distribution, and use of the content by anyone, without needing to obtain permission beforehand or pay royalties. The concept of a Christian Commons is not new—it is profoundly Biblical, being rooted in Old Testament principles and lived out in the New Testament church. The Christian Commons provides the necessary content and legal freedom for believers from every people group to openly collaborate in the completion of the Great Commission. Because the content is open-licensed, speakers of any language—even those with the smallest numbers of speakers—can legally translate and use the content without hindrance.

Note that a number of sections in this book are expanded upon in a corresponding appendix. The intent is to cover the topics succinctly in the text, while also providing further information for those interested in them.

Finally, it must be noted that there is a real risk of miscommunication when writing a book like this. When suggesting a new alternative to a usual means of doing anything, it is easy to come across as being against the standard approach. In this book, specifically, there is a risk of sounding anti-copyright or antagonistic toward those who hold the copyrights on Bible translations and other discipleship resources. This is not the case. My intent in this book is to explain the need of the global church, the opportunities we have to meet that need, the obstacle that hinders it, and a solution to the problem, in the form of the collaborative creation of the Christian Commons.

PART 1

THE SPIRITUAL FAMINE
OF THE GLOBAL CHURCH

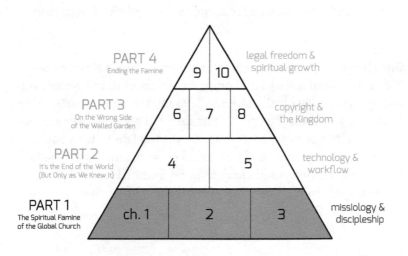

PART 4
Ending the Famine

9 | 10

legal freedom &
spiritual growth

PART 3
On the Wrong Side
of the Walled Garden

6 | 7 | 8

copyright &
the Kingdom

PART 2
It's the End of the World
(But Only as We Knew It)

4 | 5

technology &
workflow

PART 1
The Spiritual Famine
of the Global Church

ch. 1 | 2 | 3

missiology &
discipleship

CHAPTER 1

"BE WARMED AND FILLED"

The mandate Jesus has given to the Church is to make disciples of all people groups. Evangelism and church planting are necessary aspects of discipleship, but neither is the ultimate goal. Accomplishing the goal of making disciples is dependent on the Word of God, translated into the languages of the world, made accessible to oral communicators, and forming the basis for other discipleship resources that explain the Word of God with clarity.

~ ~ ~

One should only trek through the swamps of Papua New Guinea in the rainy season if they truly enjoy relentless heat, unbearable humidity, and endless trails of knee-deep mud. I am not particularly fond of any of these, but my teammate and I only discovered what we had gotten ourselves into after it was too late to turn back. So we made the most of it and continued on as planned with the language survey that would help determine the need for a Bible translation project in the language of the people group native to that area.

Many days later, as we slogged along behind our guide through the rain and mud in yet another swamp, we came across a long tree trunk lying in the direction we were going. Instead of continuing through the mud, we crawled up on the tree trunk and walked along it. As we got to the end of the log, our guide stopped so suddenly I nearly ran into him. He waited there, perfectly still in the falling rain. Finally, he said to us, "Get off the log." So we got down and walked around the end of the log to continue on our way. As we passed the end of the log, I glanced over and saw the reason for the detour. A clump of grass had been cut off neatly at the roots and laid across the end of the log. It had obviously been placed there by someone, but we had seen no one on the trail so far that day.

I asked our guide what the clump of grass was all about. He did not answer right away and when he did, there was concern in his voice. "It is witchcraft," he said. "Someone is trying to use black magic to kill another person. If we had stepped over the grass, the curse would have fallen on us and we would soon die."

We walked on in silence for a few minutes and then, quietly at first but growing louder, our guide started singing a traditional chant, one of the songs of his ancestors. The haunting melody was unlike anything I had ever heard before, and seemed to be an eerie flashback to the ancient history of that people group. The song was presumably sung as a white magic "antidote" to the curse we had encountered, in the hope that it would protect him from harm.

This was intriguing, because in the villages we had visited on that trek, we kept asking the people if they would sing us some of their traditional songs. "Oh no," they replied, "We do not know the traditional songs anymore. We are Christians now and we only sing hymns."

The first Christian churches had been planted in that people group over a century before, and most of the larger villages had a church building. It was true that in their church services they only sang

Christian hymns. But now we realized that the traditional songs were, in fact, quite well-known. They were still used in situations like these, when faced with spiritual warfare and the possibility of demonic attack.

Our guide was one of the most spiritually alert people we met in that entire people group. He was the one who had made the all-day hike multiple times to the nearest village with a two-way radio, to ask for missionaries to come and help them translate the Bible into their language. But though they knew the right words to say, even had church buildings and sang hymns, it appeared that little had changed at a heart level for most of the people in that language group. They did not know that "white magic" is a lie, or that Jesus has won the victory over Satan and his demons, or that faith in His Name is the only real protection against demonic attack.

A little later, we stayed in a village that was near the border of the language group. In the course of the conversation, some of the people mentioned that one of the villages in a neighboring language group had converted to the Bahá'í religion. As the story unfolded, we learned that the village had for decades been known as a Christian village. But recently, the advancing Bahá'í cult had swept through that part of the country and, with little opposition, consumed the village and claimed its allegiance.

What had happened? Why was it so easy for an entire village of "Christians" to be swept away by a cult? Why had the people pretended not to know the traditional songs when, in reality, they were well-known and were used in spiritual (but not "Christian") contexts?

These are difficult questions that we will attempt to answer—both in this situation and in many other situations like it. God alone knows the hearts of the people involved, and care must be taken not to assume what cannot be known. But there is one crucial lesson that comes through in countless stories like this one: making disciples of all nations involves more than merely evangelism and church planting.

The Goal of Missions Is Discipleship

Evangelism and planting churches among the unreached and least-reached people groups of the world are extremely important.[1] But evangelism and church planting *must* be seen for what they are: a means to an end. The end toward which we have been commissioned by Jesus to work is not making converts to the Christian faith. The end goal is not "x number of churches in y number of years." The end goal is not a Bible translation or Biblical storying or any of the many other important missions tasks. These are all intermediate steps to the end goal—the same unwavering goal that Jesus first commissioned His disciples to reach, nearly 2,000 years ago:

> "All authority has been given to Me in heaven and on earth.
> Go, therefore, and *make disciples* of all nations, baptizing
> them in the name of the Father and of the Son and of the
> Holy Spirit, teaching them to observe everything I have
> commanded you. And remember, I am with you always, to
> the end of the age."
>
> —Matthew 28:18b-20, emphasis added

The purpose of world missions, according to Scripture, is singular: make disciples of all nations. Accomplishing this task in a people group usually involves evangelism, church planting, Bible transla-

---

1   "Unreached people groups" refers to people groups without any known converts to Christianity. The term "least-reached people groups" is not as easily defined, but is used here to refer to people groups in which there may be small numbers of Christians, but they are lacking in crucial elements of mature discipleship, namely adequate discipleship resources in their own language to sustain spiritual growth, and a self-supporting, self-propagating and self-governing indigenous church.

tion, and many other activities. But the goal itself must not become redefined according to one's own particular area of focus, lest the means become the end. If the only tool I have is a hammer, everything really does start to look like a nail. In the same way, if I am a church planter then my natural inclination may be to see every need in world missions as a need that would best be solved by planting a church. If I am an evangelist, I may tend to perceive the definition of the end goal in terms of evangelism. A Bible translator must take care not to lose sight of the fact that the actual goal is "make disciples" not "finish the translation."

This is not criticism; all of these are important components in making disciples of all nations. But, as Dr. John Piper puts it:

> ...making disciples means more than getting conversions and baptisms. "Teaching them to observe all that I have commanded you . . ." Conversion and baptism are essential, but so is the on-going teaching of what Jesus taught. The new life of a disciple is a life of obedience to Jesus' commandments, or it is not a new life at all. It is worthless to acknowledge the lordship of Christ in baptism and then ignore his commandments. So all disciple-makers must be teachers, and disciples must be continual learners.[2]

Why does it matter? What could possibly go wrong by inadvertently redefining the ultimate goal? In the short term, maybe not much. People come to Christ and churches are planted. But in the long term, the results of aiming for the wrong goal are often disastrous.

---

2   John Piper, "Go and Make Disciples, Baptizing Them...," nov 1982, http://www.desiringgod.org/resource-library/sermons/go-and-make-disciples-baptizing-them

Falling Short of Discipleship

Even a brief survey of world missions suggests that we as a church have historically been quite effective at evangelism and church planting, but relatively weak at discipleship. Discipleship—the "teaching them to obey" part of the Great Commission—is hard work and does not generate quantifiable numbers. This tends to make it a less attractive aspect of the task.

Conversions and church plants—the "baptizing them" part of the Great Commission—are much easier to count, and they make for great reports and emotional pictures to send back to supporting churches and organizational leadership. Sadly, the tendency in world missions is often to focus on evangelism and church planting and hope that discipleship happens automatically after that. History and Scripture both suggest this is not what happens. Paul told the church in Corinth:

> "I planted the seed in your hearts, and Apollos watered it,
> but it was God who made it grow. It's not important who
> does the planting, or who does the watering. What's impor-
> tant is that God makes the seed grow. The one who plants
> and the one who waters work together with the same pur-
> pose."
>
> —1 Corinthians 3:6-8a, NLT

According to this passage, making disciples of every people group includes the distinct aspects of "planting" and "watering." These correspond to the "baptizing them" and "teaching them" aspects of the Great Commission in Matthew 28:18-20. Historically, the seed has often been planted but not watered. The world is littered with fragile, poorly-equipped, and sometimes broken churches in people groups all over the world—churches that have lacked discipleship teaching, making them "a mile wide, and an inch deep."

Although we may never know for sure, I suspect that what I encountered on that language survey in Papua New Guinea was the result of inadequate discipleship. The evangelists had come through decades before, and churches were planted with leadership installed. The churches may have been strong and vibrant at the outset, and there were probably true believers in them. But the evangelists moved on and, though the young churches were able to hold on for a season, they eventually faltered. They did not have the Word of God in their language or the discipleship resources they needed to grow in knowledge and spiritual maturity. So they were unprepared for the testing of their faith that lay ahead. The result was disaster.

Satan is patient. When young churches are not trained and equipped as disciples of Christ, the devil only needs to bide his time and he will often be able to turn the tables and uproot the young plants that were planted. If he succeeds, what remains is often the hollowed-out shell of a Christian church, with little or no spiritual life (though they may still sing hymns). The people may still profess the Christian faith, and some of them may be believers, but Christianity to most of them will have become a thin veneer that whitewashes the outside, while on the inside their hearts still cling to their former beliefs and way of life. And they may cling to those beliefs more tightly than ever before.[3]

So what is the solution? We need to continue evangelism, church planting, Bible translation, and other related missions work. But it is crucially important that we, the global church, focus on follow-

---

3   While my focus here is world missions and making disciples of all nations, anyone who has looked objectively at churches that have been established for some time in nearly *any* culture can often see the same thing. External appearances may all be in order, but it is often not accompanied by a meaningful change in heart or worldview. In many cases, though, the "former beliefs and way of life" that lurk under the gloss of the "Christian" surface have less to do with chanting traditional songs in an effort to dispel black magic and more to do with blatant materialism and the love of money. But the problem is essentially the same.

ing through, and "making disciples." Thankfully, the Bible is full of instruction and examples of how the process of discipleship works.

Biblical Discipleship

A disciple in the Bible is a "learner" or "student" who is taught by a teacher. Making disciples involves the person-to-person living of life together in which younger Christians are taught by more mature Christians. The process is similar to the way that an apprentice learns a skill by direct observation of, and involvement with, the master craftsman.

In the New Testament, Paul says to the Corinthians that they may have many "guides" (or "teachers") but that Paul was their spiritual "father" (1 Corinthians 4:15). Paul laid the foundation and others were building on that foundation as guides and teachers (1 Corinthians 3:10) in the process of discipleship.

The objective of the discipler, according to Mathew 28:20, is to teach the new believer to obey all that Jesus has commanded. This is intended to be a multiplicative process, where disciples go on to disciple others, as Paul instructed Timothy:

> "...what you have heard from me in the presence of many witnesses entrust to faithful men who will be able to teach others also."
>
> —2 Timothy 2:2

This takes time and perseverance, and there is no substitute for the personal, relational aspect of it. The rise of the Internet and mobile phones does not mean that we can now stay home and make disciples over Skype. Tools such as these are useful in many aspects of equipping the global church to grow spiritually as disciples of Christ. But they are not replacements for the mandate to "Go" and live incarnationally among least-reached people groups, testifying of the risen Christ, and living out God's love to them in tangible ways.

One of the most helpful stories in the Bible for understanding Biblical discipleship is the story of Ezra. The Babylonians had defeated the kingdom of Judah 140 years before, but now, finally the walls of Jerusalem had been rebuilt and some of the exiles had returned. All the people in Jerusalem gathered into the square and Ezra, together with the other leaders, read to the people from the Law.

> They read out of the book of the law of God, translating and giving the meaning so that the people could understand what was read.
>
> —Nehemiah 8:8

Note some key aspects of Ezra's approach: it was centered on the Word of God, translated into the language of the hearers, communicated orally, and explained so they could understand it.

The Word of God Is the Foundation for Discipleship

Ezra knew that God's Word is the only basis for truth and spiritual instruction. The purpose for his return to Jerusalem was to teach God's Word to the people:

> Now Ezra had determined in his heart to study the law of the LORD, obey it, and teach its statutes and ordinances in Israel.
>
> —Ezra 7:10

As with Ezra thousands of years ago, so it is today. The teaching of the Word of God is the foundational aspect of "making disciples of all nations." The end-goal of world missions is disciples of Christ in every language and people group—disciples who are spiritually complete and equipped to equip others. Apart from the Word of God, this cannot happen.

> All Scripture is breathed out by God and profitable for teaching, for reproof, for correction, and for training in righteousness, that the man of God may be complete, equipped for every good work.
>
> —2 Timothy 3:16-17

It is no surprise, then, that the greatest felt need of new believers in any people group is to learn the Word of God. David Platt tells the story of meeting with believers in a country where it is illegal for Christians to gather. He had to wear dark clothes and they smuggled him into the village in the dead of night. Finally, he arrived at the house where Christian brothers and sisters were waiting to be taught from the Bible. These believers were so hungry for God's Word they asked him to teach them about all the books of the Old Testament, though he only had limited time with them. "We will do whatever it takes," they said. "Most of us are farmers, and we worked all day, but we will leave our fields unattended for the next couple of weeks if we can learn the Old Testament."[4] So they studied the Old Testament and then, on the last day he was with them, did a twelve-hour study of the entire New Testament as well.

More than anything else, disciples of Christ need the Word of God. But the Bible is not magic. It is "living and active, sharper than any two-edged sword" (Hebrews 4:12, ESV) *when it is understood*, at both the cognitive and spiritual level. Often, the Holy Spirit uses people as teachers and disciplers to help the human mind comprehend the Word of God. In Acts 8:26-40, we see that the Ethiopian eunuch was reading the Word of God, but unable to understand what he was reading. After Philip helped him understand the Word of God, it

---

4   David Platt, *Radical: Taking Back Your Faith From the American Dream* (Multnomah Books, 2010), 24.

brought about change in the life of the Ethiopian. He believed, was baptized, and went on his way rejoicing.

In order for there to be understanding, it is important that the Word of God be translated into the language the hearers know best and that communicates most deeply to them—their "heart language." The heart language is the vehicle through which the Word of God brings about real and lasting change at a deep, worldview-altering level.

The Word of God, Translated

When Ezra read aloud from the Word of God (Nehemiah 8:8), he made every effort to enable the people to clearly understand what was read. The exact details of how he and the Levites did this, especially to a crowd that may have numbered nearly 50,000 people (Nehemiah 7:66–67), is not stated in the narrative. Many of the people in that gathering had been raised in exile and probably spoke Aramaic as their heart language. Because of this, the Law, written in Hebrew, may not have been understandable to them without translation. So it is likely that part of the communication process used by Ezra and the Levites involved translation of the Law from Hebrew to Aramaic so that everyone could understand. The result of this clear communication of the Word of God in the language of the hearers went far beyond mere intellectual assent. It cut all the way to their hearts:

> Nehemiah the governor, Ezra the priest and scribe, and the Levites who were instructing the people said to all of them, "This day is holy to the LORD your God. Do not mourn or weep." *For all the people were weeping as they heard the words of the law.*
>
> —Nehemiah 8:9, emphasis added

The people heard the Word of God and understood it, not just academically, but at an emotional, life-changing level. This pattern repeats itself all over the world. When the Word of God is communicated in a trade language or language of wider communication, there may be some life change and spiritual awakening in some people. But a worldview-altering, people group-awakening "heart change" that lasts most readily occurs when the Word of God is communicated in the heart language of the hearers.

The story of the translation of the Bible into the Kabuverdianu language of the Cape Verde islands is a classic example of the kind of impact the Word of God in the heart language can have.[5] The Kabuverdianu translation team had completed a draft of the first chapters of Luke and had given it to the pastor to review. On the first Sunday in December, the pastor started his sermon by announcing the reading from God's Word. But instead of reading from the Bible in the national language, Portuguese, he read from the verses that had been translated into Kabuverdianu.

> "Our reading will be from Luke 2, verses 1 through 7," he announced.

> As the congregation listened intently, he read the passage. Pausing, he exclaimed, "It tastes so good, it tastes so good!" Then he started reading again and didn't stop until he'd finished the entire chapter, reading with the confidence and expression of someone who understood and cherished every word.

> The translation team began to sob. A row of teenage girls stared at each other in wide-eyed wonder and then dissolved into a group hug. Eyes glistened with tears. As the last word was read, a spontaneous cheer erupted: "Amen! Hallelujah!" The service closed with many hugs for those who had worked on the translation.

---

5   Bob Creson, "Hearing the Christmas story again—for the first time," n.d., http://www.wycliffe.net/Stories/tabid/67/Default.aspx?id=2086

A woman who had been educated in Portuguese had started to follow along in her Portuguese Bible, but then stopped and just listened to the Word of God in her language.

> "I let the words fall over me," she said. "For the first time in my life I felt washed by the Word. I thought I knew the Christmas story by heart, but I must confess that today I feel like I've heard it for the very first time."

It is clear that part of the process of "making disciples of all nations" must include the translation of the Bible into the languages that are spoken by these people groups. But merely translating the Bible as a written text is not sufficient for people groups who are primarily oral (not text-based) in their means of communication.

The Word of God, Heard

The Bible tells us that "faith comes from hearing, and hearing through the word of Christ" (Romans 10:17, ESV). When Ezra instructed the people from the Word of God, he did so out loud, speaking to them the Word of God. Jesus also used an oral approach when he taught his disciples, frequently using stories as the means of teaching:

> "He taught them by telling many stories in the form of parables..."

> —Mark 4:2, NLT

The significance of this should not be missed. Hearing the Word of God results in faith. The oral communication of the Word of God also removes the need for literacy as a prerequisite for ingesting and comprehending the Word of God in oral communities. This is significant because, according to missiologists in the International Orality Network, oral communicators are found in every cultural group in the world, and they constitute approximately two-thirds of the world's population.[6]

Traditionally, however, the process of "making disciples" cross-culturally has tended to use text-based, linear teaching approaches that are usually encountered in academic environments. These teaching materials and techniques are usually not well-suited for oral patterns of communication. These patterns often include the telling of stories, drama, song and dance, and are used in most people groups around the world. As a result of the disconnect between a text-based means of communication and a people group that communicates orally, comprehension of the content by the target audience is often very limited.

The effectiveness of using oral strategies among people who are oral communicators is illustrated in the story of a pastor in India who came to Christ through the work of a cross-cultural missionary.[7] He went to a Bible college where he received two years of theological training, after which he returned to his village to preach the Gospel.

But not all went according to plan. "To my surprise," he said, "my people were not able to understand my message. A few people accepted the Lord after much labour. I continued to preach the gospel, but there were little results. I was discouraged and confused and did not know what to do."

Then he attended a seminar where he learned how to communicate the Gospel using oral methods. At this point, he realized that his problem was that the communication style he had been using was based on lecture methods with printed books, like he had learned at the Bible college. He returned to the village and started using

---

6   Avery Willis and Steve Evans, *Making Disciples of Oral Learners* (ILN, 2007), 3. Some estimates suggest this may be a conservative estimate and put the total number of oral communicators closer to 85% or more of the world's population.

7   Ibid, 2-3.

oral methods to communicate the Gospel, and the people were more responsive:

> After the seminar I went to the village, but this time I changed my way of communication. I started using a story-telling method in my native language. I used gospel songs and the traditional music of my people. This time the people in the villages began to understand the gospel in a better way. As a result of it, people began to come in large numbers. Many accepted Christ and took baptism.

The prevalence of oral communicators in the world does not mean the printed Word of God or other text-based materials are obsolete and no longer of use. On the contrary, they will continue to be foundational to the task of making disciples. But effective discipleship strategies among least-reached people groups also take into account the reality that most people in the world will best learn to become disciples of Christ through primarily oral means.[8]

So we see that the Word of God must be translated for effective use and also made accessible to oral communicators. But "making disciples of all nations" also includes explaining the Word of God and contextualizing the message for accurate communication within the culture of the disciple.

---

8   A common concern regarding the "orality" approach in world missions has to do with the potential for degradation of the message through imperfect oral communication. Given the ease with which orally-communicated messages can change, it would seem to suggest that oral approaches might not be reliable for communicating the eternal and unchanging Truth.

This is a valid concern, but it does not take into account the significant advantages that are unique to primarily oral cultures, or the techniques used in reaching oral communicators that mitigate this potential problem. Those of us from literate cultures may assume that everyone else is as dependent on written methods of communication and data transfer as we are. But oral communicators do not have these same dependencies, because of the significant advantages they have in the realm of memory and retaining information.

The Word of God, Explained

In addition to communicating the translated Word of God orally, Ezra and the Levites "gave the meaning" of what was read. The Law was originally given by God directly to the Jewish people, written in Hebrew and applied directly to their culture. But for many in Ezra's time, this may have been the first time they had heard the Law. Others may have heard the Law many times, but they needed it explained and applied to their context. Nearly a thousand years had passed since the giving of the Law, and much had changed in the daily lives of the Jewish people. Even though the Law had been written to them, it was important for it to be explained and the meaning clearly communicated in order for the people to understand it.

The cultures of the vast majority of the people groups in the world are far removed from the Jewish and Greco-Roman cultures of the original audiences of the Old and New Testaments. In addition, the languages spoken today by these thousands of people groups are usually very linguistically different from the Hebrew language of the Old Testament and Greek of the New Testament. The more distinct the culture and language of a people group are from the culture and language of the original audience of the Bible, the more likely the need for explanation of what is written in the Bible, to bridge the gap between the two contexts.

Consider, for example, the challenge in communicating crucial Biblical themes like "eternal life", "faith", "forgiveness", "sin", and "mercy" in cultures where such concepts are unheard of, and in languages for which there is no vocabulary to describe them? How do you explain the significance of John's statement regarding Jesus: "Here is the Lamb of God, who takes away the sin of the world" (John 1:29) in a culture that does not have sheep or a sacrificial system? If you have never heard of the Romans, or that they occupied Judah many years ago, or that during that time a Roman soldier could require anyone to carry loads for them, how will you understand the significance of Jesus' audacious statement, "If anyone forces you to go one mile, go with him two" (Matthew 5:41)?

Additionally, certain aspects of the culture and language of the original audiences of the Scripture were implicitly understood by them, even though they are not explicitly stated in the Biblical texts. The absence of this implicitly understood information can create confusion or misunderstanding for people in other cultures who are not aware of the differences between the contexts of the original audience and their own.

Bruce Olson, in the book *Bruchko*, tells of challenges he faced when communicating the stories of the Bible to the Motilone people in the Amazon jungle. One story, the parable of the wise man who built his house on the rock, was especially problematic. In the story, Jesus says, "Everyone then who hears these words of mine and does them will be like a wise man who built his house on the rock" (Matthew 7:24, ESV). But this created such problems that Bruce's friend and language helper at first wanted to skip it.

> "That's not right, Bruchko. A house that is solid must be built on sand. Otherwise the poles won't go deep enough, and the house will fall apart."[9]

In the Motilone context, a direct, word-for-word translation of the parable would have communicated exactly the opposite of what Jesus had communicated to the original hearers. In Jesus' context, buildings that were built on sand collapsed, so wise men built their houses on rock. In the Motilone context of the Amazon river basin, only a fool would build his house on a rock, because the flooding rivers would wash it away with the first rain. Instead, jungle houses were built on poles that ran deep into the sand where they would be firm and not collapse in any flood.

In the end, they translated the parable with the wise man building his house on the sand, in order to accurately communicate to the

---

9   Bruce R. Olson, *Bruchko* (Creation House, 1989), 160.

Motilone people what Jesus' story was intended to communicate. But regardless of how they translated it, the Motilone (and any) disciple of Christ needs to know at least three things in situations like these. They need to know what Christ actually *said*, what he *meant*, and *why there is a difference* between the two.

The Motilone needs to know that Jesus said "everyone... who hears these words of mine and does them will be like a wise man who built his house on the rock [because he is wise and wants his house to stand firm]" (Matthew 7:24). But they also need to know what Jesus actually *meant*, as it applies in their own context: "everyone... who hears these words of mine and does them will be like a wise man who built his house on the sand [because he is wise and wants his house to stand firm]"). They also need to understand why there is a difference between what Jesus said and how it is accurately communicated in their own culture. In this case, the explanation would describe the different geography, climate, and cultural factors that affected the building of houses in Israel in the 1st century.

Without explaining the context of a Biblical text and matching its intent to the context of the target culture, much of the Bible may be confusing and unclear to disciples of Christ, even though it is translated and accessible to them in their language. This does not in any way imply that the Scriptures alone are inadequate for "life and godliness"—far from it! The Word of God is "living and active", and it effectively communicates when it is clearly *understood* by the hearers in any culture and language.

This is why Ezra and the Levites took great care to read the Word of God *and provide explanation*. This is also why well-prepared sermons that exposit a portion of Scripture carefully draw out the crucial linguistic, historical, and cultural aspects of the text. The goal of good exegesis in the exposition of Scripture is to help the hearer come to a correct understanding of the text as it would have been understood by the original hearers. In this way, the meaning of the text can be accurately and consistently applied to the unique context of the hearer today.

Needed: Discipleship Resources

There are many different factors that contribute to the spiritual health of any church, but in general, there are two key factors that seem to be especially important in the task of "making disciples": disciplers and discipleship resources. Disciplers, as we have seen, are those who do the difficult, day-to-day work of teaching converts to obey everything Jesus has commanded us. Discipleship resources are materials that sustain, teach, and continue to spiritually nourish the disciples, even when the discipler is not present.

The most important and foundational discipleship resource is the Word of God. Other resources are, necessarily, built on the Word of God and are significantly more effective when they are translated and adapted into the language and culture of a people group. These discipleship resources provide explanation and Biblical instruction, enabling young believers to grow spiritually and withstand the all-out spiritual assaults and the subtle deceptions that will continue to come their way. Even though there may be a growing number of churches and believers in a people group, the task of making disciples is not finished until disciples are equipped with the discipleship resources they need to continue to learn and grow spiritually on their own.

> The task of making disciples is not finished until disciples are equipped with the discipleship resources they need to continue to learn and grow spiritually on their own.

Discipleship resources include text, audio, and video materials that help to explain and clarify the Word of God in the social, cultural, and historical context of the consumer. In some contexts, these resources may include things such as Bible study notes, commentaries, concordances, leadership training courses, children's ministry materials, Bible story videos, and so on. Depending on the context and need, however, they also might look nothing like the kinds of resources with which we are familiar. Regardless, the purpose of discipleship resources is to enable believers in a given culture and language to grow in their understanding of the Word of God, and so to grow in spiritual maturity and obedience to "everything that Jesus has commanded" (Matthew 28:20).

Discipleship resources can be thought of as being complimentary to "evangelistic resources" (like tracts, videos, etc.) which are specifically intended to lead an unbeliever to faith in Jesus Christ. Historically, much focus and effort has been given to the creation of translated and contextualized evangelistic resources. But apart from Bible translation, relatively little has been done in most languages of the world to provide adequate translated and contextualized discipleship resources for the global church. This lack of spiritual "meat" to strengthen them (by making it possible for them to increase in their understanding of the Word of God and solid doctrine) is one of the most crucial needs facing the global church today.

The value of discipleship resources in the life of the Christian has been clearly understood throughout much of the history of the Church:

> If he shall not lose his reward, who gives a cup of cold water to his thirsty neighbour, what will not be the reward of those, who, by putting good works into the hands of their neighbours, open to them the fountains of eternal life![10]
>
> —Thomas à Kempis

---

10   à Kempis, Thomas. *The Imitation of Christ - In Four Books*. Translated by Right Rev. R. Challoner, D.D., V.A. McGlashan and Gill, 1873. vii. Interestingly, given the topic of copyright addressed later in this book, the translator Challoner says this about Thomas à Kempis: "...his favourite occupation appears to have been the copying of useful books; and he warmly exhorted others to the same occupation."

The Reformation itself seems to be almost unthinkable without taking into consideration the printed pages of Luther's sermons, essays, addresses, and biblical translations. Indeed, the Reformation went hand in hand with book and press.[11]

—Richard Cole

Reading, when it is an exercise of the mind upon wise and pious subjects, is, next to prayer, the best improvement of our hearts; it enlightens our minds, collects our thoughts, calms and allays our passions, and begets in us wise and pious resolutions.[12]

—William Law

[Paul] is inspired, and yet he wants books! He has been preaching at least for thirty years, and yet he wants books! He had seen the Lord, and yet he wants books! He had had a wider experience than most men, and yet he wants books! He had been caught up into the third heaven, and had heard things which it was unlawful for a man to utter, yet he wants books! He had written the major part of the New Testament, and yet he wants books! The apostle says to Timothy and so he says to every preacher, "Give thyself unto reading."[13]

—Charles Spurgeon, on 2 Timothy 4:13

No agency can penetrate Islam so deeply, abide so persistently, witness so daringly, and influence so irresistibly, as the printed page.[14]

---

11   Cole, Richard G. "Reformation Printers: Unsung Heroes." *Sixteenth Century Journal* 15, no. 3 (1984): 327. doi:10.2307/2540767.

12   Law, William. *A Practical Treatise Upon Christian Perfection*. Repr. [of the 1726 Ed.]., 1734.

13   Spurgeon, Charles. "Paul—his Cloak and His Books." November 29, 1863.

14   Wilder, et al. *The Missionary Review of the World*. Funk & Wagnalls, 1912. 779.

In many lands the post-office has become an evangelistic agency. It carries Christian literature unobtrusively into the homes of all classes, and those who have tried this method are enthusiastic regarding its effectiveness and comparative economy.[15]

—Samuel Zwemer

Books may preach, when the author cannot, when the author may not, when the author dares not, yes, and which is more, when the author is not![16]

—Thomas Brooks (Puritan author)

There are two things in the entire history of missions that have been absolutely central. One, obviously, is the Bible itself. The other is the printed page. There is absolutely nothing else, in terms of mission methodology, that outranks the importance of the printed page. Meetings come and go and personalities appear and are gone. But, the printed page continues to speak.[17]

—Ralph Winter

The leader who intends to grow spiritually and intellectually will be reading constantly... Spiritual leaders should also read for intellectual growth. This will require books that test

---

15   Harper, et al. *The Biblical World*. University of Chicago Press, 1918. 300-304. The authors make this important observation about the importance placed by Zwemer on Christian literature: "He would not make it a substitute for the living voice, but he insists that its power as an evangelistic agency has never been realized. In this form the message is often more persuasive, more permanent, and reaches a larger audience than that spoken by human lips. It is the ubiquitous missionary, often entering closed lands and penetrating into the most secluded villages."

16   Brooks, Thomas. *Heaven on Earth*, 1667.

17   Ralph Winter, quote for "Friends of Bible Pathway Ministries." Accessed November 24, 2011. http://www.biblepathway.org/English/Friendsof-BP.html.

wits, provide fresh ideas, challenge assumptions, and probe complexities... The leader should read, too, to acquire new information, to keep current with the time, to be well informed in his or her own field of expertise... The leader should read to have fellowship with great minds. Through books we hold communion with the greatest spiritual leaders of the ages.[18]

—Oswald Sanders

Clearly, the value of discipleship resources is in the *content* itself ("what it communicates"), not only in the *format* in which it is delivered ("how it is communicated"). There is value in reading discipleship resources that are available in the format of a book. There is also value in discipleship resources available in media formats for those who do not (or cannot) read.

If we, as part of the global church, are serious about truly fulfilling Christ's mandate to make mature disciples in each people group, we need to do more than evangelism and church planting. Just as James tells us it is no good to see a needy brother and send him off without meeting his physical needs, so also it is imperative that we do more than simply tell believers in other people groups, "Go in peace, be [spiritually] warmed and [theologically] filled," (James 2:15-16, ESV). It is imperative that every people group have access both to the Word of God and to other contextualized discipleship resources—in their own languages and in formats that are accessible to oral communicators.

This presents us with a significant challenge, because there are a *lot* of people groups in the world, and they speak a *lot* of different languages.

---

18   Sanders, Oswald. *Spiritual Leadership*. Second Revision. The Moody Bible Institute of Chicago, 1994. 102-103.

CHAPTER 2

REACHING THE LINGUISTICALLY "LEAST OF THESE"

Making disciples of all people groups requires using their "heart languages" in order to teach them to "obey everything Jesus has commanded." The magnitude and complexity of this task is immense, and much remains to be accomplished. Merely "working harder" in world missions is an inadequate approach for accomplishing the Great Commission. Equipping every people group with adequate discipleship resources in their own language requires a fundamental shift in our approach to world missions.

~ ~ ~

In July 1974, Christian leaders from around the world gathered in Lausanne, Switzerland for the International Congress on World Evangelization. One of the significant outcomes of that gathering came from Ralph Winter's indictment of the missionary movement for "people blindness":

The shattering truth is that four out of five non-Christians in the world today are beyond the reach of... evangelism. Why is this fact not more widely known? I'm afraid that all our exultation about the fact that every country of the world has been penetrated has allowed many to suppose that every culture has by now been penetrated. This misunderstanding is a malady so widespread that it deserves a special name. Let us call it "people blindness"—that is, blindness to the existence of separate peoples within countries... In the Great Commission... the phrase "make disciples of all ethne (peoples)" does not let us off the hook once we have a church in every country—God wants a strong church within every people![1]

The realization that four out of five non-Christians were still cut off from the gospel because of cultural and linguistic barriers, not geographic ones, resulted in a significant missiological change in the global world missions community. The task of missions came to be (correctly) understood as requiring a focus on unreached *people groups*, not merely evangelism in every country. A people group is defined as:

A significantly large sociological grouping of individuals who perceive themselves to have a common affinity with one another. For evangelization purposes, a people group is the largest group within which the Gospel can spread as a church planting movement without encountering barriers of understanding [i.e. linguistic differences] or acceptance [i.e. sociocultural differences].[2]

---

1   Ralph D. Winter, "The New Macedonia: A Revolutionary New Era in Mission Begins," in *Perspectives on the World Christian Movement: A Reader* (Pasadena, Calif.: William Carey Library, 1974), www.joshuaproject.net/assets/TheHighestPriority.pdf, 346.

2   This definition is used by the Joshua Project ("Definitions and Terms Related to the Great Commission," n.d., http://www.joshuaproject.net/definitions.php) and is based in part on the 1982 Lausanne Committee Chicago meeting.

The exhortation by Winter to focus on people groups (or "ethnic groups") as opposed to countries in the task of world missions was not a new, trendy idea of the 70s. It was, as Winter points out, a return to Biblical missiology and a more accurate understanding of Matthew 28:18-20. In *The Supremacy of God among "All the Nations"*, John Piper agrees, saying this about Christ's command to the Church:

> These words of the Lord are crucial for deciding what the missionary task of the church should be today. Specifically, the words "make disciples of all nations" must be closely examined. They contain the very important phrase "all nations", which is often referred to in the Greek form *panta ta ethne* (*panta* = all, *ta* = the, *ethne* = nations). The reason this is such an important phrase is that *ethne*, when translated "nations," sounds like a political or geographic grouping. That is its most common English usage. But... this is not what the Greek means... the focus of the command is the discipling of all the people groups of the world.[3]

This task of making disciples of all people groups will someday be completed. A vision of the completed Great Commission is given in Revelation 7:9:

> "After this I looked, and behold, a great multitude that no one could number, from every nation, from all tribes and peoples and languages, standing before the throne and before the Lamb, clothed in white robes, with palm branches in their hands..."[4]

The renewed focus on reaching every people group with the Gospel has resulted in encouraging progress toward the completion of the Great Commission in the last thirty years. However, there is still

---

3   John Piper, "The Supremacy of God among 'All the Nations,'" *International Journal of Frontier Missions* 13 (mar 1996), http://www.ijfm.org/PDFs_IJFM/13_1_PDFs/04_Piper.pdf, 16-17, 22.

much work that remains to be done before this task is complete. The total number of people groups in the world is somewhere between about 11,000 and 16,000 (depending on the criteria used), and the number of "least-reached" people groups is over 6,500.[5]

Least-reached people groups are not distributed evenly among the countries of the world. For instance, the Joshua Project lists Papua New Guinea as having 3 least-reached people groups, Mexico has 15, China has 428, and India has a staggering 2,216. Some least-reached people groups are comprised of millions, but many of them have only a few thousand people. Some of these people groups may be found in large, easily accessible urban areas, but many are among the most geographically distant, remotely located people in the whole world. Many of these people groups are economically disadvantaged, politically oppressed, and resistant to the Gospel. But the mandate to the Church is, as it has always been: make disciples of *every* people group.

---

4   The great multitude in heaven is from every people group and language, but the text does not suggest that they will lose their ethnic identity or language in heaven. This notion of many different cultures and "people groups" in heaven is consistent with Revelation 21:3, where Piper points out that "the standard Greek texts of the New Testament now agree that the original wording of Revelation 21:3 requires the translation: 'and I heard a great voice from the throne saying, Behold the dwelling of God is with men, and he will dwell with them and they will be his peoples,' and not 'his people' (singular)." Ibid, 23.

5   Two excellent sources of information and statistics regarding people groups are the International Mission Board: "Research Data," n.d., http://public.imb.org/globalresearch/Pages/ResearchData.aspx and the Joshua Project: "Great Commission Statistics about Peoples, Countries and Languages," n.d., http://joshuaproject.net/great-commission-statistics.php. At the time of writing, the IMB data lists the number of least-reached people groups as 6,651 (excluding the U.S. and Canada) and the Joshua Project lists the number of least-reached people groups as 6,997.

The Spiritual Famine of the Global Church

Can you imagine spiritual life without the Word of God in your own language? Try to picture your bookshelves empty, no Christian radio, no sermon podcasts, no Bible on the coffee table, no Bible app on your smartphone, no devotionals, or study guides. Nothing. How would you grow spiritually? What if, in this context of total lack, you are trying to raise your children as believers who resist the advances of the dominant religion in your culture? What if you are the pastor of a church in a language that has nothing?

This kind of context is difficult for many of us to comprehend or even imagine, especially if we speak a language that has had access to a seemingly infinite number of discipleship resources for centuries. A total lack of discipleship resources in one's own language, however, is the daily reality for followers of Jesus in many, if not most, people groups of the world today.

These Christians may have become believers through the preaching of an evangelist yesterday. But today they are watching the evangelist walk down the trail to the next village, knowing they may never see him again. As the evangelist leaves, so does their only source of theological guidance and spiritual instruction, because they have no discipler and no discipleship resources in their language. They desperately want to add to their faith, virtue and to their virtue, knowledge (2 Peter 1:5), but they have no means of doing so. Their spiritual famine is absolute.

It is all but impossible to accurately quantify the spiritual famine of the global church. Objectively proving that adequate discipleship resources do not exist in a given language is difficult to accomplish, because complete statistics do not exist. Perhaps the best way to begin to understand the breadth and severity of the spiritual famine of the global church is to see it firsthand.

Visit Christians in other parts of the world and ask to see what discipleship resources are available in their own languages. Ask Christians in China, for example, to take you to their local Christian bookstore (if one even exists) and see what is available. Ask them what Christian programs are broadcast on local TV or radio stations. Consider the hundreds of languages spoken in that country, and compare it with the number of languages in which discipleship resources are available.

Or go to other parts of Asia and ask pastors there how the Christians in their churches study the Word of God. Ask Christians how they grow spiritually and what resources they have available to help them grow in the knowledge of the Word of God. Then find out that as many as 80% of the people in the church are illiterate, and that the Word of God is either not available in their own language or, if it is, it is only available in print. You may discover that they have no other discipleship resources in their own language and only receive occasional spiritual nourishment from the pastor, and he has not had the opportunity to receive any formal training in theology or Biblical studies.

If you were to visit other parts of the world and assess the situation on the ground for Christians, here is what you could expect to find:

- Some discipleship resources *are* available in some languages—almost always the national language, or the very largest languages having the most speakers.

- Discipleship resources that exist in other languages are often very costly and beyond the means of the average Christian.

- If discipleship resources exist in a given language, they are often intended only for pastors. In terms of access to the Word of God and having the ability to study and understand it for themselves, much of the global church is still in the Dark Ages. They are often dependent on those with a formal role and special training in the church to access the

Word of God and mediate it to them. This is not to denigrate the role of these church leaders in any way! There is, however, a great need for both trained church leaders *and* discipleship resources that are accessible to everyone in the church, for their spiritual growth and maturity.

- For Christians who speak the vast majority of the smaller languages, adequate discipleship resources in their own languages simply do not exist.

When I was in Papua New Guinea—a "Christian" country with over 800 languages—I remember noting that the shelves of the local Christian bookstore only contained the Bible in English, the Bible in Tok Pisin (the national language) and maybe one or two other materials. These are important first steps, but is nowhere near providing adequate discipleship resources in the hundreds of languages spoken by Christians in that country.

On a recent trip to India, I attended a pastors' conference and had the opportunity to interact with church leaders from all over India. They came from many different provinces, and spoke many different languages. These men love God and serve Jesus Christ with their whole heart. Interestingly, however, the concept of "discipleship resources" (theological content to promote spiritual growth and increase Biblical knowledge) was almost unheard of. Few had access to a Bible in their own language, much less additional resources to help them study it effectively.

I had a chance to visit the library on the campus of the training institute where the conference was held and was delighted to see row upon row of books, covering many topics. I asked what languages the books were in, and was told that they were all in English. For pastors who are able to read English (and live in proximity to the library), it is helpful to have access to discipleship resources in English.

The problem is that English was not the first language of any of the pastors there. The services were conducted in English, but were simultaneously translated into as many five other languages, because *English was an inadequate means of communication* for most of the attendees. They need their own discipleship resources in their own languages—books in English are not enough.

The need for discipleship resources in the languages of India has been observed by others, like author Tim Challies:

> The church there is growing quickly, but it is lacking in depth. There are a growing number of leaders there who love the Lord, who are eager to serve him, and who are doing this very well. Yet *they are lacking in training and in resources...* This is their self assessment and by all appearances it is true. [Churches in the larger cities] have available to them all the teaching and training the English language offers; the church in northern India has only what is available in Hindi.[6]

Others have pointed out:

> Christianity is growing at a staggering rate [in India]. Despite rising resistance and persecution, these new believers are also starting to take responsibility for the Great Commission. There are more churches being planted in this region of the world than ever before.
>
> Good news, certainly, but it also presents a unique challenge. Young Christians are working to plant and multiply churches, *reproducing new churches ahead of Bible training.* Over 90% of them have no formal instruction and will never have the opportunity to get that kind of education.[7]

---

6   Challies, Tim. "Reflections on Leaving India." *Challies Dot Com*, 16 nov 2012. http://www.challies.com/articles/reflections-on-leaving-india. Emphasis added.

7   "Missiologist Confirms Great Commission Trends for Ministry." *Mission Network News*, 1 feb 2012. http://mnnonline.org/article/16768. Emphasis added.

The immense lack of discipleship resources in other languages is not unique to India. Lack of adequate training and materials to promote spiritual growth and Biblical knowledge is the norm for most Christians who do not speak English as their first language. For them, there is no Amazon.com where they can instantly order even basic resources in their own language to help them grow spiritually.

Complete numbers to quantify this famine are not available, but these statistics may help paint the picture:

- More than 1.2 billion people worldwide have no access to the Bible in their heart language, and there are 2,000 languages that have no Scripture translation efforts underway.[8]

- Eighty-five percent of churches in the world are led by men and women who have no formal training in theology or ministry.[9]

- If every Christian training institute in the world operated at 120 percent capacity, less than 10 percent of the unequipped leaders would be trained.[10]

- The Jesus Film project is available in 1,168 languages, with over 5,500 languages remaining to reach the goal of sharing Jesus "with everyone in his or her own heart language."[11]

---

8   "Major Bible Translation Ministries Unite to Eradicate 'Bible Poverty'." *OutreachMagazine.com*, 13 dec 2012.
http://www.outreachmagazine.com/news-and-stories/5110-Major-Bible-Translation-Ministries-Unite-to-Eradicate-%E2%80%98Bible-Poverty%E2%80%99.html.

9   Livermore, David A. *Serving with Eyes Wide Open*. Baker Books, 2006. 44.

10   Ibid.

11   "Languages Completed." *The JESUS Film Project*, 13 jan 2013. http://www.jesusfilm.org/film-and-media/statistics/languages-completed.

- *The Imitation of Christ* by Thomas à Kempis is generally considered to be the most widely read Christian book after the Bible and has reportedly been translated into hundreds of languages, leaving thousands without (precise numbers are not available).[12]

- *The Pilgrim's Progress* by John Bunyan—one of the most popular books in Christian history—has been translated into only 200 languages, leaving the vast majority of the world's languages without.[13]

- *Systematic Theology*, which has sold more than 450,000 copies and is used as a theology textbook all over the world is available in 8 languages, with 8 more underway.[14]

Listing statistics like these is not criticism in any way. Many people and ministries are focused on helping end the spiritual famine of the global church and they are to be commended for their efforts. Numbers like these merely indicate that there is much still to be done in the task of "making disciples" of all people groups and equipping them with adequate discipleship resources.

People Groups and Their Languages

Making disciples of every people group includes equipping believers in these people groups with adequate discipleship resources in their own languages. Interestingly, the relationship between people groups and languages is not 1:1. There are "multi-ethnic language groups", where many people groups speak the same lan-

---

12   "The Imitatio Christi Through Six Centuries." Accessed January 14, 2013. http://www.smu.edu/Bridwell/Collections/SpecialCollectionsandArchives/Exhibitions/ImitatioChristi.

13   Bunyan, John. *The Pilgrim's Progress.* Edited by W. R. Owens. Oxford University Press, 2003.

14   Grudem, Wayne. "Systematic Theology." Accessed January 14, 2013. http://www.waynegrudem.com/systematic-theology/.

guage. According to Operation World, Hindi is an example of this, as there are 297 different people groups in India who speak Hindi.[15] In other situations, there are "multi-lingual ethnic groups", where one people group with a common ethnic identity speaks many different languages. The Dinka people group of Sudan is an example of this, as the Dinka people group is comprised of five different languages.[16]

The global linguistic situation that forms the context for the mandate "make disciples of all people groups" is complicated, to say the least. Regardless of how the lines are drawn between ethnic identities and language groups, every people group needs access to the Word of God, translated into whatever languages they speak, accessible to oral communicators, and explained with clarity through discipleship resources that communicate the Word of God accurately in their culture. In order to understand the magnitude of this task, it may be helpful to survey the linguistic complexity of the world.

---

15 Jason Mandryk, *Operation World: The Definitive Prayer Guide To Every Nation* (IVP Books, 2010). Note that the number of people groups worldwide who speak Hindi as their primary language is higher. The Joshua Project lists 533 such people groups. "Hindi Bibles, facts, materials and people groups that speak Hindi," n.d., http://www.joshuaproject.net/languages.php?rol3=hin. This number includes the four varieties of Hindi listed in the Ethnologue: "Ethnologue report for language code: hin," 2009, http://www.ethnologue.com/show_language.asp?code=hin.

16 Some suggest that the languages are actually dialects of the same language, which they may be—the distinction between "dialect" and "different language" is often not a clear one. In the case of the Dinka, the languages (or dialects) are sufficiently dissimilar that three of the five language variants (Northeastern, Southeastern, and Southwestern) are listed as having their own translation of the New Testament. "Ethnologue report for language code: din," 2009, http://www.ethnologue.com/show_language.asp?code=din

The Linguistic Aftermath of Babel

Following the Flood, mankind spoke only one language. In addition to being united by language, they were united in their desire to make a name for themselves and keep from being scattered throughout the whole earth (Genesis 11:4). So God "confused the language of the whole earth, and from there the LORD scattered them over the face of the whole earth" (Genesis 11:9). But God's confusing of the languages and His scattering of mankind over the face of the earth—where they gathered as groups according to the languages they spoke—was not merely judgment on the pride and willfulness of mankind. It was, and still is, God's sovereign purpose to bring glory to Himself through each and every one of the people groups of the earth, and to receive praise in every one of the languages spoken by these people groups.

We are now thousands of years removed from Babel. Through the ongoing process of language change and shift, there are now nearly 7,000 living languages spoken in the world.[17] The total population of the world is over 7 billion people, but the 7,000 languages spoken in the world are not evenly distributed among the 7 billion people of the world. This creates a complex global picture of "who speaks what, where."

One of the best resources for helping to make sense of the linguistic complexity of the world today is the Ethnologue (www.ethnologue.com). It provides specific details about every known language in the world, from languages with huge numbers of speakers (like Mandarin, with over 845 million speakers[18]) to languages with rela-

---

17   The Ethnologue lists 6,909 languages in M. Paul Lewis, ed.*Ethnologue: Languages of the World* (Dallas, TX, USA: SIL International, 2009), http://www.ethnologue.com. More recent statistics put the number of living languages at 6,877, see "Scripture Access Statistics 2012," 2012, http://www.wycliffe.net/resources/scriptureaccessstatistics/tabid/99/Default.aspx.

tively few speakers (like the Boor language of southern Chad, with a grand total of 200 speakers[19]).

In addition to providing details on specific languages, the Ethnologue also provides a means of better understanding the "big picture" of language use in the world. In order to break down the linguistic complexity of the world's languages, it may be helpful to group the languages of the world into population brackets, as shown here:[20]

---

18 "Ethnologue report for language code: cmn," 2009, http://www.ethnologue.com/show_language.asp?code=cmn. Note that Mandarin is part of the Chinese macrolanguage (ISO 639-3 zho) that also includes Gan, Hakka, Huizhou, Jinyu, Min Bei, Min Dong, Min Nan, Min Zhong, Pu-Xian, Wu, Xiang, and Yue, and has a combined population of over 1.2 billion. "Ethnologue report for language code: zho," 2009, http://www.ethnologue.com/show_language.asp?code=zho.

19 "Boor of Chad Ethnic People Profile," n.d., http://www.joshuaproject.net/people-profile.php?peo3=10945&rog3=CD. Note that the Ethnologue lists the language population as being 100 in 1999 "Ethnologue report for language code: bvf," 2009, http://www.ethnologue.com/show_language.asp?code=bvf. It is assumed that the information in the Joshua Project profile is more recent.

20 The data and tables used in this chapter reflect the number of first-language speakers for each language and are taken from "Ethnologue: Statistical Summaries," 2009, http://www.ethnologue.com/ethno_docs/distribution.asp?by=size. Note that the total population for all speakers of all languages in this data is listed as 5,959,511,717. The discrepancy between this figure and the 7 billion world population figure is due in part to the data being based on the 16th version of Ethnologue, which is the most current at the time of writing, but published in 2009. The smaller population size is also affected by the 277 languages for which the number of speakers is not known. It is likely, although not certain, that most of these languages are on the smaller end of the spectrum of language size, as information for languages with greater numbers of speakers is often more readily available. In the interest of simplicity, the numbers and calculations in this chapter do not take into account these languages for which the number of speakers is not known. Finally, it should also be noted that counting languages and speakers is a notoriously complicated task, and the numbers here should not be taken as absolutes, but rather as a very close approximation of the linguistic context in the world today.

Number of speakers per language	Languages	Total speakers
100,000,000+	8	2,308,548,848
10,000,000 to 99,999,999	77	2,346,900,757
1,000,000 to 9,999,999	304	951,916,458
100,000 to 999,999	895	283,116,716
10,000 to 99,999	1824	60,780,797
1,000 to 9,999	2014	7,773,810
100 to 999	1038	461,250
10 to 99	339	12,560
1 to 9	133	521

Table 1: Languages and Speakers (source: Ethnologue.com)

This data is visualized in Chart 1 which follows, showing the number of languages in each of the above population brackets, as well as the number of speakers in each bracket. Note that the chart further divides the nine population ranges into 3 simplified population ranges to provide a clearer overview of the data:

- Languages having greater than 1,000,000 speakers
- Languages having between 10,000 and 1 million speakers
- Languages having fewer than 10,000 speakers

Languages and People

The top half of Chart 1 (labeled as "number of speakers") shows the total population of the world, distributed according to the number of speakers of each language.

Note how the vast majority of people in the world speak languages that have more than 1 million speakers (columns 1-3). By contrast, there are a relatively minuscule number of people who speak languages that have fewer than 10,000 speakers each (columns 6-9).

The bottom half of Chart 1 (labeled as "number of languages") shows the number of languages in each of the language population ranges. Note that the vast majority of languages in the world have fewer than 1 million speakers (columns 4–9). Note also that there are only 8 languages in the world that have 100 million speakers or more (row 1)[21] and there are fewer than 400 languages that have more than 1 million speakers (columns 1–3). By contrast, there are more than 3,500 languages that have fewer than 10,000 speakers (rows 6-9).

---

21   These languages are, in descending order: Chinese, Spanish, English, Arabic, Hindi, Bengali, Portuguese, and Russian. Note, however, that Table 3 on "Ethnologue: Statistical Summaries" lists a ninth language (Japanese) as having more than 100 million speakers. The reason for this discrepancy is not explained and the numbers in the charts here follow the numbers in Table 2 of the Ethnologue data.

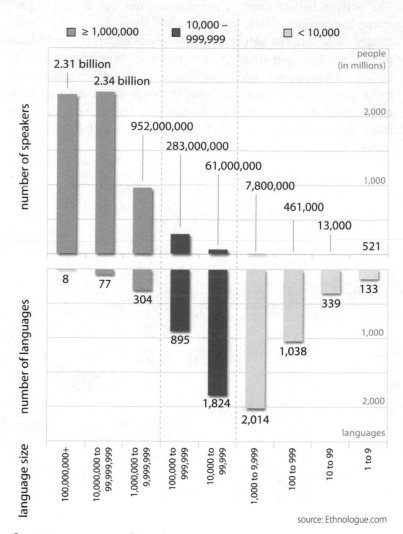

Chart 1: Languages and People

Languages and People, Simplified

The chart which follows (Chart 2) shows these same numbers, but merges the data into the 3 meta-brackets mentioned above: languages having more than 1 million speakers, languages having between 10,000 and 1 million speakers, and languages having fewer than 10,000 speakers.

Chart 2 shows the extreme imbalance between the large number of speakers of the 389 most populated languages and the relatively few number of speakers of the thousands of least populated languages. More than half of the languages of the world (3,524 languages) have fewer than 10,000 speakers each. By contrast, almost 95% of the people of the world (5.6 billion) speak approximately 5% of the world's languages (389). To put it more simply: the majority of people in the world speak a tiny fraction of the world's languages, and a small fraction of the people in the world speak the vast majority of the world's languages.

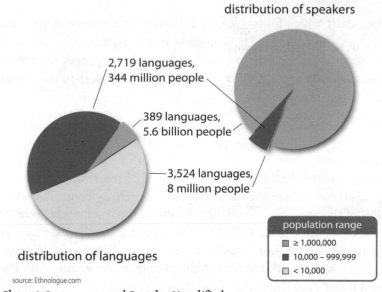

distribution of speakers

2,719 languages,
344 million people

389 languages,
5.6 billion people

3,524 languages,
8 million people

distribution of languages

population range
- ≥ 1,000,000
- 10,000 – 999,999
- < 10,000

source: Ethnologue.com

Chart 2: Languages and People, Simplified

The Danger of Playing the "Numbers Game" in Missions

If the languages of the world were distributed evenly among the people of the world, we might approach the task of translating the Bible and other discipleship resources with a degree of balance. If the number of speakers of each of the world's language were somewhat similar, every language would logically appear to be relatively "equal" in terms of strategic importance, as defined by language size.

But because of the extreme imbalance between the number of speakers of each of the thousands of languages in the world today, there is a natural tendency to consider languages having more speakers as more missionally strategic and relegate languages with fewer speakers to the lowest priorities.

This tendency to focus only on the largest languages is often stated something like this: "If we can translate <our discipleship resource> into 25 languages, we can reach nearly 80% of the population of the world with solid Bible teaching." This may be true, but it begs the question: "What will the other 20% of the world's population do?" The people who speak those 25 languages may be blessed to receive the resource in their language, but 25 languages is *less than 0.4% of the languages in the world*. How will the millions who do not speak those languages receive solid Bible teaching? Often, no provision is made for the linguistically "least of these" and the assumption is (apparently) that either they do not need discipleship resources or that someone else will account for them.

The sheer number of languages in the world and the massive amount of time, effort, and financial resources traditionally re-quired to translate even one resource into another language presents an immense challenge. Organizations are required to make difficult choices and logically tend to choose the largest lan-guages first. This is understandable, but it tends to create a prob-lem in that the people groups who have the fewest number speak-ers of their languages are often overlooked *by everyone* when it comes to the creation and translation of discipleship resources.

We live in a world that wants to see results. Churches that support missionaries usually want to know that their financial "investment" is a good one. If the missionary works in a language with, for example, 200 million speakers, and 5% of the people in that language group get "reached" by the missionary's work, the total "reached" is 10 million people. By contrast, if 5% of the people in a language having 10,000 speakers are reached, the total is 500 people. Which is a better use of resources? Are the people who speak these less-populated languages of different value? What fac-tors do we use to answer these questions?

In the digital realm, this approach correlates to tracking analytics such as "number of hits", "app downloads", "video plays", etc. If your website/app/video in a large language gets *20,000 times* more use than your website/app/video in a small language, that not only feels good, it could also result in much more funding, as donors hear about how many millions of people your project is reaching. The economics of traditional missions favors the larger language, and all too often the smaller language is forgotten or left waiting, literally for thousands of years.

It makes sense that larger languages often get the missionaries and the discipleship resources first. After all, if 95% of the people of the world speak only about 5% of the world's languages, then it makes sense to target the mega languages in that 5% first. But implicit in this logic is the assumption that "more Christians" is the highest goal of missions. Scripture suggests that God's purpose in the world is not necessarily tied to the numbers of "people reached" or "conversions."

To be sure, we all want to see the greatest possible number of people come to salvation in Christ. But we need to remember that God cares about the smallest, the least, and the forgotten. Jesus says he is the Good Shepherd, and that one of the things the Good Shepherd does is leave the ninety-nine to go find the one. The parable of the lost coin shows the same aspect of God's heart. It was not enough that the woman had all the other coins, because there was one missing. She moved heaven and earth to find that lost coin and rejoiced greatly when she found it. In the same way, God cares deeply for the "least of these."

God's purpose, as put forward in His mandate to the Church in Matthew 28:18-20 ("make disciples of *all* people groups") and evidenced by the vision in Revelation 7:9 (the great multitude from *every* nation, tribe, people and language) is that the Bride of Christ be comprised not just of massive numbers of the redeemed, but that it include redeemed from even the smallest people group, speaking the least-significant language. The linguistically "least of these" are as precious in God's sight as the massive mega-peoples comprised of hundreds of millions.

In light of this, there is a subtle danger in "playing the numbers game" in missions, as it can begin to corrupt our missiology. By emphasizing practicality in mission strategies ("biggest bang for the buck" or "return on investment") over Biblical mandate (a mandate that is, by its very nature, highly *impractical*), we open the door to additional and more severe error. We *should* seek to be "shrewd as serpents" and make good use of resources in our missiology, but not at the risk of elevating our economic model for world missions above God's sovereign purpose in world missions: bringing to His flock people from *every* nation, tribe, people and language. Even those with fewer than 10,000 speakers.

Translation and the Languages of the World

Many mission organizations, publishers, and churches realize the importance of translating discipleship resources into other languages so they can be used effectively by the speakers of those languages. So they hire translators or assign some of their people to start translating their materials, usually starting in a handful of the most widely-spoken languages of the world. As many different entities do the same thing with their own content, it results in many "parallel" translation projects in larger languages. The smaller languages of the world continue to wait for their first discipleship resource while larger languages continue to acquire more translated materials. It is a good thing that larger languages continue to get more discipleship resources! But the absence of even one discipleship resource in each of the smaller languages of the world perpetuates a significant hindrance to the spiritual growth of speakers of those languages who are (or will soon be) followers of Christ.

Given that many (probably most) discipleship resources are rarely translated into even one other language, it is a noteworthy accomplishment when one is translated into, for example, 500 languages. In the standard approach to translation of discipleship resources, it often takes considerable expense and *decades* to translate a resource into 500 languages. But even though it is a noteworthy accomplishment, 500 languages is only about 8% of the world's languages. After all the effort, time, and expense of translating a resource into 500 languages, followers of Jesus who speak 92% of the world's languages still do not have access to it.

Not only would the bulk of the world's languages be left lacking in this scenario, but given the usual approach of targeting the largest languages first, one could reasonably argue that the remaining languages would be the hardest ones into which to translate. The speakers of these smaller languages are more likely to be geographically remote, with fewer potential translators who speak both the source language and the target language.

To illustrate this, consider the examples of Mandarin (845 million speakers worldwide) and the Boor language of Chad (200 speakers). Translating a discipleship resource from English into Mandarin might be relatively easy to accomplish because there are hundreds of thousands (maybe millions) of people who speak both languages and many of them could conceivably translate the work from one language to the other. Of this large pool of potential translators, some of them might be found in any large city anywhere in the world, given how common English and Mandarin are today.

But this is not at all the case when translating into the Boor language. It is unlikely that even one speaker of a language as small as Boor is sufficiently bilingual in English to be able to serve as a translator for a discipleship resource written in English. If that is the case, then translating a discipleship resource into their language would need to involve a different approach. Either an outsider would need to learn their language well enough to translate directly into it, or the resource would first need to be translated into a language of wider communication, like French or Arabic. This would enable bilingual Boor speakers to translate from the translation in the common language into Boor. Translating discipleship resources into languages like Boor—the smallest, most geographically isolated languages of the world—will often be a much more intensive and complicated task than translating into larger languages.

So where does all of this leave us and the task of making disciples of all people groups? There does not yet exist a single discipleship resource (including the Bible itself) that is available in every language of the world. Or to look at it from a different perspective: there still exist thousands of people groups that have never received even one discipleship resource in their own language—not even a portion of the Bible.

Not only that, existing translations of discipleship resources are gradually losing their effectiveness over time.

CHAPTER 3

DISCIPLESHIP RESOURCES AND THE MARCH OF TIME

Disciples of Jesus in every people group of the world need adequate discipleship resources in their own languages. Although the discipleship resources needed may be different for each people group, they are necessarily dependent on a complete translation of the Bible. Bible translations and other discipleship resources are static works. They reflect the usage of a language at a point in time. Languages change over time, and smaller languages tend to change more rapidly. Discipleship resources must be revised periodically in order to maintain their usefulness.

~ ~ ~

When faced with a seemingly impossible situation, it is easy to inadvertently redefine the end goal in order to make it more achievable. This is especially the case when we consider the task of making disciples of all nations, and the kinds of discipleship resources that are needed in each language of the world in order to accomplish it. People who speak one of the handful of languages with vast numbers of discipleship resources are especially prone to making this mistake. We can easily take for granted how much we have in our own language that we use on a consistent basis for our own spiritual nourishment.

English speakers, especially, have access to more discipleship resources and sources of theological training than we can count. We enjoy the luxury of a nearly endless supply of commentaries, concordances, lexicons, interlinear Bibles, Strong's numbers with original language assistance, study guides, books on every Biblical theme, books on systematic theology, books on how to evangelize your neighbor, books on how to witness to people of other religions, exegetical helps, maps of Biblical lands and events in Bible times, illustrations of life and culture in Bible times, hundreds of different versions of the Bible in English (some specifically for teens, mothers, young adults, etc.), Christian broadcasts on television and radio, and so on.

This abundance of discipleship resources is a wonderful thing and a tremendous help to spiritual growth! But it may be quite difficult for us to comprehend the immense spiritual need experienced by speakers of smaller languages who cannot fathom the richness of discipleship resources we enjoy. We must be careful not to take such blessings for granted or implicitly suggest that other languages in the world should make do with meager rations, while we enjoy a seemingly endless spiritual feast.

Is an Evangelistic Movie and a New Testament Enough?

Encouraging progress is being made in Bible translation and the translation of films about the life of Christ. Seeing this progress, it is easy to start thinking that the task of "equipping the global church to grow in spiritual maturity" is approaching completion. The default assumption is often that if we just keep plugging away at things and work harder, we will get there. This assumption needs to be reconsidered.

These *are* tremendous steps in the right direction. But the completed translation of some Scripture portions and an evangelistic movie in a given language does not mean we have finished the task of making disciples of that particular people group—there is still far more to be done. Look at it this way: would you be able to survive spiritually and grow to maturity as a follower of Jesus if the only discipleship resources you ever had available to you in your language were an evangelistic movie and a New Testament? No teaching courses, no study guides, no Bible handbook, no concordance, no seminary, no systematic theology, and no pastor who has any of these. A movie and a New Testament would certainly be valuable and useful. But would they be enough to grow in knowledge (2 Peter 1:5; 3:18) as mature disciples of Christ (not just converts to Christianity)?

Of the nearly 7,000 languages in the world, just over 1,200 have a complete translation of the New Testament.[1] Having a translated New Testament is a good starting point for equipping the believers who speak these languages to grow in spiritual maturity. But some concerning trends can occur in people groups who have only received a New Testament in their language, because they have a critically incomplete understanding of the whole Word of God.

One area of concern is that the missing context of the Old Testament can tend to result in a lack of understanding of God's holiness and wrath against sin. The realization of mankind's absolutely desperate need for His grace can thus become muted. There may also be a lack of understanding about God's purposes in the Old Testament in general and in the nation of Israel, specifically. The pivotal events of the Exodus, the detail of the Law, the purpose of the sacrificial system, the imagery of the Temple, the richness of the

---

1   The current total is 518 languages with a complete Bible, 1,275 with the New Testament, and an additional 1,005 languages that have some Scripture portions. "Scripture Access Statistics 2012."

Psalms, the wisdom of the Proverbs, the prophecies of the Messiah, the promises of the Prophets, the shock that Gentiles are now included as the people of God by faith—all of this and everything else in the Old Testament is lacking for people groups who only receive a translation of the New Testament.

Of the nearly 7,000 languages in the world, about 500 have a complete Bible.[2] Having a Bible in their own language is the essential foundation for spiritual maturity among believers in any people group. But even a translation of the complete Bible is not the sum total of discipleship resources needed for the spiritual growth and maturity of a people group. We are quick to affirm the Reformation rallying cry of *sola scriptura*, and this is correct—the Word of God alone is the authority on all matters of "life and godliness" (2 Peter 1:3). But the Word of God is to be correctly understood and applied in each ethnolinguistic context, and then the "living and active" Word of God (Hebrews 4:12) will bring about spiritual maturity. Discipleship resources help transfer this important knowledge, fulfilling an important function in the spiritual growth of the global church.

Let's Be Unrealistic for a Moment

In a perfect world, every language would have a translation of the whole Bible and key discipleship resources that help teach and contextualize the Bible so that it can be accurately understood by speakers of that language. Given the reality of nearly 7,000 languages in existence and the sheer amount of time it takes to translate just the New Testament into these languages, the notion of every language having the entire Bible and other additional discipleship resources can seem completely unrealistic. After all, translation alone is not the only aspect to be considered. There are other complicating factors that are also part of the equation.

---

2   Ibid

In the first place, we have already established the fact that the majority of people in the world are not "text-based" learners, but oral learners. So merely translating discipleship resources as printed books will not adequately meet their need for effective and accessible discipleship resources. We may not even know what discipleship resources that are effective for oral communicators look (or sound) like. What would an "oral Bible commentary" be like? How would "oral Bible study notes" work? The tendency is to be dismissive of the idea from the outset. But just because it may not have been done before and we—from text-based, academically-oriented cultures—may not be able to envision how oral discipleship resources could work does not mean they are not needed.

The Life and Death of a Language

Languages are not static. Over time, they can split, merge, change, and even die. This dynamic nature of languages is often overlooked, although it is a significant factor in world missions and has important implications for the translation of discipleship resources.

Languages Change

Speakers of common world languages that have millions of native speakers are often unaware that languages change over time. This is because languages that have many speakers and a strong written tradition tend to change very slowly. Some languages, like Icelandic, have changed very little in the last thousand years. But all living languages change, as the speakers of each language are affected by dynamic and varied forces. Changes in technology, social pressures, education, immigration, and many other factors can all play a part in bringing about language change.

English tends to change slowly, but we can see evidence of language change in just the last twenty years. New words have been added to the English language in recent years due to the rise of technology, like "Internet", "blog", "smartphone", etc. Meanings of certain words in politically charged contexts (often having to do with sexual orientation) have changed because of the social and political forces affecting them. We may not like or agree with the changes that happen, but the reality is that language change happens.

Throughout the centuries, hundreds of versions of the Bible in English have been created. A primary motivator for the creation of new versions of the Bible in English is to improve the clarity of the Bible in the English language, even as the English language changes. This kind of change can be seen by comparing the translation of John 3:16 from different points in history:

New Living Translation (1996): "For God loved the world so much that he gave his one and only Son, so that everyone who believes in him will not perish but have eternal life."

King James Version (1611): "For God so loued the world, that he gaue his only begotten Sonne: that whosoeuer beleeueth in him, should not perish, but haue euerlasting life."

Tyndale (1534): "For God so loveth the worlde, that he hath geven his only sonne, that none that beleve in him, shuld perisshe: but shuld have everlastinge lyfe."

Wycliff (1380): "for god loued so the world; that he gaf his oon bigetun sone, that eche man that bileueth in him perisch not: but haue euerlastynge liif."

Anglo-Saxon Proto-English Manuscripts (995): "God lufode middan-eard swa, dat he seade his an-cennedan sunu, dat nan ne forweorde de on hine gely ac habbe dat ece lif."

The significance of language change and the need for revision of Bible translations is illustrated by Tyndale's version of 1534 and the

King James Version of 1611. It is often assumed that the King James Version was created as a brand new translation directly from the original languages without influence from other translations. In reality, it could probably be considered to be a revision of Tyndale's original translation, seventy-seven years earlier.

Brian Moynahan, in *God's Bestseller*, points out that an analysis of the translations in 1998 showed that Tyndale's translation accounts for 84% of the King James Version New Testament and 76% of the Old Testament books that he translated. According to Moynahan, "the fifty-four divines appointed by James I to produce the final work provided marginal notes and scholarly revisions to Tyndale's existing translation, but the King James itself is, so *The Oxford Companion to Literature* states, 'practically the version of Tyndale with some admixture from Wycliffe'."[3]

Generation Change → Language Change

When I first began work in Papua New Guinea, I was part of a language survey team involved in sociolinguistic research. The team's responsibility was to help determine which languages were the highest priorities for new Bible translation projects. The priorities assigned to different languages depended on many factors that were researched and written up in reports.

Many of the languages in Papua New Guinea have fewer than 10,000 speakers each. Our language survey team was well aware of the potential for language change in languages having so few speakers. Because of the likelihood of language change, our organization had a policy that the reports we wrote about a language had a shelf-life of only ten years. After ten years had passed since the original survey of a given language, the report was considered obsolete and the survey needed to be redone. The reason for this is

---

3   Brian Moynahan, *God's Bestseller: William Tyndale, Thomas More, and the Writing of the English Bible—A Story of Martyrdom and Betrayal* (St. Martin's Press, 2003), 1-2.

that a lot can happen to a small language in ten years, and the language itself could change rapidly in that amount of time.

External factors often bring about language change, but not always at a slow, steady rate. Significant language change can often be observed at the turnover of a new generation. The language that parents speak may be noticeably different from the language their children speak.

I first encountered this while visiting with people in their villages during language survey trips in Papua New Guinea. We would ask them for a list of words in their language, so that we could compare it with the same list of words elicited in other villages. Many times, when we asked the people if they could help us as we tried to write down these words in their languages, they would say, "Wait! I'll go get one of the old men who speaks our language the right way." The way they talked, I expected that they would return with an ancient sage from a prehistoric era who spoke their language the way it was when dinosaurs walked the earth.

But almost without exception, the man they brought back was not an ancient, wizened guru from a long-forgotten era. He was an older man that was only *one generation* older than the people with whom I was speaking. Their language had changed so significantly in just one generation that they could readily perceive a significant difference in the way their parents spoke compared to the way they themselves spoke. And the way they spoke the language and the way their own children spoke it was also different.

Languages Die

Not only do languages change, they also die. More than half of the languages in the world have fewer than 10,000 speakers, and many of these languages have fewer than 1,000 speakers. Because of their small size (and a number of other factors), languages with relatively few speakers are at risk of dying out. Language death can happen in contexts where there is a dominant national language (like French in some West African countries) or an influential language that is more prestigious than the smaller, "minority" language. Parents who speak both languages may choose to use the dominant, more prestigious language with their children. When the children grow up, they may not even speak the minority language their parents grew up speaking. In as little as a generation or two, the smaller language can disappear, having no more speakers left.

The potential for the death of a minority language has significant implications for making disciples of the people who speak it. People who speak minority languages experience the same urgent spiritual needs as people who speak common languages. In the traditional way of approaching the task of creating and translating discipleship resources, the languages spoken by the smaller numbers of people are often ignored or left until the end. This raises some difficult questions. Is making the smallest language communities wait for contextualized discipleship resources until larger languages are served first an acceptable strategy in the task of making disciples of *every* people group? It is logical, but is it right? Is waiting for language death—thereby diminishing the number of languages into which translation is needed—a good strategy for making disciples of these people groups?

In many situations, speakers of these minority languages specifically want to undertake a Bible translation project to increase the status of their language and hopefully preserve its existence. The perception is often that "real languages" have the Bible in them. Translation projects in languages like these may be considered "high risk" and may only serve a few thousand (or even just a few hundred) people. What should be done in such situations? Should these people be denied the Word of God or other discipleship resources in their language because their language is too risky or, if we are honest, not important enough due to the small number of speakers? If so, what does that say about our missiological strategy as a global church?

But if we agree this is not an acceptable approach, then who is going to do the work, especially when translation of discipleship resources can take decades to complete? Maybe more to the point: how hard will it be to get funding for a multi-year translation project that serves a relatively minuscule fraction of the world's population, who speak a language that might be extinct in ten years? What kind of missiological and economic strategy will be able to go the distance and not exclude a language based on its relatively tiny number of speakers and the intrinsic risk of translation projects in it? Who decides what languages need discipleship resources, how many discipleship resources, and what those discipleship resources should be?

Teaching Them to Fish

There is a well-known proverb that goes: "Give a man a fish and you feed him for a day. Teach a man to fish and you feed him for a lifetime." This proverb is especially true when it comes to making disciples of every people group. A lot of work and expense that has been put into traditional missions has gone into "giving them a fish." The "fish" may have been a church, a church building, a translated New Testament, or even the introduction to Jesus, the Lamb of God who takes away the sin of the world. But merely "giving a fish" is a deficient strategy for making disciples of every people group, for two crucial reasons: first, it creates dependency and second, it critically limits the scope of what is possible in world missions.

Creating Dependency

A few years ago, I attended a conference and heard a veteran missionary tell of his work overseas. He had, like all the other missionaries at that conference, been given 5 minutes to present about his ministry. His enthusiastic slideshow lasted nearly an hour (of course) and was meant to provide an exciting update of "the missions work." Instead, it told a sad story of a weak, crippled church that had only ever known dependence on the missionary himself. Decades after it first came into existence, that congregation was still almost completely reliant on him for leadership and spiritual nourishment.

It is a tragic story, but do not miss the point. The missionary was *right* to go and plant the church in obedience to Christ's command. His intentions were probably noble and his motivations were probably right. But unless care is taken from the outset, it is all too easy to create a dependent relationship between the church and the church planter. Sadly, it can often turn into a co-dependent relationship, where the church cannot function without the church planter, and the church planter's reason for existence becomes wrapped up in the church that was planted.

The apostle Paul is an excellent example of "making disciples" done right. He was an evangelist who led many to Christ, and he planted many churches. But his goal was discipleship: believers growing in spiritual maturity, dependent only on the Word of God and the Holy Spirit who worked in them and in the local leadership of the church. Even a brief reading of Paul's journeys in Acts leads to the conclusion that Paul was reticent to stay in one place too long. He was quick to put the leadership of new churches in the hands of the people themselves. He was a pioneer whose aim, he said, "is to evangelize where Christ has not been named, so that I will not build on someone else's foundation" (Romans 15:20). Paul's approach to missions had the significant advantage of not creating dependency on himself.

The point is this: in world missions, it is imperative that we strive to "teach the global church to fish." Believers in a people group may be blessed for a season by being "given" a church building and ecclesiastical structure. But what they really need is to be taught how to grow spiritually and to obey everything Jesus has commanded us. They may benefit greatly from being taught the Word of God. But their real need is to be taught *how to teach themselves* the Word of God.

Believers in every people group need to grow in spiritual maturity and be able to continue feeding themselves from the Word. Those who answer the call to serve a people group must do so with the intent of equipping believers in that people group to equip themselves for spiritual growth. This may not happen immediately, but it is vitally important that the global church not be put in a position where they are necessarily dependent on others for an ongoing string of handouts. They "have not" but must not be put in a position where they are dependent in any way to the good graces of those who "have." They may need an immediate "fish" to help them today. But the task of making disciples is not complete until they have been taught "how to fish" and so be able to feed themselves spiritually for a lifetime.

Limiting the Scope of World Missions

Church planting is not the only area where we can have the tendency to create dependence. The traditional approach to the translation and provision of discipleship resources has, until recently, been modeled almost exclusively on a "give them a fish" approach. Missionaries learned the language and culture, developed an alphabet, taught reading and writing, translated the Word of God, and eventually gave the people a finished book. This is not an indictment or criticism of Bible translation. Millions of people in the last centuries have been eternally blessed by the work of Bible translators and those who have translated other discipleship resources for them. Up until recently, there was absolutely no other way to get the job done.

But there is an intrinsic problem with this model of "giving them a fish" rather than "teaching them to fish" in the context of creating discipleship resources. The problem is that the model is not capable of finishing the missions task adequately or efficiently. If everything depends on "us" (established churches and missionaries) giving "them" (new believers in least-reached people groups) translated discipleship resources, we put ourselves in the distasteful position of being the ones who decide which languages get resources, what resources they get, and when they get them. These decisions must be made for the simple reason that it takes a lot of time, money, and personnel to do a traditional translation project. There are far too many people groups, speaking far too many languages, needing far too many discipleship resources, for the "give them a fish" model to be an effective approach for completing the Great Commission. In spite of the significant progress made in translation projects of past decades, thousands of the smallest languages—which may prove to be among the most difficult translation projects—still have no discipleship resources. Less than 8% of the world's languages have the single most crucial discipleship resource: a translation of the Bible.

My point is not to find fault or exhort anyone to "work harder." My point is to suggest that we have assumed a "give them a fish" model in world missions for so long that we may have tended to minimize the severity and magnitude of the need. Tremendous advances are being made in the spread of Christianity in some parts of the world. But equipping these new believers with translated discipleship resources and teaching them to teach themselves the Word of God has not kept pace. The truth is, the situation among these thousands of people groups is desperate.

All Is Not Lost

Earlier in this chapter, we left a question unanswered: Who decides what languages need discipleship resources, how many discipleship resources they need, and what those discipleship resources should be? The answer is: the people themselves decide. Believers in each people group should be the ones who make those decisions for themselves. If they want the full Bible translated in their language along with dozens of other discipleship resources as well, they should be able to have them. There is no theological or missiological rationale for any element of the Church to say to any other element, "Your language is too insignificant and the expense too great —make do with less."

This notion may seem out of touch with reality. At least, it may seem that way when we look at the magnitude of the task without seeing the new and unprecedented opportunities that God has given the Church to accomplish it. If we look at the impossibility of the task in light of "giving them a fish", then it is indeed hopelessly idealistic. But the traditional way of doing missions is in significant need of reassessment in light of Biblical missiology and changes in the world in the last twenty years. There is an urgent need for a large-scale shift in world missions to "teaching the global church to fish." Our focus in missions needs to include teaching believers in other people groups how to translate and create their own discipleship resources. Instead of trying to do it all for them, they need to be equipped to do the work for themselves. Some of them will also become teachers of believers in other languages, joining together in the task of equipping the global church to grow in spiritual maturity.

Nearly thirty years ago, Ralph Winter exhorted the Church to not be content with having established Christianity in every country. Instead, he argued, God wants a strong church from every people group. In keeping with his challenge to the Church, we must also not be content to merely give some of the major people groups some translated Bible portions and an evangelistic video in their own language. Instead, the entire global church in every people group needs to be equipped with all the discipleship resources they need to grow spiritually.

Achieving this vision *is* possible, but it might only be possible if our goal is to "teach the global church to fish." The next step in teaching them to fish is to gain a better understanding of the new opportunities before us and how they can be used to finish the task of making disciples in all nations more effectively and efficiently. Two key factors create unprecedented opportunities for equipping the global church and the fulfillment of the Great Commission: the rise of the mobile phone, and the potential for the open collaboration of the global church.

~ ~ ~

Conclusion of Part 1: *Fulfilling the Great Commission requires equipping the global church to translate, adapt, build on, revise, redistribute, and use adequate discipleship resources in their own language.*

IT'S THE END OF THE WORLD
(BUT ONLY AS WE KNEW IT)

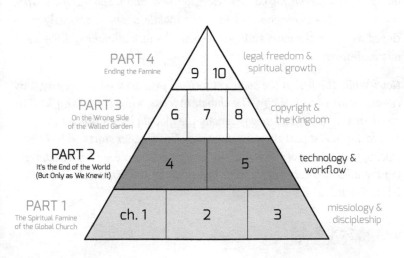

PART 4
Ending the Famine

9 | 10

legal freedom &
spiritual growth

PART 3
On the Wrong Side
of the Walled Garden

6 | 7 | 8

copyright &
the Kingdom

PART 2
It's the End of the World
(But Only as We Knew It)

4 | 5

technology &
workflow

PART 1
The Spiritual Famine
of the Global Church

ch. 1 | 2 | 3

missiology &
discipleship

CHAPTER 4

THE RISE OF THE MOBILE PHONE

The mobile phone has rapidly become the most widely used technology in the world. It is far more common than traditional computers, the Internet, and even traditional media like television and radio. Spanning cultures, countries and socioeconomic classes, the mobile phone is uniquely positioned as one of the most strategic tools in the task of making disciples of all people groups.

Note: While the first three chapters focused primarily on missiology, this chapter is about technology. The change in focus, while stark, is difficult to avoid, as the rise of technology among the global church is a very important factor in 21st century world missions. This chapter starts off by briefly tracing the "wiring of the world" for computer technology before addressing the missiological opportunities presented by the worldwide rise of mobile technology.

~ ~ ~

A few years ago, I found myself standing on a sidewalk in Thailand slowly coming to the realization that the world had passed me by. Overnight, it seemed, nearly everyone had acquired a mobile phone and was using it constantly. Talking in the mall. Streaming videos in noodle shops. Listening to MP3s while installing air conditioners. Texting while walking. Texting while waiting for the bus. Texting while riding motorcycles. The mobile phone was everywhere.

The explosion of mobile phones in popularity is not limited to Thailand. In only a few years, the mobile phone has gone from a technological novelty enjoyed by a few to an indispensable aspect of life nearly everywhere on earth. People that live on less than $2/day and have, until recently, been on the other side of the "digital divide" are now on the web, updating their Facebook status from their mobile phone in their village. What happened? And how did it happen so rapidly? The chain of events that leads to the ongoing mobile phone revolution starts with what is arguably one of the most significant developments in history: the dawn of the digital age.

From Atoms to Bits

The 20th century (and many centuries before it) was about tangible, physical goods. Industries and business dealt in atoms: manufacturing, transporting, and selling physical goods. Even sectors of society that dealt with intangible goods like education, information, and entertainment were dependent on physical objects for the storage and transfer of information. Books were printed on paper (i.e. the "paper" world). Music and other content was recorded on vinyl discs and magnetic tapes. In order to get access to the content, like a book or a song, it was necessary to have a physical object with an actual physical imprint of the content on it. In the case of a book, the physical imprint was ink on paper. For record albums, the physical imprint was the groove cut into the vinyl. For video, it was the spool of tape with the print of each frame in the film (or, in the case of video cassettes, the magnetic patterns in the tape).

But everything changed with the invention of digital technology. Digital technology made it possible to represent the same content (like a song, movie, or book) as "bits" of digital information—a string of virtual 0s and 1s that a computer could interpret. Instead of needing a physical copy of the song, movie, or book, you could give a computer a "file" containing the digital representation of the content and there you were: reading a book or listening to your favorite song on a computer.

This may seem like a trivial change, and at first it did not change much in the day-to-day life of anyone except the computer scientists who invented it. But it would soon prove to be a development of historic proportions, one that would change the lives of virtually everyone in the world in just a few short decades.

The Computer Gets Personal

In the January 1975 issue of Popular Electronics, the cover story introduced a computer called the MITS Altair 8800, billing it the "World's First Minicomputer Kit to Rival Commercial Models." Most commercial computers in those days were huge and extremely expensive, putting them beyond the reach of most people. Two young computer scientists, Bill Gates and Paul Allen, realized that the Altair 8800 computer was practically useless to hobbyists without an easy programming language. So Gates and Allen got their version of a popular programming language to run on the computer and convinced MITS to sell it. This event was the beginning of the company known today as Microsoft.

In 1980, IBM designed a new computer, but it needed an operating system. Microsoft got the contract to provide it and the IBM "Personal Computer" running Microsoft's operating systems (DOS, later Windows) eventually became one of the most common computing platforms for the next decades. The IBM PC and Microsoft's software made it possible for anyone—not just technically skilled people—to join in the digital revolution.

In the years that followed, computer users became accustomed to a standardized graphical interface for word processing and spreadsheets. But the real revolution was still to come. The IBM PC was originally a stand-alone computer and transferring digital content like a word processor document from one computer to another required physically moving a floppy disk with the data from one computer to another. There was no alternative, until the computers were connected together on a network.

The Personal Computer Gets Networked

Computer networks had been invented many years before, but the technology on which the Internet of today is built was not developed until the 1980s. The invention of the "Internet Protocol Suite" enabled large, commercial computers to communicate with each other over a network. But large-scale "inter-networking" of those networks together—the Internet—had not yet taken place.

Gradually, the technology for networking computers together was also included in personal computers. In 1991, the standardized protocols of the "World Wide Web" were invented, which enabled anyone with a computer to "browse" to any website in the world and retrieve information. At the time, however, "browsing the web" remained outside the reach of average people using average personal computers, because of the lack of a functional web browser. That changed with the release of Netscape Navigator.

The Networked Personal Computer Gets a Web Browser

Marc Andreessen was studying computer science at the University of Illinois around this time. He had a vision of creating software that would enable anyone to browse the Internet. He wanted to "level the playing field" among the different computer operating systems by providing a consistent web browsing experience across all of them. He and his team of programmers built a web browser called Netscape Navigator, with the motto "the web is for everyone."

When Netscape went public on August 9, 1995 their stock price exceeded everyone's expectation, and by the end of the day, Netscape was valued at 2.9 billion dollars. Two weeks later, Microsoft released Windows 95, the first version of their operating system that had built-in support for accessing the Internet. The combination of a user-friendly web browser and an Internet-ready operating system was an idea whose time had come.

In very little time, Netscape became the fastest-growing software firm in history.[1] Up until the release of the Navigator web browser and Netscape's astronomical rise, major technology companies like Sun, Oracle, SGI, and Microsoft had been focused on interactive television. Now, these large companies as well as thousands of new startups began focusing on the Internet. Netscape had not only made web browsing possible for average people, it had also inadvertently set the stage for what came to be known as the "dot-com bubble."

---

1   David Sheff, "Crank It Up," aug 2008, http://www.wired.com/wired/archive/8.08/loudcloud.html, 4.

The World Gets Connected

From 1995–2000, hundreds of new Internet companies were started, called *dot-coms*. In the hope of finding another company as successful as Netscape, venture capitalists were quick to fund these new startups, often long before conventional wisdom suggested they were worth the risk. Some of the startups were extremely successful, like Amazon and Google. But the "dot-com bubble" started to collapse in on itself in 2000. Many of the startups went bankrupt after burning through their venture capital, often without ever having turned a profit.

Before the collapse of the bubble, however, something very significant happened. Some of the dot-com startups that specialized in laying fiber optic cable had laid cables underneath oceans and connected together many countries on every continent. Thomas Friedman, in *The World is Flat* explains it this way:

> The Internet boom led everyone to assume that the demand
> for bandwidth to carry all that Internet traffic would double
> every three months—*indefinitely*. For about two years that
> was true. But then the law of large numbers started to kick
> in, and the pace of doubling slowed. Unfortunately, the tele-
> com companies were not paying close attention to the de-
> veloping mismatch between demand and reality. The mar-
> ket was in the grip of an Internet fever, and companies just
> kept building more and more capacity. And the stock mar-
> ket boom meant *money was free! It was a party!* So every one of
> these new telecom companies got funded. In a period of
> about five or six years, these telecom companies invested
> about $1 trillion in wiring the world.[2]

So the world had been wired for the Web and the spread of the Internet around the globe accelerated rapidly in the years that fol-

---

2   Thomas L. Friedman, *The World Is Flat: A Brief History of the Twenty-first Century* (Farrar, Straus and Giroux, 2005), 72-73.

lowed. In 1995, the year Netscape went public, there were fewer than 40 million Internet users worldwide. By the end of 2011, there were nearly 2.3 billion Internet users worldwide.[3]

As significant as the Internet and personal computers were in the digital age, the mobile phone was on track to become an even more significant development. In 1995, at the start of the dot-com boom, there were only 2 mobile phone subscriptions for every 100 people worldwide. But that number was about to skyrocket. If current growth rates continue (and it appears they will), there will be more than 100 mobile phone subscriptions for every 100 people worldwide in 2013.[4]

The World Goes Mobile

Part of the reason I was surprised by the prevalence of the mobile phone in Thailand was because before moving there, I had been living in Papua New Guinea. That part of the world had not yet experienced the same surge of growth in the availability and affordability of mobile phones. When I lived there, mobile phones were so rare and costly that only the most wealthy could afford them. That changed rapidly, thanks to innovative mobile phone companies.

Bridging the Digital Divide

Digicel is a company that provides mobile phone service in impoverished and politically unstable countries. The approach used by Denis O'Brien, the founder of Digicel, in challenging contexts like

---

3   "World Development Indicators" (2010), http://data.worldbank.org/data-catalog/world-development-indicators *Internet World Stats*, 2011. http://www.internetworldstats.com/stats.htm.

4   Ibid; "World Internet Usage Statistics News and World Population Stats," 2011, http://www.internetworldstats.com/stats.htm

these is: Give phones to the masses and they will fight your enemies for you.[5]

This strategy, which had proven successful in many other countries, succeeded brilliantly in Papua New Guinea as well. Within a few months, Digicel made mobile phones available to hundreds of thousands of people who had never owned one before. By the end of 2010, there were more than 1.7 million mobile connections in Papua New Guinea.[6]

This same story is repeating itself in many other parts of the world. Entrepreneurs and large businesses alike are realizing that the so-called digital divide is a massive untapped market. They are scrambling to take advantage of this opportunity by making mobile phones and mobile services available to the developing world. People in remote parts of Asia and Africa are using mobile phones long before the electric grid makes its way to their villages. In most parts of the developing world, people are bypassing the intermediate technologies of personal computers and landlines by going directly from no digital technology to Internet-capable mobile phones in one short step. The mobile phone is bridging the digital divide.

Huge and Growing Fast

The mobile industry is the fastest growing industry in the world and one of the few trillion dollar industries.[7] It is growing so fast that statistics are often obsolete by the time they are published.

---

5   Bernard Condon, "Babble Rouser," jul 2008,
     http://www.forbes.com/forbes/2008/0811/072.html

6   "Asia Pacific Mobile Observatory 2011," 2011, http://www.gsma.com/mobile-observatory/

7   Tomi Ahonen, "The State of the Union blog for Mobile Industry - all the
     stats and facts for 2012," feb 2012, http://communities-dominate.blogs.
     com/brands/2012/02/the-state-of-the-union-blog-for-mobile-industry-
     all-the-stats-and-facts-for-2012.html

That said, these numbers may help to paint the picture of the phenomenal growth of the mobile phone at the time of writing:

- In 2006 there were 2.7 billion mobile phone subscriptions worldwide, with 1.6 billion of them in the developing world. By the end of 2012, there were approximately 6.7 billion mobile phone subscriptions worldwide. Around 5 billion of those subscriptions were in the developing world, primarily India and China. In five years, nearly 3 billion mobile subscriptions were activated in the developing world![8]

- 9 out of 10 mobile phones sold worldwide in 2011 included a web browser and were capable of accessing the Internet. (Note that this includes all phones, not just "smartphones.")[9]

- Smartphones accounted for only 25% of the phones in use worldwide in 2012.[10]

- Nearly 3/4 of all mobile phones sold worldwide in 2011 included a memory card slot and had media playing capabilities.[11]

---

8   Ahonen, Tomi. "Latest Mobile Numbers for End of Year 2012 - This Is Getting Humongous." *Communities Dominate Brands*, 19 dec 2012. http://communities-dominate.blogs.com/brands/2012/12/latest-mobile-numbers-for-end-of-year-2012-this-is-getting-humongous.html.; "Key Global Telecom Indicators for the World Telecommunication Service Sector," nov 2011, http://www.itu.int/ITU-D/ict/statistics/at_glance/KeyTelecom.html.

9   Tomi Ahonen, "Communities Dominate Brands: Latest Annual Edition of TomiAhonen Almanac 2012 is now released. Lets share some data from it," feb 2012, http://communities-dominate.blogs.com/brands/2012/02/latest-annual-edition-of-tomiahonen-almanac-2012-is-now-released-lets-share-some-data-from-it.html

10   Ahonen, Tomi. "Latest Mobile Numbers for End of Year 2012 - This Is Getting Humongous." *Communities Dominate Brands*, 19 dec 2012. http://communities-dominate.blogs.com/brands/2012/12/latest-mobile-numbers-for-end-of-year-2012-this-is-getting-humongous.html.

- Africa has the highest rate of growth in mobile subscriptions among major world regions. By the end of 2012, Africa had more than 750 million mobile subscriptions and was predicted to reach 1 billion by the end of 2015.[12]

- China has more than 1 billion mobile phone users, with India not far behind (nearly 900 million in 2011), bringing the total mobile connections in the Asia-Pacific region to over 3 billion.[13]

- China has more people using the mobile web than the U.S. has people. Over 538 million Chinese use the Internet and 72% of them (388 million) access the Internet from their mobile phones.[14]

- 100% mobile phone penetration worldwide—when the number of mobile phone subscriptions equals the population of the world—will occur sometime in 2013, if current growth rates continue. More than 100 countries already

11 Tomi Ahonen, "Preview of Mobile Stats to End of Year 2010: 5.2 Billion subscribers, 350M people got their first phone this year.," nov 2010, http://communities-dominate.blogs.com/brands/2010/11/preview-of-mobile-stats-to-end-of-year-2010-52-billion-subscribers-350m-people-got-their-first-phone.html

12 Reed, Matthew. "Press Release: Africa Mobile Subscriptions Count to Cross 750 Million Mark in Fourth Quarter of 2012." *Informa Telecoms & Media*, 12 nov 2012. http://blogs.informatandm.com/6384/press-release-africa-mobile-subscriptions-count-to-cross-750-million-mark-in-fourth-quarter-of-2012/.

13 "China mobile phone users exceed 1 billion," mar 2012, http://www.shanghaidaily.com/nsp/Business/2012/03/30/China%2Bmobile%2Bphone%2Busers%2Bexceed%2B1%2Bbillion/; "Information Note to the Press (Press Release No. 05/2012)" (Telecom Regulatory Authority of India, jan 2012), http://www.trai.gov.in/WriteReadData/trai/upload/PressReleases/859/Press_Release_Nov-11.pdf; "Analysis — Mobile Asia Congress 2011," 2011, http://www.wirelessintelligence.com/analysis/2011/11/mobile-asia-congress-2011/

14 "Mobile Web Overtakes PC Web in China." *mobiThinking*, 17 oct 2012. http://mobithinking.com/blog/mobile-web-overtake-in-china.

have more mobile phone subscriptions than people, and some already have twice as many mobile phone subscriptions as people.[15]

■ 4 out of every 5 mobile connections is in the developing world.[16]

■ In 2013, mobile phones are expected to overtake PCs as the most common Internet access device worldwide.[17]

Numbers like these often raise a question: What is it about the mobile phone that has resulted in such phenomenal growth in just a few years, even in the developing parts of the world?

The mobile phone is unlike any other technology in that it provides unprecedented opportunities and functionality at a relatively low price. One of the most basic and essential advantages of the mobile phone is that it enables people to communicate and stay socially connected at a very personal level. At the same time, the mobile

---

15   Ahonen, Tomi. "Latest Mobile Numbers for End of Year 2012 - This Is Getting Humongous." *Communities Dominate Brands*, 19 dec 2012. http://communities-dominate.blogs.com/brands/2012/12/latest-mobile-numbers-for-end-of-year-2012-this-is-getting-humongous.html.; "Asia Pacific Mobile Observatory 2011.", 10. There are many reasons why the number of mobile subscriptions may outnumber people. In many parts of the world, people have more than one SIM card for their mobile phone, often because it is cheaper to make calls to contacts using the same mobile service. Some people travel to other countries and have different mobile phone subscriptions in each country. Some people have multiple mobile devices (e.g. a smartphone and a tablet), each with its own mobile subscription. In addition to scenarios like these ("multiple subscriptions per person"), it should also be noted that in some parts of the world it is not uncommon for a single mobile subscription to be used by an entire extended family ("multiple people per subscription").

16   "Snapshot: Developing world accounts for four in every five mobile connections" (2010), https://www.wirelessintelligence.com/print/snapshot/101021.pdf

17   "Gartner Highlights Key Predictions for IT Organizations and Users in 2010 and Beyond," jan 2010, http://www.gartner.com/it/page.jsp?id=1278413

phone also provides significant economic and educational opportunities.

Economic Opportunities

The classic example is of the fisherman coming in from the sea with his catch and phoning ahead to the various ports to find the best price for selling his fish. In other parts of the world, a betel nut seller can continue selling in the marketplace and use his mobile phone to ask his suppliers if a new shipment has come in yet. Before the mobile phone, he would have needed to leave the market (losing sales) in order to check on the shipment. Now he can accomplish both tasks simultaneously.

The mobile phone enables opportunities like these all over the world, by connecting every point in the business "chain" in ways that were not previously possible. The usefulness of the mobile phone also extends beyond merely making phone calls to business contacts. It is increasingly being used in the management and transfer of money. In fact, the development and use of mobile banking and financial services is one of the areas where the developing world has surpassed the developed world.

In 2007, Safaricom launched a financial service in Kenya for mobile phones called M-Pesa ("pesa" is Swahili for "money"). The service enabled Kenyans to transfer money to friends, merchants, and others simply by sending them a text message. Taxi drivers could receive payments without carrying cash. Vendors could be paid without money changing hands. The service grew rapidly and reported over 14 million users by the end of 2011. According to the International Monetary Fund, "M-Pesa now processes more transactions domestically within Kenya than Western Union does globally, and provides mobile banking facilities to more than 70 per cent of the country's adult population."[18]

Educational Opportunities

The mobile phone also provides educational opportunities that would not otherwise be available to people in the developing world. An article in the *The Economist* describes how mobile phones facilitate education in developing countries like China:

> Jim Lee, a manager at Nokia's Beijing office, says he was surprised to find that university students in remote regions of China were buying Nokia Nseries smart-phones, costing several months of their disposable income. Such handsets are status symbols, but there are also pragmatic reasons to buy them. With up to eight students in each dorm room, phones are often the only practical way for students to access the web for their studies. And smart-phones are expensive, but operators often provide great deals on data tariffs to attract new customers.[19]

This kind of scenario is becoming increasingly common in developing countries all over the world. In many countries, access to the Internet over a mobile phone is billed by how much you download, rather than requiring an expensive monthly subscription. Because of this, people living in countries where land lines and broadband connections are far beyond their means can often access information over the Internet on their mobile phones at minimal cost.

---

18   "M-Pesa transactions surpass Western Union moves across the globe - Business News," oct 2011,
http://www.nation.co.ke/business/news/-/1006/1258864/-/4hyt6qz/-/index.html

19   "Monitor: The meek shall inherit the web," *The Economist* (sep 2008),
http://www.economist.com/node/11999307

Personal Technology

In addition to being an indispensable tool for communication, economic advancement, and educational opportunities, the mobile phone is a very personal technology. It is the hub that connects many aspects of a person's life, including who they know, how they communicate, what music they listen to, what videos they watch, what they have scheduled, and where they are going.

It may be due in part to the highly personal nature of the mobile phone that it is accepted as an "insider" in cultures all over the world. Indians in the Amazon rainforest who still hunt with bows and arrows now also carry their cell phones with them. People visiting the most barren parts of the African wilderness are surprised to hear the familiar ringtone of a Nokia mobile phone, miles from the nearest town. The richest of the rich have mobile phones. The poorest of the poor, living in slums in some of the most destitute parts of the world often have mobile phones too.

Keeping these personal tools charged up can be a challenge in some parts of the world, but necessity is proving to be the mother of invention. Some people charge their phones off car batteries, inverters on bicycles, and solar panels. The back of some phones have a built-in solar panel to charge the phone. People in some African villages that do not have electricity send their mobile phones with the driver of the local "bush taxi" into the nearest town, where he drops them off at the local phone-charging kiosks. At the end of the day, the driver pays the kiosk owner and returns the phones to their respective owners in the village, who then pay him for the service. The process is repeated whenever the phones need charging.

Daily life for people all over the world is being shaped by the mobile phone. Keith Williams, founder of Mobile Advance, worked for many years with nomadic people groups of North Africa. He notes that mobile technology has become such an important factor for these people that they no longer decide where to set up camp on the basis of where they can find water. Rather, campsites are determined by where they can get mobile phone coverage. In *The Little Phone That Could*, Williams writes:

> It took meeting Abu Mohammed at my neighbor's funeral to realize just how far things had developed. As it turned out, he was a man who fulfilled all the noble ideals of his people —living in the remote desert in a black goat hair tent, having a reputation for hospitality and generosity, and excelling as a big-game tracker and hunter. After the commemorative dinner in the mourning tent, Abu Mohammed took the role of emcee for the evening, regaling us with tales of his hunting exploits and the skills he had used to track down and kill his prey. I was amazed when he produced a mobile phone from his pocket and pulled up a video showing him brandishing his scoped hunting rifle as he posed next to various animals he had bagged. Wow! Not only had this forty-something "man's man" embodying the ideals of his people taken his video clips and assembled them into an impressive show on his phone, but he had even added a popular local tune in the background. Yes, I had known that the mobile phone was making tremendous inroads among these people, but this meshing of all that was truly and agelessly representative of their culture with the latest and greatest of the 21st century took my breath away![20]

The Digital Library of the Global Church

The worldwide rise of the mobile phone and its adoption by people groups all over the planet presents an unprecedented opportunity for the advance of the Gospel. In a very short amount of time, ev-

---

20   Keith Williams, "The Little Phone That Could: Mobile-Empowered Ministry," *International Journal of Frontier Missiology* 27 (2010): 139–145, http://ijfm.org/PDFs_IJFM/27_3_PDFs/mobile_williams.pdf

eryone, everywhere in the world will own (or have access to) an Internet-capable mobile phone with a built-in media player. Never
before in history have people in nearly every people group in the
world equipped themselves with the technology to read, hear, and
experience the Word of God. The mobile phone is becoming the
digital library of the global church.

Some ministries are starting to realize the incredible potential of
the mobile phone for getting multimedia evangelistic content into
the pockets of the people they are seeking to reach. A Christian
evangelist in India tells the story of trying to witness to Hindu students at a university. The young man he spoke to was not interested in hearing about Jesus. So the evangelist pulled out his phone
and started watching an evangelistic video on it. The Hindu student
was curious and came over to see what he was watching. "Here,"
the evangelist told him, "you can have your own copy." Using his
phone's Bluetooth radio, he
wirelessly transferred a copy
of the video to the other phone
and told him to watch it and
share it with his friends.

> Never before in history
> have people in nearly
> every people group in
> the world equipped
> themselves with the
> technology to read,
> hear, and experience
> the Word of God.

Later that day, the student told
the evangelist that he had
shared the evangelistic video
with 40 of his colleagues, who
were also Hindus. These university students frequently
share videos from phone to
phone, rapidly spreading the
latest interesting media among themselves. By using the students'
own patterns of social media sharing, the evangelist was able to
gain a hearing for the Gospel where one was not possible before.

The mobile phone is more than just a library for consuming content, however, and its usefulness as a tool for the advance of God's
Kingdom is not limited to evangelism. One of the most important

qualities of mobile phones is that *they are devices to create content*, as well as consume it. The capabilities built into many mobile phones today make them ideally suited for creating audio, video, and even text content. It is the Gutenberg press of the oral and developing world.

The mobile phone makes possible the open collaboration of the global church in the task of making disciples of all nations.

CHAPTER 5

OPEN COLLABORATION AND THE GLOBAL CHURCH

In the pre-digital "paper" era, large, complex projects could only occur in industry (private production) or government (public production). With the advent of the digital era, where content is comprised of "bits" of digital data, a new means of accomplishing such projects has emerged. Social production, using computing devices connected via the Internet, enables a geographically-distributed team of self-selecting individuals to accomplish complex objectives by collaborating openly toward a common goal. Compared to traditional models, these objectives can often be achieved in less time, with better results, and at a near-zero marginal cost. Open collaboration is a model that can go the distance and meet the need for adequate discipleship resources in every language of the world.

~ ~ ~

In the middle of the 15th century, Johannes Gutenberg invented the movable type printing press. Printing presses were already in use, but they required carving out each page of text from a block of wood. The movable type printing press made it possible to arrange carvings of individual letters into any words you liked. Books, indulgences of the Roman Catholic Church, and eventually the writings of the Reformers could be printed on Gutenberg's press in a fraction of the time that it would have taken using the older printing technology.

In addition to the speed of printing, Gutenberg's press also significantly lowered the cost of printing. By the end of the 15th century, a printer with a movable type press could print over three hundred copies of a book for the same price that a scribe could make a single copy of the same book. This rapid and less expensive means of printing books resulted, not surprisingly, in an abundance of books.

The financial cost of producing books was lessened using Gutenberg's press, but the cost was still a significant one. The risk of printing hundreds of copies of a book that no one wanted to read could be disastrous for a printer. At first, the printers alone bore all the risk for the quality of the books they printed. Eventually, publishers became the ones who took on the risk of printing an unpopular book and incurring financial loss to their business.

In the five hundred years since Gutenberg's era, many new media have been created, including radio, television, records, video tapes, CDs, DVDs, etc. The technologies behind these media may be quite different from each other in some ways. But they are all built on the same core of "Gutenberg economics": massive investment costs.[1]

A "Scarcity" Model

Gutenberg economics are rooted in the "paper" era, where industries and businesses largely revolved around the creation and dis-

---

1   The concept of Gutenberg economics used here is borrowed from Clay Shirky, *Cognitive Surplus* (New York, NY: Penguin Press, 2010), 42–45.

tribution of physical objects. Dealing in physical objects is costly and time-consuming. Since both time and money are scarce, the cost of production is high.

For instance, it costs a lot of money to professionally publish a book. Not only are there massive costs associated with creating and distributing it (e.g. editing, formatting, typesetting, designing, printing, etc.), the cost of correcting errors is prohibitively high as well. If an error is found in the book, the publisher has to absorb the cost of recalling the offending books, correcting the error, reprinting, and redistributing the book a second time. If this happens too often, the publisher could find himself in serious financial trouble.

To minimize the risk of losing money due to poor quality (or poor content), the traditional means of creating media is tightly controlled at every point in the process by a small group of people in positions of power at the top of the industry. In the world of books, the content creation process is controlled by the publishers. In the realm of music and television, the content creation process is controlled by the music labels and movie studios. Regardless of the media, the pattern is the same: a small group controls every step of the process in order to maximize the revenue stream back to the ones at the top who control the process.

An "Abundance" Model

With the rise of the digital age and the ability to encode content as "bits" of information, what used to be scarce became abundant. Creating and distributing content became virtually free and almost instantaneous. Instead of requiring a massive financial investment to create content and distribute that content to the general public, anyone could now create whatever they wanted from any computer and instantly distribute it on the Internet for free. Correcting errors in an article published on an online weblog was as simple as clicking "edit", making the needed change, and clicking "save". The massive cost of creating and distributing content in the "paper" era had been reduced to virtually zero marginal cost in the "bits" era.

Not surprisingly, this reduction in marginal cost to virtually zero had massive implications for industries and people everywhere. Chris Anderson, in *Free: The Future of a Radical Price*, lists some of the differences that resulted from this massive shift:[2]

	Scarcity	Abundance
Rules	"Everything is forbidden unless it is permitted"	"Everything is permitted unless it is forbidden"
Social model	Paternalism ("we know what is best")	Egalitarianism ("you know what is best")
Profit plan	Business model	We will figure it out
Decision process	Top-down	Bottom-up
Management style	Command and control	Out of control

The rise of computers and digital technology paved the way for the monumental shift from a "scarcity" mentality to one of "abundance." But it also enabled another significant change: the potential for massively distributed, open collaboration among self-selecting individuals. Before looking at open collaboration, we first need to understand the context in which it came into its own.

---

2   Chris Anderson, *Free: The Future of a Radical Price* (Hyperion, 2009). This table, while generally helpful, can be easily misconstrued. For example, the management style in the abundance model (listed as "Out of control") could seem alarming to some, as it is not really out of control. Social production (discussed in the next section) is not anarchy. Successful projects that are built on an "abundance" model have management, leadership, organization, and control. But they are quite different from their counterparts in the "scarcity" world. For those who only understand the "scarcity" model, projects that are built on an "abundance" model often look as though they are out of control.

Social Production

Some tasks are so large and complex that they are best accomplished by teams of people working together, instead of by an individual. Building a road, for instance, is a large and complex undertaking. The building of roads is best accomplished by teams of people instead of one individual attempting to do the whole thing alone. Building cars is also a large and complex undertaking and is best accomplished by teams of people instead of an individual attempting to do everything alone.[3]

It used to be that accomplishing a large, complex task as a team of people could only be done in one of two sectors: the private sector or the public sector. In the private sector, accomplishing a task is governed by market forces and the task is accomplished if the financial compensation (sales) of the finished task is greater than the cost of assembling the team and completing the task (expenses).[4] Most cars are built in the private sector. In the public sector, a task is accomplished when it is deemed to be beneficial to the society, but is not compensated through the sale of the product. Most roads are built in the public sector.

The rise of digital technology (namely, computers and the Internet) has enabled a third means of undertaking large and complex tasks:

social production.[5] People who accomplish tasks through social production are driven primarily by intrinsic motivations (e.g. "having fun") rather than extrinsic motivations (e.g. "getting paid").

---

3   The analogy of roads, cars, and picnics is borrowed from Clay Shirky in *Cognitive Surplus*.

4   As we will see, the same pattern holds true for "free of charge" resources that are restricted by licenses in order to preserve revenue from donations.

5   Social production is also called "commons-based peer production" or just "peer production".

Most picnics happen through social production, as do neighborhood music recitals, and church potlucks.

Social production has always been an important aspect of society, but before the digital era, it had been necessarily limited in its scope. The primary constraint on social production in the "paper" era was that it was almost completely dependent on physical proximity. People who shared the same interest or wanted to accomplish the same task had to be in the same geographic vicinity for social production to happen. If they could not meet together in person, they were severely limited in what they could do together. It was still possible to make phone calls and coordinate some elements of a task or event, but the task or event *itself* could not happen. What the Internet and personal computers enabled was the possibility for social production to happen virtually instantaneously among people who were distributed all over the world, for free.

Some forms of social production (like the music recital and church potluck) still require being physically in the same location as other participants. It is hard to have a potluck over the Internet (something for which we can all be grateful). But other forms of social production have flourished in the online world. Hobbyists of the most esoteric strain can compare notes and interact with anyone else who shares the same interests using web forums. People who enjoy posting humorous captions on pictures of cats ("lolcats") can do so from all over the world. Citizens can join together in online mailing lists to discuss their concerns and bring about political change.

The ability to work together from anywhere in the world with others who share the same objectives has proven to be extremely compelling. The number of websites and web services that depend on this capability continues to grow rapidly. Today, social production is the foundation on which some of the most popular websites are built, including YouTube (for sharing videos), Wikipedia (for sharing knowledge), Open Street Maps (for mapping the world), and even some aspects of commercial websites like Amazon (their ratings and comments system) and eBay (establishing the trustworthiness of a buyer or seller).

According to Yochai Benkler, a professor at Harvard Law School, social production is the critical long-term shift caused by the Internet. It is, in some contexts, more efficient than either public production (governments) or private production (firms and markets). Social production in the Internet era is sustainable and is moving fast, but it is a threat to—and threatened by—existing industrial models.[6]

Open Collaboration and Crowd-Sourcing

Open collaboration is built on the model of social production, as opposed to production in the private or public sectors. This is the definition of "open collaboration" used in this book:

> An approach to accomplishing an objective that encourages and depends on contributions of self-selecting individuals or entities who are not formally associated (such as project staff and partners) with the particular cause or initiative.

An openly collaborative project, then, is one that anyone can join and to which anyone can make meaningful contributions without first being formally inducted into it. The only prerequisites for involvement in openly collaborative projects are the desire of the individual to join the project and the existence of a means to contribute to it. As we will see later, the possibility for anyone to be involved in an openly collaborative project does not minimize the role of "experts" in that project or result in anarchy.

---

6   Yochai Benkler, "Yochai Benkler on the new open-source economics" (Oxford, England, jul 2005),
http://www.ted.com/talks/yochai_benkler_on_the_new_open_source_ec
onomics.html

It should be noted that open collaboration is not synonymous with another frequently encountered term in the online world: crowd-sourcing. Crowd-sourcing is:

> The act of outsourcing tasks, traditionally performed by an employee or contractor, to an undefined, large group of people or community (a crowd), through an open call.

Open collaboration includes elements of crowd-sourcing, but crowd-sourcing certain aspects of a task does not make the task one that is openly collaborative. Crowd-sourcing can happen in tasks that are not built on a social model of production. An example of this is the comments and rating system used by Amazon. Amazon is clearly in the private sector, but they use a crowd-sourcing model very effectively to improve the quality and value of their online store. By encouraging and enabling anyone to submit their comments and ratings on a product, potential buyers of that product benefit by finding out in advance what purchasers of the product think of it.

The crowd-sourced ratings and comments on Amazon are one of the aspects of the online merchant's website that has made it very successful. But Amazon itself is not an openly collaborative project. For an example of an openly collaborative project, we will look at one of the most well-known software projects of the digital era: the Linux operating system.[7]

The Story of Linux

In 1991, Linus Torvalds, a Finnish student at the University of Helsinki, posted a message to an online computer newsgroup, inform-

---

7   Technophiles will rightly point out that Linux is actually only the kernel of an operating system and is incomplete without other utilities and software programs that run on it. In the interest of simplicity, we will not attempt to nuance the definition but refer to it as the Linux operating system.

ing the community that he was working on a new operating system for personal computers. He specifically invited feedback from the computer users and included a copy of the source code that he was writing.[8] Five of the first ten people who wrote back included improvements to the code Torvalds had written. The openly collaborative Linux operating system had launched.

At first, Linux was intended only as a hobby. But it gradually attracted more "hackers" who continually improved it. Soon Linux began to be used by commercial companies to power their computer servers. Eventually, these companies began to assign their own programmers to help improve the open-source Linux operating system. It steadily increased in popularity and soon became one of the most widely-used operating systems for computer servers that power the Internet.

Today, Linux is a massive operating system, comprised of over 13 million lines of source code. It powers everything from supercomputers (more than 450 of of the 500 fastest supercomputers in the world run Linux[9]) to mobile phones (Android is Linux-based and is one of the fastest growing mobile operating systems worldwide). Since 2005, over 6,000 contributors from over 600 different companies have helped to improve the Linux operating system.[10] These companies are fierce competitors in the economic arena, but they

---

8   The "source code" of a computer program or operating system is the set of instructions that tells the computer what to do. This code is written in plain text files and then compiled into a "binary" (0s and 1s) computer file that is used directly by the computer. It may be helpful to think of the source code being to the computer what a recipe is to a finished cake. If you know what the recipe is, you can tweak and improve it ("a little less salt, a little more vanilla"). But if all you have is the finished cake, you either like it or you don't—you do not know how it was put together. In the same way, if computer programmers have access to the source code of a program, it is possible for them to make improvements to the software. But if all they have is the finished program, they either use it or don't use it—improving it is not an option (apart from reverse-engineering the software, which we will not address here).

9   "TOP500 - Statistics," nov 2011, http://i.top500.org/stats

collaborate together in the creation of the operating system that benefits them all. They implicitly agree that "a rising tide raises all boats."

Why has Linux been so successful and impervious to attacks by vendors of commercial operating systems who have been severely threatened by it? One reason is that Linux is free of charge, so anyone who wants to can download the entire source code, build it, and install the operating system on any computer without paying for a license. There is no financial barrier preventing access to the operating system. Not only can anyone use it for free, they can also give away copies of it to anyone else as well. Free access to the operating system has been an important factor in the success of Linux. But even more important than "free of charge" access to Linux is the license under which the source code to the operating system is released.

Early on, Torvalds released the source code to his operating system under the GNU General Public License. This license gives anyone the freedom to see the source code, modify the source code, and redistribute their modifications to the source code (with or without financial compensation), as long as their modifications to the source code are also released under the same license. This makes it possible for computer programmers all over the world to openly and legally collaborate in the creation of the Linux operating system. It also ensures that the work they have done cannot be improved by others without those improvements being freely shared with the rest of the community as well.

The General Public License was specifically written to ensure that "what was intended to be open, stays open." Because of this, no commercial entity can buy the rights to Linux and shut it down to

---

10   Jonathan Corbet, Greg Kroah-Hartman, and Amanda McPherson, "Linux Kernel Development: How Fast it is Going, Who is Doing It, What They are Doing, and Who is Sponsoring It" (The Linux Foundation, nov 2010), https://www.linuxfoundation.org/sites/main/files/lf_linux_kernel_development_2010.pdf

prevent competition with their own operating system. The Linux operating system has been legally locked open.

Linux is not the only open-source software project built on the model of open collaboration. Many other highly successful software projects (like the Apache webserver, the Firefox web browser, and the LibreOffice office suite) provide additional examples of how effective open collaboration can be in the development of computer software. But open collaboration is effective for more than the development of software. It is also a highly effective model for the creation of content—massive amounts of content.

The Story of Wikipedia

Almost ten years after the launch of the Linux operating system, an Internet entrepreneur named Jimmy Wales and a philosopher named Larry Sanger started an online encyclopedia, one that would be completely free. They assembled a team of contributors and began writing content. But they quickly ran into a significant obstacle. Before potential authors could write articles, they had to pass an elaborate screening method, greatly limiting the number of contributors. The actual creation of content involved a tedious, seven-step process before content could be published online:

1. Assignment

2. Find lead reviewer

3. Lead review

4. Open review

5. Lead copyediting

6. Open copyediting

7. Final approval and markup

Not surprisingly, their encyclopedia progressed very slowly. Many months after the launch of their encyclopedia, called Nupedia, they realized something needed to change.

About that time, a new technology was invented: the wiki. Wiki software (from the Hawaiian word for "quick") puts an "edit" button on every page, enabling anyone to quickly edit a web page while also preserving a log of the edits made to each page. This makes it possible for large numbers of people to collaborate together over the Internet to create content, using only the web browser on their computer.

In January, 2001, Wales and Sanger set up a wiki version of their encyclopedia, called Wikipedia, where anyone could join and edit any article. By the end of January, seventeen articles had been created. By the end of February, Wikipedia had 150 articles, then 572 in March, and over a thousand articles by the end of May. The trickle of content was turning into a stream and then into a deluge. By the end of the year, 350 "Wikipedians" had joined the project and the site had more than 15,000 articles.[11]

In little more than 10 years, Wikipedia would come to have more than 20 million articles in over 270 languages, created by more than 15 million contributors. The open collaboration of geographically distributed, self-selecting people continues to create an immense encyclopedia that is the equivalent of more than 1,600 volumes of the *Encyclopedia Britannica*.[12]

Open collaboration is an effective means of creating vast quantities of content. But what about the quality of the content? There are many examples from Wikipedia's history showing that, at times, it has contained significant errors. The fact that errors exist in an en-

---

11   Marshall Poe, "The Hive," *The Atlantic* (sep 2006), http://www.theatlantic.com/magazine/archive/2006/09/the-hive/5118/

12   Wikipedia Contributors, "Wikipedia:Size in volumes" (Wikimedia Foundation, Inc., jun 2012), http://en.wikipedia.org/w/index.php?title=Wikipedia:Size_in_volumes&oldid=462112380

cyclopedia built openly by the collaboration of the masses, rather than small numbers of experts behind closed doors can give rise to concern.

This potential for error can be especially concerning when considering open collaboration as a model for creating discipleship resources. It is one thing to have misinformation and inaccuracies in an encyclopedia. It is altogether something else when they are included in discipleship resources where the eternity of those who use those resources may rest in the balance.

Can Open Collaboration Be Trusted?

Wikipedia is, for better or worse, one of the most widely-known examples of open collaboration in the digital age. This can be a good thing, because the success of Wikipedia points out the strengths of the openly collaborative model, especially in its potential for engaging massive numbers of people in the creation of vast amounts of content. But there is also a downside. It is all too easy to unnecessarily attribute the problems in Wikipedia to the model of open collaboration itself. There can be a knee-jerk reaction against what some have termed "the wiki model" as a whole because of the concerns with Wikipedia, specifically.

It follows, then, that any discussion of open collaboration as a model for equipping the global church to grow in discipleship must address this misunderstanding. The objective is not to defend Wikipedia, but to attempt to uncouple the model (open collaboration) from one of the most visible examples of that model (Wikipedia), in an attempt to allow the model itself to rise or fall on its own merits. To begin with, we will address one of the most common concerns about Wikipedia—the notion that it is untrustworthy because it is not created exclusively by experts.

When the Experts Are Wrong

The *Encyclopædia Britannica* was first published in 1768 and is considered by many to be the pinnacle of encyclopedic perfection. Written by over 4,000 experts—including some Nobel laureates—in various fields, it is widely regarded as one of the most authoritative sources of information on a broad number of topics.

In 2005, the science journal *Nature* published an article entitled "Internet Encyclopaedias Go Head to Head." In it, they compared the accuracy of Wikipedia and Britannica on a number of articles.[13] The question they were seeking to answer was this: if anyone can edit articles in Wikipedia, how do users know if Wikipedia is as accurate as established sources such as *Encylopaedia Britannica*?

To answer this question, *Nature* selected entries from both encyclopedias on a broad range of scientific disciplines. They had relevant experts review the articles without being told which article came from which encyclopedia. The results of the reviews were surprising.

Of the 42 entries tested, the difference in accuracy between the two encyclopedias was not as significant as might have been expected. The average science entry in Wikipedia contained about four inaccuracies, while Britannica's entries had about three. Of all the articles reviewed, only eight serious errors were encountered: four in each encyclopedia.[14]

When the results of this peer reviewed comparison were published, some immediately pointed out that the study confirmed what they had suspected all along: an encyclopedia written by volunteers is less trustworthy than one written by the experts. More discerning readers, however, made two very significant observations. The first is this: *Encyclopædia Britannica* had errors! Many people had been

---

13   Jim Giles, "Internet Encyclopaedias Go Head to Head," *Nature* 438 (dec 2005): 900–901,
     http://www.nature.com/nature/journal/v438/n7070/full/438900a.html

led to believe that it was unassailable "truth" on all topics that it addressed. The assumption is often that whatever is written in it is true *because it was written by experts*. But the evidence suggests that merely being written by experts does not mean it is free of errors.

Given the evidence that Britannica is not without errors in the 42 articles reviewed, some questions arise: What other errors are in Britannica, about which we do not yet know? What process does Britannica have in place for reviewing the remaining articles in their encyclopedia and providing timely corrections to errors encountered in them? Will Britannica provide a list of errata for the errors they do find, so that readers can know what the errors were?

It must be noted that Britannica, Inc. has never claimed their encyclopedia is error-free. But this points out a disturbing trend: it is

---

14 A few months after the comparison was published in Nature, Britannica published a blistering criticism of it and suggested *Nature* should retract it. They said it was "so poorly carried out and its findings so error-laden that it was completely without merit"("Fatally Flawed - Refuting the recent study on encyclopedic accuracy by the journal Nature" (Encyclopædia Britannica, Inc., mar 2006), http://corporate.britannica.com/britannica_nature_response.pdf, 14). They published their rebuttal in order to set the record straight, and "to reassure Britannica's readers about the quality of our content."

At this point in history, Britannica's business model was being decimated. In the "paper" era when printed encyclopedias were the only option, Britannica enjoyed significant profit margins and a healthy business model. With the rise of significantly less expensive digital encyclopedias (like Microsoft's Encarta) and free online encyclopedias (like Wikipedia), Britannica was experiencing significant economic turmoil at the time the article was published. This does not mean their criticism of the comparison is without merit. But it does mean that Britannica, Inc. was not immune to strong financial motivations for attempting to refute the article.

Nature responded to their criticism ("Nature's Responses to Encyclopaedia Britannica," mar 2006, http://www.nature.com/nature/britannica/index.html), asserting that their process for reviewing the encyclopedias was open, honest, and unbiased, and that they did not intend to retract their article. They pointed out that some of the allegations made by Britannica were unfounded, and that others applied equally to Wikipedia as well as Britannica. They also noted that Britannica took issue with less than half the points that were raised by reviewers of the articles.

very easy to begin implicitly assuming that if something comes from "the experts" then it is free of error (i.e. "truth") and need not be further researched. Studies like the one in *Nature* show that this is an unwise approach to "truth", because even the experts can be wrong. Sometimes, the error is due to honest error, without bias or ulterior motives. But if error or bias were to be introduced into the content created by "the experts" (which, by virtue of the fact that it came from them, is usually accepted as fully reliable), it would be much harder to correct. The centuries-long spiritual darkness of the Middle Ages bears witness to this.

A second observation about the results of the comparison between Britannica and Wikipedia is equally significant. Both encyclopedias contained errors in the articles reviewed. But only one of the encyclopedias was able to correct these errors within days of their discovery: Wikipedia.

> Both encyclopedias contained errors in the articles reviewed. But only one of the encyclopedias was able to correct these errors within days of their discovery: Wikipedia.

Wikipedia is built on an "abundance" model—creating and editing content is easy to do and takes minimal time to accomplish. The end-goal of Wikipedia is a web page that is easily published and corrected, as needed. Wikipedia's rapid editing framework (wiki technology) made it possible for volunteer contributors to quickly update the reviewed articles with accurate information from *Nature's* study, in very little time.

Britannica, however, is built on a "scarcity" model. It has a much more involved editing and review process, resulting in a much slower error-correction process. The model on which *Britannica* is built has a centuries-old goal of producing a printed book, although it is also available online (for a fee). The articles in the online version of Britannica were corrected as a result of the peer review, but there are still some pressing questions: How long will it take for the known errors in these articles to be corrected in the printed volumes of *Encyclopedia Britannica*? What do the people who purchased those volumes—in the belief that they were written by experts and so contained only "truth"—do now? Do they need to repurchase the encyclopedia? Do they get their money back?

Contributions, not Contributors

The goal here is not to glorify openly collaborative projects like Wikipedia or denigrate traditional projects like Britannica. Nor is it to suggest that the contributions of "experts" are no longer needed now that the masses can collaborate together—far from it. The point is that open collaboration, as exemplified by Wikipedia, Linux, and other "open" projects like them, levels the playing field by enabling a contribution to a project to rise or fall *on the basis of its own merit*, rather than on the credentials of the contributor.

In openly collaborative projects, the hierarchy of authority is not determined by the credentials of the participants. Rather, such projects are built on a "meritocratic hierarchy" where what matters is not the degrees a contributor possesses, or the title they hold, but the work they do. Critics of open collaboration often fail to understand that although this change in structure is significant, it is *not* a shocking slide into "radical egalitarianism." It is merely living out the Biblical principle of "by their fruits you will know them" (Matthew 7:15-16).

In an openly collaborative project, a contributor who consistently creates content of good quality, treats others graciously, and advances the project's purpose will rise in credibility and authority, regardless of their age, gender, experience, or education. Conversely, someone who does not contribute quality content to the project and is antagonistic toward other contributors will not be trusted or given authority in the community, even if they have vast education and experience in the topic at hand.

> In an openly collaborative project, a contributor who consistently creates content of good quality, treats others graciously, and advances the project's purpose will rise in credibility and authority, regardless of their age, gender, experience, or education.

This should not be a threatening situation to "the experts" who contribute to openly collaborative projects. The contributions of experts greatly increase the value and quality of the project. But the value and quality increases because *experts tend to contribute content that is of greater value and quality*, not because they have credentials stating they are experts. The shift is subtle, but crucial: the focus is no longer *who* created the content (thereby proving or disproving quality) but *what* the content is that was created. The proof of the content's quality is in the content itself, rather than the identity of the content's creator. If the contributor is an expert, their contribution to the project can stand on its own merit. But if they are masquerading as experts, their concern about the new way is not without basis. In meritocratic hierarchies, what matters is what you do, not who you think you are.

Shallow Errors

A significant advantage of creating content using a wiki platform is, to borrow a phrase from the open-source software community, "to many eyes, all errors are shallow." That is, not only can errors in the content be spotted by anyone, they can also be easily corrected by anyone. The wiki technology itself makes it easier to create good content than to create bad content. Given enough collaborators, a well-managed wiki tends to incrementally progress toward better, more reliable content.[15]

This aspect of wikis can seem illogical—it is hard to make the theory of it "work." Because of this, Wikipedia has been dismissed by many as a joke—an absurd project that could only ever result in unreliable content of inferior quality. But many people, once they understand the technology itself and see the result, have changed their minds. Kevin Kelly, former editor of *Wired*, was one of these skeptics who found that, over time, his view about Wikipedia changed:

> Much of what I believed about human nature, and the nature of knowledge, has been upended by the Wikipedia (sic). I knew that the human propensity for mischief among the young and bored—of which there were many online—would make an encyclopedia editable by anyone an impossibility. I also knew that even among the responsible contributors, the temptation to exaggerate and misremember what we think we know was inescapable, adding to the impossibility of a reliable text. I knew from my own 20-year experience online that you could not rely on what you read in a random posting, and believed that an aggregation of random contributions would be a total mess. Even unedited web pages created by experts failed to impress me, so an entire encyclopedia written by unedited amateurs, not to mention ignoramuses, seemed destined to be junk...

---

15   I use the term "well-managed" to refer to a wiki that is sufficiently open and permissive to provide its contributors the freedom to join the project easily, contribute directly to the content, and correct errors that arise in the content. The tendency can be to stifle the inherent advantages of the openly collaborative model by creating too many obstacles in the configuration of the software. As we will see, the definition of a "well-managed wiki" is entirely dependent on the wiki's purpose and its pool of contributors.

How wrong I was. The success of the Wikipedia keeps sur-
passing my expectations. Despite the flaws of human nature,
it keeps getting better. Both the weakness and virtues of individuals are transformed into common wealth, with a minimum of rules and elites. It turns out that with the right tools
it is easier to restore damage text (the revert function on
Wikipedia) than to create damage text (vandalism) in the
first place, and so the good enough article prospers and continues. With the right tools, it turns out the collaborative
community can outpace the same number of ambitious individuals competing...

Wikipedia is impossible, but here it is. It is one of those
things impossible in theory, but possible in practice. Once
you confront the fact that it works, you have to shift your
expectation of what else that is impossible in theory might
work in practice.[16]

What happened to Kevin Kelly continues to happen to many people. The "theory" of a wiki is hard to grasp—it has to be seen and
experienced in practice before it can be fully understood.

It is not just the theory of a wiki that is difficult to grasp. One of the
most frequently encountered misunderstandings about wikis is the
assumption that all wikis function in exactly the same way. Sometimes, those who do not understand the technology make blanket
statements about how the "wiki model" is deficient as a means to
create reliable content of the highest quality. They have concerns
about Wikipedia and assume that all wikis look and work like
Wikipedia.

The concept of a single wide-open, free-for-all "wiki model" is inac-
curate. There are actually many ways to configure wiki software. A
wiki can be completely open for anyone to edit anonymously (like
Wikipedia) or locked down so tightly that only a limited number of

---

16   Kevin Kelly"The World Question Center 2008," 2008,
     http://www.edge.org/q2008/q08_6.html#kelly

known contributors can edit the content, and then only over highly secure connections and with full names and datestamps logged on each edit. Want an example? Meet the wiki used by a U.S. intelligence agency: Intellipedia.

A Wiki Is Not a Wiki Is Not a Wiki

For decades, one of the primary goals of one of the top U.S. intelligence agencies was to find answers to relatively static questions about a relatively static enemy. The kinds of questions needing answers had to do with things like the number of missiles the Soviet Union had in Siberia. But the world changed rapidly after the decline of the Soviet Union. The terrorist networks the agency now faced were much more complicated and decentralized. This required the development of a more efficient means of collecting and processing intelligence on an increasing number of topics. This was a task much more complicated than their traditional, hierarchical model could accomplish.

So, in 2006, Intellipedia was launched. It uses the same open-source software used by Wikipedia, enabling the same ease of creating and editing content as the online encyclopedia. But that is where the similarities end. Intellipedia is, not surprisingly, on a highly secure, private network that is not publicly accessible. The only contributors to it are those who have the necessary security clearances, and all contributions are tagged with the name of the contributor. Because of the strengths of wiki technology, however, vast amounts of information have been rapidly assembled and collectively organized by the members of the agency. Within just a few years of launching the wiki, nearly a million articles had been created in Intellipedia.

This brief comparison of Wikipedia and Intellipedia suggests that the notion of a uniform "wiki model" where all wikis are alike is deficient. The same software can power a wide-open, anonymously-editable wiki (like Wikipedia) or it can power a highly secure, restricted-access wiki where all users are known and all edits are tagged with the author's name (like Intellipedia). The difference is all in how the wiki is configured.

So it follows that a wiki should not be considered an inherently scary thing and content on a wiki should not be assumed to be unreliable, just because it is in a wiki. All a wiki does is make creating content on the web much easier. The reliability of the content and usefulness of the wiki for a given purpose is entirely dependent on the processes implemented by the configuration of the wiki software.

Wiki technology provides distinct advantages for creating reliable content that is easily corrected when errors are discovered. The configuration of wiki software is an important key to ensuring the reliability of the content produced by the contributors. In the next section we will step back from addressing wikis specifically and look at what makes open collaboration work. Or, to put it another way: What makes the crowd wiser than the experts?

The Wisdom of Crowds

The research & development departments of many companies are in a difficult position. Year after year, they need to invest more in R&D to develop innovative products, but the profits are not there to support it. Not only that, some of the research problems have the R&D departments completely stumped and continually throwing money at the problems is not making them go away.

InnoCentive is a "knowledge broker" company that addresses this problem. InnoCentive connects freelance problem-solvers with the R&D departments of major companies like NASA, Boeing, DuPont, and Procter & Gamble. The R&D departments post their most challenging research problems on InnoCentive's website, and anyone who wants to can attempt to solve the problem, with a cash prize being awarded for a successful solution. Over 250,000 "solvers" from nearly 200 countries are in the InnoCentive network and have collectively solved more than 50 percent of the problems on InnoCentive's website—problems that have already bested the brightest minds in the R&D departments that posted them.[17] And this is where things get interesting.

The people who make up the InnoCentive network of problem-solvers come from a wide variety of backgrounds and fields of expertise. It is this diversity that is the single greatest factor contributing to the successful solution of problems posted on the website. A study conducted by Karim Lakhani made some interesting discoveries about the solutions made and the people who made them. His study found that the odds of a solver's success increased significantly when the problem was in a field *in which they had no formal expertise.* For instance, successful solvers of problems in chemistry or biology often had a background in physics and electrical engineering. The farther the problem was from their specialized knowledge, the more likely they were to be able to solve it.[18]

A second finding is equally intriguing: nearly 75% of successful solutions were made by solvers *who already knew the solution to the problem.* The solution already existed, it just needed to be connected to the problem. Connecting the solution to the problem simply required broadcasting the problem to a large enough group of people ("crowd-casting") such that the pre-existing solution known by the crowd could be identified. The key was not acquiring new knowledge, but in aggregating and utilizing the knowledge already available in the crowd.

---

17   "Facts & Stats," n.d.,
     https://www.innocentive.com/about-innocentive/facts-stats

18   Karim R. Lakhani et al., *The Value of Openness in Scientific Problem Solving,*
     2007

Diversity

InnoCentive illustrates a crucial aspect of the wisdom of crowds: diversity at a cognitive level is one of the most significant advantages of the crowd. The people who comprise the R&D departments of most companies tend to be homogeneous in their training and expertise. A pharmaceutical company tends to have chemists in their R&D department, while an aerospace company tends to have physicists, and a technology company tends to have electrical engineers.

Because the members of each R&D department contain a largely identical set of skills and training, they are limited in their ability to "think outside the box." The individual abilities and training of each member of the group may be extremely high, but what they are lacking is the diversity that would enable them to see solutions to the problems that are outside of their area of expertise.

James Surowiecki, in *The Wisdom of Crowds* explains it this way:

> Diversity helps because it actually adds perspectives that would otherwise be absent and because it takes away, or at least weakens, some of the destructive characteristics of group decision making... Adding in a few people who know less, but have different skills, actually improves the group's performance.[19]

When faced with a complex and involved task, the tendency may be to assemble a small team of the brightest experts with skills and training to accomplish the task. As heretical as it may sound, the best way to accomplish these tasks is actually to assemble a diverse group of people with varying skills and different degrees of knowledge, rather than having a smaller team with greater expertise but less diversity. Surowiecki explains why:

---

19   James Surowiecki, *The Wisdom of Crowds* (New York: Anchor Books, 2005), 29-30.

Groups that are too much alike find it harder to keep learning, because each member is bringing less and less new information to the table. Homogeneous groups are great at doing what they do well, but they become progressively less able to investigate alternatives... Bringing new members into the organization, even if they are less experienced and less capable, actually makes the group smarter simply because what little the new members do know is not redundant with what everyone else knows.[20]

To better understand why diversity is so crucial in achieving the best solution to a problem, consider MATLAB, the name of a programming contest started in 1999.[21] Contestants attempt to solve a classic "traveling salesman problem," submitting a solution in the form of an algorithm (computer code) that directs the salesman to accomplish the objectives of the problem in the fewest number of steps. The algorithms are graded in real-time and the results are posted on the contest website, with the leaders ranked by the efficiency of their algorithm.

But there is a twist in the contest: contestants can steal each other's code. Not only are leaders ranked on the leader board, but the algorithm they use to solve the problem is available for anyone else to see and reuse, either completely or in part. If a contestant can improve the efficiency of the algorithm, it could vault them into first place, where others can see and improve on their algorithm.

Rather than being threatened by this "plagiarism" of their algorithms, contestants are inspired by the challenge. The ultimate goal is not to win so much as it is to be the one who develops a brilliant tweak to a good algorithm that makes it a great algorithm and im-

---

20   Ibid, 31.

21   MATLAB is also a programming language used by mathematicians and engineers to solve massively complex problems. Both the MATLAB programming language and the MATLAB programming contest were created by a company called Mathworks.

presses the other contestants. There is a good deal of prestige associated with being the one who develops the key algorithm that everyone else copies.

The MATLAB competition illustrates the importance of diversity as one of the key factors that make the crowd "wiser" than the experts. Jeff Howe, in *Crowdsourcing* observes:

> The best coders have generally all learned the same tricks
> and shortcuts from years of using the MATLAB computer
> language. It is the inexperienced coders—the outsiders who
> have to come up with their own shortcuts—that make possi-
> ble the giant cognitive leaps that allow the winning solution
> to improve on the initial solution by so many degrees of
> magnitude... A diverse group of solvers results in many dif-
> ferent approaches to a problem.[22]

Shared Information

The MATLAB competition illustrates another important aspect of enabling the crowd to collectively create the best solution to a problem: being able to reuse the content created by others in the crowd. In MATLAB, the rules are thrown out and anyone can reuse anything without legal implications. This results in a tremendous increase in the speed of the problem-solving process and an exponentially greater quality in the resulting solution to the problem. Howe explains:

> The extraordinary aspect of MATLAB isn't the fervor it in-
> spires, but the fact that the ten-day hurly-burly—in which
> all intellectual property is thrown into the public square to
> be used and reused at will—turns out to be an insanely effi-
> cient method of problem solving... On average... the best al-

---

22   Jeff Howe, *Crowdsourcing: Why the Power of the Crowd Is Driving the Future of Business* (Crown Business, 2008), 145.

gorithm at the end of the contest period exceeds the best algorithm from day one *by a magnitude of one thousand.*[23]

This idea of specifically allowing anyone to reuse the work that has been done by others is one of the most crucial aspects of openly collaborative projects. It is a common factor in every open project that is successful. In Linux, the source code to the operating system is legally reusable. In Wikipedia, all the content is released under an open license that enables anyone else to use and reuse the content. In MATLAB, anyone can see and improve on the algorithms used by the leaders.

The importance in openly collaborative projects of being able to reuse and build on the content created by others cannot be overstated. Without this freedom, *open collaboration cannot happen.* When a diverse crowd of people works together toward a common goal and is able to build on and reuse the work that has been done by others, it is capable of accomplishing incredible feats—ones that would otherwise never have been possible.

When the Global Church Collaborates Together

God is raising up His Church, from thousands of people groups all over the planet. In people groups that were completely unreached with the Gospel as little as a month ago, there are now believers and young churches. These believers are different from each other in many ways: they live in different parts of the world, speak different languages, and come from different cultures. But they are alike in their fervent desire to grow spiritually. They are highly motivated and many are starting to translate discipleship resources into their own languages.

---

23   Ibid, 137-138.

It used to be that translation of a discipleship resource could only be done by a small team of experts. They would work together to create a translated draft of the content (like a passage of Scripture) then present it to a subsection of the community for review. This approach to translation was constrained by the fact that the technology to collaborate openly on a large scale had not yet been invented. The traditional translation process is firmly grounded in the "paper" era, with all its requisite challenges and limitations. The only way for people to collaborate in a traditional translation process is to be in the same physical vicinity. This necessarily limits how many people can work together on the project.

In the "bits" era of the 21st century, large numbers of self-selecting people can work together at any point in a translation project, using computer technology. All the strengths of the openly collaborative model can be employed in the creation and translation of discipleship resources in any language. We are in the earliest stages of what may prove to be one of the most pivotal eras in the spiritual growth of the global church.

Open collaboration is a model that is able to "go the distance" and produce translated discipleship resources in every language of the world. Open collaboration is the future of the global church. Pioneering mission organizations are already developing and testing software platforms that enable the global church to work together to translate discipleship resources into their own languages.

One of these organizations is The Seed Company. In 2011, they published an article introducing the Ganbi translation project in South Asia. This Bible translation project uses custom web software to enable anyone who speaks the Ganbi language to join in the process of drafting and checking the translation. The results, according to Gilles Gravelle of The Seed Company, were astounding:

> Within months, over 3,000 people participated via their own custom-designed Web site where the translation work resides. About 78 people were confirmed by the community as

quality drafters. Over 100,000 votes were cast, answering essentially the same questions: Is the translation clear? Does it accurately convey the meaning of the original texts? And does it sound natural?

All segments of the community participated. Significantly, women and youth were able to participate, adding their perspectives which are typically missing because of cultural constraints. Non-literate people were able to participate because the people chose to work in groups. People from seven regions, across denominational boundaries, worked together with surprising unity and harmony. And most importantly of all, they view the translation work as their own from the very start, and it is already making an impact in their community in ways we could not have guessed.[24]

Given the deep, spiritual motivation experienced by Ganbi believers, results like these are not surprising. And the Ganbi are not alone. Believers in thousands of other people groups experience the same earnest need for discipleship resources in their own languages, and they are ready to work together to help make it happen.

The Future is Bright! (Or Is It?)

Think of the vast numbers of discipleship resources that could be translated for effective ministry in every language of the world! The Word of God, leadership training materials, Bible study guides, commentaries, children's ministry resources, evangelistic materials —the list is massive. Think of the hundreds of millions of believers, in people groups all over the planet. Many of these brothers and sisters in Christ, who are desperate to grow in spiritual maturity,

24   Gilles Gravelle, "What Happens When A Crowd Translates the Bible?," dec 2011, http://blog.theseedcompany.org/bible-translation-2/what-happens-when-a-crowd-translates-the-bible/

are ready to start today to equip themselves with discipleship resources in their own languages.

The technology to openly collaborate in translation of these resources is spreading all over the world, even to the most remote villages of the least-developed countries. As the global church—from experts in Biblical languages to speakers of a minority language—openly collaborates together, with each participant using their God-given gifts and abilities, we could see an incredible surge forward in equipping believers in even the smallest languages with what they need to grow spiritually. The rapid development of adequate discipleship resources for the spiritual growth of every believer in each one of the nearly 7,000 languages in the world, *is possible.*

But there is a problem, and it is a significant one.

If we consider discipleship resources as a garden, the vast majority of that garden is surrounded by a wall and the gate is locked shut. Copyright law, in this analogy, functions as a padlock that enables rights holders to maintain legal restrictions that effectively lock the global church in thousands of languages out of this "walled garden."

Copyright law is not inherently a problem, nor should it be abolished or declared immoral. Copyright serves a good purpose and its use is both legal (government-sanctioned) and ethical (Biblically-sanctioned). The reality, however, is that the laws governing copyright were not designed to facilitate the openly collaborative translation of a large corpus of discipleship resources into every language of the world.

Many discipleship resources exist in some major languages of the world. There are, however, thousands of languages into which discipleship resources have not been translated and the speakers of those languages do not have the legal freedom to translate, adapt, build on, redistribute, and use existing discipleship resources for themselves. *This* is the problem, because this lack of legal freedom perpetuates the spiritual famine of the global church. Copyright law is merely the framework that makes it possible to restrict the global church in this way. Before proposing an alternative, we will seek to better understand what copyright is, why it was invented, and how it works.

~ ~ ~

Conclusion of Part 2: *The global church is already acquiring the tools and developing the capability to translate, adapt, build on, revise, redistribute, and use discipleship resources in their own language.*

ON THE WRONG SIDE
OF THE WALLED GARDEN

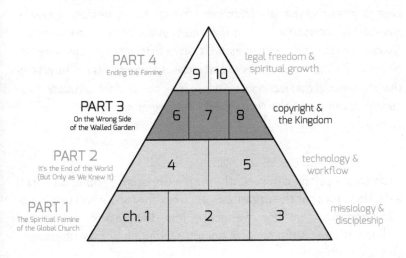

PART 4
Ending the Famine

9 10

legal freedom &
spiritual growth

PART 3
On the Wrong Side
of the Walled Garden

6 7 8

copyright &
the Kingdom

PART 2
It's the End of the World
(But Only as We Knew It)

4 5

technology &
workflow

PART 1
The Spiritual Famine
of the Global Church

ch. 1 2 3

missiology &
discipleship

CHAPTER 6

"ALL RIGHTS RESERVED"

Modern copyright law was invented to encourage the creation of content by granting exclusive rights to owners of creative works, restricting the distribution and use of the content by others. This creates an artificial scarcity of the content, which preserves a higher price for the content and maximizes the revenue stream from it. This revenue stream is preserved even for resources that are given away free of charge, because the exclusive right of distribution enables the content owner to use distribution statistics in an effort to procure donations. Given that copyright law has as its objective the limiting of access to and reuse of content, it is not surprising that it is a model that has been unable to meet the need for adequate discipleship resources in the thousands of languages spoken by the global church.

~ ~ ~

I received a phone call recently from a Christian brother in South Asia. He knew that the organization I work for focuses on using mobile phones as tools for evangelism and discipleship and he was calling with a specific need. "Can you send me a library of evangelistic videos that I can use on my phone to share the Gospel with Hindus?" he asked. "I want to be able to give copies of the videos to others so they can become followers of Jesus too."

As exciting as it was to receive a request like this, I was disappointed that I did not have any videos I could send him. "The videos exist and we have some access to them in English," I explained, "But they are encumbered by copyright restrictions and so it is illegal for others to redistribute them without permission. We are trying to get permission, but we do not have it yet."

There was a very long pause in the conversation. Finally, this brother in Christ said, "I do not know about this 'copyright restrictions' of which you speak. All I know is that I need discipleship videos on my mobile phone, but I do not have them."

A mission leader told me of the frustration they are experiencing as they attempt to make a book available to Christians in India. This discipleship resource is available on Amazon for $10, but getting large quantities into India incurs many additional expenses, including: shipping, import fees, and in-country shipping. The difficulties continue, as the books are unlikely to make it across provincial borders in India without paying bribes to border officials. If the border officials (who are usually Hindus) discover that the books are Christian resources, they might not let them across the border at all. Republishing the books in-country is not allowed, because the owner of the copyright on that book is not interested. Merely making the book available as a digital eBook does not solve the problem either, because the license under which it is released does not permit translation or redistribution of the content.

These are not isolated cases. There are many, many more like it, from all over the world. In the introduction to this book, we encountered the Bible translation team unable to use the translation software because of the restrictions on the discipleship resources included with it. In another part of the world, a classic book on systematic theology is only legally available to believers in that country when it is imported through official means at vastly inflated prices. In another country, a large ministry is unable to use cutting-edge technology for the advance of the Kingdom because it is denied a license to make the legally-restricted discipleship resources available.[1]

In other situations, ministry websites that collect and redistribute discipleship resources for the benefit of the global church have been shut down because they were not legally permitted to redistribute the resources. In other situations, individuals who need access to discipleship resources in their own language are legally prevented from using them as they need to for ministry, because they are unable to obtain a license that would remove the legal restrictions preventing their use of those resources. The list goes on, and on. Every day, in countless situations all over the world, the lack of legally unencumbered discipleship resources hinders the global church from growing spiritually. Stories like these are the *norm*—not the exception—in the world today.

What is going on? What are "copyright restrictions" anyway? And how have they become an obstacle to evangelism and the spiritual growth of the global church?

These are important questions that deserve answers. Finding the answers requires understanding how copyright law came into existence and how it works today. And doing that requires stepping back a few short years to Ireland in the 6th century and what may be the earliest documented case of copyright restrictions.

---

1   This matter of obtaining a license for legal use of a discipleship resource can be deceptively complicated. As we will see later on, it can be a very involved process even when transacted between entities with shared language and culture, and in direct contact with each other. When transacted across linguistic, cultural, and geographic boundaries, often without direct contact between the entities, the possibility of requesting and gaining legal permission to translate, adapt, build on, and redistribute someone else's discipleship resource tends to be greatly minimized. In this regard, the likelihood of being granted a license in such contexts is akin to winning the lottery.

To Every Cow Belongs Her Calf

Saint Columba, the Apostle to the Picts, had a problem. He had borrowed a book—a psalter, containing several Psalms—from Saint Finnian and made a written copy of it, intending to keep the copy for his own use. Presumably, Columba needed the Psalms for his ministry and assumed there would be no problem if he copied it.

Saint Finnian, however, did not see things that way. He argued that as he owned the original, the copy also belonged to him. Columba disagreed, maintaining that since he had gone to the effort of making the copy, the copy should be his.

In an effort to resolve the conflict, King Diarmait Mac Cerbhaill imposed this ruling: "To every cow belongs her calf, therefore to every book belongs its copy." Instead of resolving the conflict, however, the problem got worse. The dispute escalated into the Battle of Cúl Dreimhne in 561, during which many people were killed. Columba, facing the prospect of excommunication, chose instead to exile himself from Ireland.[2]

It is ironic that what may be the first documented dispute regarding copyrights had to do with making copies of the Word of God, and that it became so intense it launched a vicious war and exiled a prominent church leader. But what may be even more ironic is that, many centuries later, we still face the same problem. Violating copyright restrictions today is less likely to lead to war and exile, but the restrictions still create impenetrable obstacles for the spiritual growth of the Church. Mattias, a speaker of the Fanson language from East Africa, recently found that out the hard way.[3]

A missionary was working with Mattias and speakers of a number of East African languages to help them translate the Open Bible Sto-

---

2   Duncan Geere, "The History of Creative Commons," *Wired UK* (dec 2011), http://www.wired.co.uk/news/archive/2011-12/13/history-of-creative-commons

3   Names of languages and people have been changed.

ries project.[4] Because of the unrestricted nature of the project, existing translations of the Bible cannot be used in it. This is because the translations of the Bible that exist in various languages are, with very few exceptions, legally restricted in such a way that they are incompatible with the total freedom of the Open Bible Stories project. (The "why" behind this problem is addressed later in this chapter.)

The missionary gave Mattias and the other translators the text of the first story in English and told them the first step was for them to write a draft of the translation in their own language. They discussed how the drafting process should go, what problems they might encounter, and the solutions to those problems. Then the translators each returned to their respective villages.

A few days later, they brought back their translation drafts. But Mattias had inadvertently run directly into the same problem that Saint Columba had run into nearly a millenia and a half earlier. The missionary gave this account:

> Mattias brought his Fanson translation to class yesterday...
> but it wasn't really his translation. He said that God told him
> he needed to copy from the Fanson Bible. I found that
> strange because it seemed last week that he understood why
> he needed to make his own translation of the English text.

---

4   Open Bible Stories (www.openbiblestories.com) is a project started by Distant Shores Media to provide a visual mini-Bible in any language. The project is comprised of fifty key stories of the Bible that can be rapidly translated and made available in text, audio, and video formats at zero marginal cost. The stories are released under a Creative Commons Attribution-ShareAlike License that permits unrestricted redistribution and reuse of the content. This license will be covered in detail in chapter 9.

Open Bible Stories is closely tied to Scripture text, with some text providing theological education and explanation. Because of the open license under which all the content is released, copyright-restricted versions of the Bible cannot be legally "copied-and-pasted" into the project. The "all rights reserved" of the Bible translations conflicts with the openness of the Attribution-ShareAlike License. This conflict will be explained in this and subsequent chapters.

He himself explained how he understood me by giving the example that if I were to travel with him to his people, and if I were to speak the Gospel to them in English, he would need to translate my words in a way that kept the same true, Biblical meaning—but using words that his people would understand. He was right on. I explained to him again why we couldn't just copy from the Fanson Bible, because of copyright restrictions, and he said he would ask God about it again.[5]

Both Mattias' and Saint Columba's approach to the problem were perfectly logical. A ministry need existed that could be easily met by using a portion of the Word of God in a discipleship resource. The Word of God, in both cases, had been translated into the target language and was available. Therefore, simply making a copy of the Word of God would have met both needs perfectly. Most of us would probably agree that using the Word of God in the ways that Columba and Mattias did *should* be permissible. After all, isn't that why we have the Bible in the first place—to share it with others and communicate it clearly? But, because of copyright restrictions and the restrictive licenses governing the translations, it is not that easy, as both Saint Columba and Mattias discovered.

The dictate of King Diarmait Mac Cerbhaill in the 6th century stating that copies of a book belong to the book's owner did not turn into a large-scale codification of copyright law. The foundations of modern copyright law did not start until more than a thousand years later with the Statute of Anne in 1710.

The Statute of Anne

Gutenberg's movable type printing press had created a problem for book publishers. It made printing books much easier and less expensive, that is true. But it also made things messier. Now any pub-

---

5   Name withheld, personal communication.

lisher could print and sell any book, creating financial problems for the established publishers.

In England, especially, publishers were feeling the pressure. Rogue "pirate publishers" from Scotland were printing the same books and exporting them to England at discounted prices. The publishers in England were not amused and looked to Parliament to pass a law that gave them exclusive control over publishing.[6] Parliament responded by enacting the Statute of Anne in 1710 which granted the publishers' request for exclusive "copyright" (the right to copy).

The act stated that all published works would get a copyright term of fourteen years, at which point the copyright would expire. The initial copyright term was renewable for another fourteen years if the author was still alive at the end of the first term. Existing works at the time the law was passed were given a one-time copyright of twenty-one years. But the act included a limitation to the copyright:

> The Statute of Anne granted the author or "proprietor" of a book an exclusive right to print that book. In an important limitation, however, and to the horror of the booksellers, the law gave the bookseller that right for a limited term. At the end of that term, the copyright "expired," and the work would then be free and could be published by anyone.[7]

Two questions need to be addressed at this point. First, why did Parliament establish copyright restrictions in the Statute of Anne in the first place? Second, looking at the situation from the perspective of the publishers, why did Parliament *limit* the term of the copyright, rather than make it perpetual?

---

6   The Licensing Act of 1662 had expired in 1695. It had given publishers a monopoly over publishing, making it easier for the government to control what was published. But since its expiration, no law had been passed that gave publishers an exclusive right to print books.

7   Lawrence Lessig, *Free Culture* (The Penguin Press, 2004), 87.

A primary consideration in the establishment of copyright restrictions in the Statute of Anne was to provide economic incentive for authors to write more books. Without a copyright law in place, an author who wrote a book could expect little in the way of a revenue stream from it. If any publisher could get their hands on a copy and could print any number of copies of the same work without providing financial recompense to the author, the price for the book would rapidly drop to near the cost of printing it. Market economics would see to that.

So Parliament established copyright restrictions as a means to encourage learned men to write books, because this was crucial to the overall benefit of society. Societies are dependent on knowledge and information, and writing books is an important means of making that content accessible to society as a whole. Parliament knew that if there were no financial reward for authoring books, the number of books would diminish and society as a whole would be worse off for it.

But Parliament also realized that a perpetual copyright on books would be equally damaging to society. These events were going on during the Enlightenment, and the notion that knowledge should be free was a very popular one at the time. The logic went like this: if the advance of a society is dependent on the dissemination of knowledge, and if that knowledge is contained in books, then a state-sanctioned monopoly on the printing and distribution of those books would create a hindrance to society as a whole. If publishers were given a perpetual and exclusive right to print books, then society—being built on the knowledge contained in and transmitted by those books—would be held in intellectual captivity to the economic interests of the publishers. Prices on books would remain high, minimizing the number of people who would be able to get access to the knowledge. Society as a whole would suffer from a perpetual lock on the Intellectual Property contained in those books.[8]

So Parliament established the Statute of Anne, which attempted to get the best of both worlds. In an effort to increase the collective knowledge and richness of society, it established copyright restrictions to preserve the economic benefit to the content creators (and distributors). But in order to prevent the abuse of those restrictions and the resulting negative effect it would have on society, Parliament limited the term of copyright.

The Statute of Anne was challenged in court in 1774. The case was taken to the House of Lords, which functioned much as the U.S. Supreme Court does. The House of Lords upheld the Statute of Anne and also established the "public domain," where works have no copyright restrictions. Legal control restricting how works in the Public Domain are used does not exist. The publishers were chagrined at the decision and predicted their pending ruin. (They did just fine, it turns out.) But the decision was hailed by the people as a great victory.

> The decision of the House of Lords meant that the booksellers could no longer control how culture in England would grow and develop. Culture in England was thereafter *free*... in the sense that the culture and its growth would no longer be controlled by a small group of publishers. As every free market does, this free market of free culture would grow as the consumers and producers chose. English culture would develop as the many English readers chose to let it develop —chose in the books they bought and wrote; chose in the memes they repeated and endorsed. Chose in a *competitive context*, not a context in which the choices about what cul-

---

8   The concept of Intellectual Property was being addressed, though the term itself had not yet been invented.

ture is available to people and how they get access to it are made by the few despite the wishes of the many.[9]

This notion of a free culture and the balance of copyright restrictions with limited terms spread to other countries as well. The U.S. Constitution provides for copyright in Article I, Section 8. The copyright system was enacted in the U.S. in 1790 and was modeled largely on the same principles embodied in the Statute of Anne. It established U.S. copyright with a term of fourteen years with fourteen-year renewal. But, over time, the limitations of copyright were diminished and the length of copyright restrictions was gradually extended to longer periods of time.[10]

Different countries adopted different lengths of time and different restrictions, increasing the complexity of copyright law. Copyrights were not enforceable across borders, so a work under copyright in England could be published and sold by any publisher in the United

---

9   Ibid, p. 94.

10   In 1831, the term was extended to twenty-eight years with a fourteen year renewal. In 1909, it was extended again to twenty-eight years with a twenty-eight year renewal. Then in 1976, U.S. copyright restrictions were extended to seventy-five years (or the life of the author) plus fifty years. In 1998, these terms were extended one more time to the life of the author plus seventy years, or 120 years after creation of a work of corporate authorship (or ninety-five years after publication—whichever comes first). These are the terms still in use today.

This lengthening of copyright has been embraced by the Church with little discussion on the implications for ministry or the theology of intellectual property ownership and discipleship resources. Interestingly, the lengthening of copyright in the U.S. and its implications for world missions may have been directly affected by Mickey Mouse. Some have speculated that the lengthening of copyright terms are directly correlated to the expiration date of Walt Disney's copyright on Mickey Mouse and other characters. The Sonny Bono Copyright Term Extension Act of 1998 is sometimes called "The Mickey Mouse Protection Act", because of the alleged lobbying for it by the Walt Disney company and the fact that its passage prevented the first Mickey Mouse cartoon from going into the Public Domain in 2003. Joyce Slaton, "A Mickey Mouse Copyright Law?," jan 1999, http://www.wired.com/politics/law/news/1999/01/17327

States. Something needed to be done to bring uniformity to copyright law around the world. In 1886, in Berne, Switzerland, a convention was enacted to fix the problem.

The Berne Convention

The Berne Convention has significant implications for world missions in the digital era. As Christians from many countries and legal jurisdictions create and distribute discipleship resources over the Internet, it is important to understand that the Berne Convention is generally considered to be the "law of the land" for matters of copyright law in most countries.

What It Does – The Berne Convention, formally the *Berne Convention for the Protection of Literary and Artistic Works*, was enacted in 1886 to protect the rights of content creators internationally, as well as to provide strong minimum standards for copyright law in member states. It requires its signatories to recognize the copyright of content creators from other signatory countries in the same way as it recognizes the copyright of its own nationals.

When Copyright Happens – A content creator does not need to register the work or apply for a copyright in order for the work to be protected. This means that the "all rights reserved" of copyright law *happens automatically*, at the point of creation of the work—whether by publishing it, recording it, posting it online, or even saving it to a computer's hard drive.

How Long Copyrights Last – The Berne Convention states that all works (with some exceptions) are copyrighted for at least the length of the life of the creator plus 50 years, but member states are free to provide longer terms. In 1998, U.S. copyright term was extended to the life of the author plus 70 years (or 95 years from the date of publication for corporate works).

What Rights are Reserved – The rights assigned to content creators by the Berne Convention cover every production "in the literary, scientific, and artistic domain".[11] There are four primary rights reserved for the content creator that are spelled out in the Convention:

- *Right of Translation* – Content creators have the exclusive right of making and authorizing the translation of their works throughout the term of protection of their rights in the original works (Article 8).

- *Right of Reproduction* – Content creators have the exclusive right of authorizing the reproduction of their works, in any manner or form (Article 9).

- *Right of Public Performance and Broadcast* – Content creators have the exclusive right of authorizing the public performance and broadcast of their works (Article 11).

- *Right of Adaptation* – Content creators have the exclusive right of authorizing adaptations, arrangements, and other alterations of their works (Article 12).

The result of the Berne Convention is that "all rights reserved" is the law regarding copyright for most countries. This means that most creative works, created in most countries by pretty much anyone in the world automatically has certain exclusive rights granted to the creator of the work at the point the work is created.

What Everyone Should Know About Copyright

So where do things stand today, after 300 years of copyright law? These are the basics of copyright law:

---

11 "Berne Convention for the Protection of Literary and Artistic Works" (World Intellectual Property Organization, sep 1886), http://www.wipo.int/treaties/en/ip/berne/trtdocs_wo001.html, Article 2.

- If you create it, you own it.[12]
- Copyright protection happens automatically, when the work is created—you do not need to register the copyright first.
- If you own it, copyright grants you exclusive rights to the work: "all rights reserved."[13]
- The rights reserved for a copyright holder include: copying & redistributing the work, creating derivatives (including translations) of the work, publicly performing or displaying the work.
- You must get permission (usually as a license) to use what someone else owns.
- Copyright law is remarkably similar around the world: by default, no one can legally do much of anything with someone else's content for many decades after the owner's death, unless they get a license from the owner (or the owner's heirs) to do so.

Copyright Restrictions and Discipleship Resources

It is important to emphasize at this point that copyrights are not evil. Copyright law can be a very good thing, as it preserves the economic incentive for creating content, including discipleship resources. This is not an unethical approach to creating and distributing spiritual content. Those who own the copyrights on discipleship resources have every right to control their use as they see

---

12   There are limited exceptions to this, such as in contexts pertaining to "work for hire" agreements and scope of employment.

13   Note that this is not true "exclusivity" in the sense that the first person to express an idea has a copyright on the idea itself. Copyright law protects the *expression* of ideas from being copied, it never protects the underlying ideas themselves. An identical expression of the same idea can legally co-exist, as long as it is independently created without reference to the "original" creative work.

fit. In fact, up until about ten years ago, there was no viable alternative to the traditional model of "all rights reserved." Until the invention of a means of legally and accurately "open-licensing" content, this traditional model for equipping the global church with discipleship resources was the only model available to us.

Painting the picture of an alternative, "open" model can be a complicated undertaking. Unless it is approached with care, attempts to contrast the classic "all rights reserved" approach with a new alternative can start to sound antagonistic. The intent is not to criticize the traditional approach or antagonize those who employ it. Rather, it is to objectively discuss the role of copyright law in world missions and how copyright restrictions affect discipleship resources and the global church. In subsequent chapters we will address the specifics of the "open" model.

Discipleship Resources and Legal Restrictions

As we have already seen, in virtually every country copyright automatically attaches to a creative work—a Bible translation, book, painting, photograph, etc.—at the point of creation. For instance, when a translation is made of the Bible into another language, the translation itself becomes the copyrighted possession of the translator (or translators, if it was made by a team of people). By default, a translation of the Word of God or any other discipleship resource, has all rights reserved for the translator, from the outset.[14]

Copyright restrictions just happen, even without applying for a registered copyright. Owners of the copyrights, however, can release those restrictions by granting permission to others, usually in the form of a license. A license authorizes a use of the work

---

14 As with much of copyright law, the statements in this paragraph come with caveats. For instance, if the translation was made as a "work for hire" or if another legal mechanism was employed that transferred the rights on the translation to another entity, then the translator would not own the translation.

(e.g. creating a translation) which would otherwise be an infringement of the copyright holder's rights.

By releasing a discipleship resource under a license that provides broad freedoms to others who encounter it, a copyright holder can legally pre-clear others to use the content in ways that would not otherwise have been possible, apart from writing a new license for each and every use. This "open-licensing" of content can only be done by the owner of the copyright.

The vast majority of discipleship resources that could be useful to the global church are under copyright, with all rights reserved for the content owner alone. Given the critical need for open-licensed discipleship resources that the global church can use and re-use without restriction, it is important to understand why there are so few open-licensed resources available. If copyright law can (and does) limit the freedom and spiritual growth of the global church, why are legal restrictions on the Word of God and other discipleship resources maintained in the first place?

No one in ministry wants to hinder the global church from growing spiritually. But releasing discipleship resources under open licenses is not always a popular idea, often for two primary reasons. The first has to do with financial considerations, and the second has to do with concerns regarding maintaining the integrity of the content.

Financial Considerations

The creation of discipleship resources, including Bible translations, has historically been undertaken in the domain of "private production," that is, business enterprises.[15] Publishing houses, individual authors, churches, or Bible translation organizations operate on a

---

15   The only other alternative up until the rise of "social production" would have been "public production," that is, government. The notion of governments undertaking the creation of discipleship resources is both unrealistic and concerning.

business model to create, translate, and sell discipleship resources. This is a good, Biblically-sanctioned approach to ministry. It is legitimate and ethical, but it is an unavoidably costly model.

Recall from chapter 5 that "Gutenberg Economics"—the model used for the creation of content that has been the default since the invention of Gutenberg's press—has remained largely unchanged through the last five centuries. The defining characteristic of "Gutenberg Economics" is significant investment costs. Creating a discipleship resource in a "private production" model costs a lot of money.

A Bible translation team may require many years to translate the Bible, resulting in significant costs associated with the translation, as salaries and other benefits need to be provided for the team members. When it comes time to distribute the finished work, the only option available up until recently was to distribute the finished work as a physical object such as a book. In the "paper" world of publishing physical books, there is the additional expense of paper, ink, and glue, then printing, binding, and distributing the book.

It all adds to up to a significant amount of overhead that needs to be recovered. In the case of some Bible translation organizations working in minority languages, these expenses are recovered by the financial donations of people who believe in the work of the translation organization. The completed translations are sometimes sold for a nominal fee, but the sale price is rarely expected to recover a significant part of the translation project's expense. For some very small people groups, even if everyone in the people group purchased a translation of the Bible in their language, they could not come close to recovering the expenses that were accrued by the translation project. So the contributions of donors and foundations are the only way to recover the expenses in these cases.

In most other cases, however, recovering the expenses incurred in the creation of a discipleship resource is accomplished by selling the finished product, or receiving royalties from others licensed to distribute it. Copyright restrictions are crucial at this point, as the primary purpose of copyright law is to preserve the economic benefit of the finished work for the creator of that work. Because the copyright holder of a work has the exclusive right to publish and distribute that work, they can control the price and keep it higher than would otherwise be the case.

This does not come without trade-offs, however. Ensuring the most revenue for the copyright holder necessarily means that the distribution of a given resource will be limited. Since there is only one distribution channel (the publisher), distribution of the resource is limited to the reach of that distribution channel. Because of the legal restrictions on the resource that prevent redistribution and maintain a higher price than would otherwise be the case, not everyone who wants a copy will get a copy of the work—especially if the price is higher than what some can afford.

The market and the restrictive licenses ("all rights reserved") afforded by copyright law attempt to maximize the *profitability* of a work, *not the number of people reached by it*. This copyright-enforced monopoly limits access to a resource and maintains an artificially higher price on it, but it is legally permitted in order to encourage the creation of additional works.

Free of Charge, But Still Restricted

Even for discipleship resources that are given away free of charge, there can be a strong incentive to not release those resources under an open license. If the resources were released under open licenses, their "competitors" in ministry would legally be able to redistribute the same discipleship resource. Instead of only being able to access the resource on one website or from one distributor, there could be dozens or even thousands of distributors of the resource. As other ministries distribute the same open-licensed discipleship resource, the owner would not necessarily have access to those numbers to include in the total. Furthermore, as people legally copy and redistribute the open-licensed resource amongst themselves, no tally of those numbers is recorded and passed on to the owner. It is likely that far more people would get access to the discipleship resource under this scenario, but there would be no way for the organization that created the resource to count the total numbers.

Who cares about numbers? Donors do. Throughout the history of donation-based ministries, donors have, understandably, wanted to see good "return on investment" for their donations. If an organization's numbers are not very impressive, it could negatively

> Generating numbers that look impressive requires severely limiting the reach of the resource.

impact the funding of their ministry. That funding might go to another organization that can show better numbers. This creates a conundrum for a ministry that wants to release copyright restrictions on a discipleship resource. By releasing it under an open license, they greatly increase the reach of that resource. But unless their donors understand that generating numbers that look impressive requires (ironically) severely limiting the reach of the resource, releasing their content under an open license might look like a bad idea from a fund-raising standpoint.

For example, imagine a scenario where an organization owns an "all rights reserved"—but free-of-charge—discipleship resource and distributes 100,000 copies of it in a year. Those numbers might look impressive to a donor, who might then be willing to provide funding for distributing another 100,000 the next year. This is a classic scenario for funding ministry. Organizations that carefully track the statistics and can show impressive numbers, increase their likelihood of receiving significant funding.

Now imagine that, instead of maintaining the "all rights reserved" on their discipleship resource—thus ensuring that they are the exclusive distribution channel—the organization releases it under an open license. By definition, an open license permits unrestricted redistribution of the content by anyone else. Now imagine that the organization distributes the resource to only two people. The next day, those two people legally distribute two copies to two other people. The following day, the four new recipients each give a copy to two others, and so on.

If this pattern continued—each new recipient giving it to two others the following day—the entire population of the earth would get a copy of that discipleship resource *in a little over one month*. While this is obviously a hypothetical example, it shows the explosive potential for redistribution of an open-licensed discipleship resource. When *anyone* can redistribute it, the potential reach of the resource is orders of magnitude greater than would otherwise be the case.

But here is the glaring problem in this example: The original organization could only show that they distributed two copies of the resource. Not thousands. Not hundreds of thousands. Not billions. Two. Never mind that the resource they released under an open license became available to every person in the world. They only have hard numbers for two, and that will not get much funding from donors operating under a traditional mindset.

This can put a ministry in a difficult position. The purpose of the organization is to build the Kingdom of God. Most would agree that they are willing to build the Kingdom of God at any cost. But it is a difficult decision to make, when releasing some of the copyright restrictions on a discipleship resource in order to not hinder the growth of the global church means the potential loss of the organization's traditional revenue streams. Are we willing to enable the entire global church to have unrestricted access to a discipleship resource we own, even if it means we lose our funding and our organization ceases to exist?

There is a "negative example" in this context as well. One could look at it like this: "We distributed 100,000 copies of our copyrighted discipleship resource last year. Show us how many people did *not* get access to our discipleship resource because it was not open-licensed."

There is, of course, no way to show how many people did not get access to a resource due to copyright restrictions. There is no way to know where it would have gone, how many people would have gained access to it, and how many lives would have been changed if it had been open-licensed. But because a ministry can show hard numbers for what *did* happen while it was under their complete control, the usual assumption is that this is the best way of going about meeting the need.

Although hard numbers for an open-licensed discipleship resource are impossible to predict, there are other sources upon which we can draw for evidence that releasing legal restrictions is a strategic move for any ministry or individual whose goal is building the Kingdom of Christ at any cost. The hypothetical example above shows how quickly a discipleship resource can blanket the earth when it is released from legal restrictions that prevent it. But we also have evidence from "open" projects in the secular world that have done the same.

If the only encyclopedia we had today was Britannica, it would be 32 volumes of information, available in one language. But because Wikipedia uses an open model for creating content, and the content itself is open-licensed, the encyclopedia contains millions of articles (1,600+ volumes), available in hundreds of languages.

Linux, the open-source operating system, is another example of how "open" is a model that is able to go much farther than comparative "closed" models. No one expected much from it when it began in 1991 as a hobby built by a handful of computer hackers. But because it was released under an open license so that anyone could use, improve, and redistribute it, Linux has become an irreplaceable component in computing today—from smartphones to Internet servers to supercomputers.

There may not be "hard facts" for how much more effective a discipleship resource will be if it is released under an open license. But the indicators from other open projects suggest that an open-licensed discipleship resource will almost certainly be used by more people, in more places, for more ministry, than would otherwise be the case.

"The Worker Is Worthy of His Wages"

The "business enterprise" model for the creation and sale of discipleship resources is both sanctioned by governments and supported in Scripture. Jesus, when sending out his disciples for ministry, affirmed that material recompense for spiritual work is right.

> Remain in the same house, eating and drinking what they offer, for the worker is worthy of his wages.
>
> —Luke 10:7a

Paul references the Old Testament principle of not muzzling an ox while it treads out the grain (Deuteronomy 25:4) in his affirmation that financial reward is appropriate for those who work in ministry.

> The elders who are good leaders should be considered worthy of an ample honorarium, especially those who work hard at preaching and teaching. For the Scripture says: 'Do not muzzle an ox while it is treading out the grain,' and, 'the worker is worthy of his wages.'
>
> —1 Timothy 5:18

To the church in Corinth, Paul made the matter explicitly clear. Those who work in the ministry "sowing spiritual things" have the right to "reap material things" as a result.

My defense to those who examine me is this: Don't we have the right to eat and drink?...Who ever goes to war at his own expense? Who plants a vineyard and does not eat its fruit? Or who shepherds a flock and does not drink the milk from the flock? Am I saying this from a human perspective? Doesn't the law also say the same thing? For it is written in the law of Moses, 'Do not muzzle an ox while it treads out grain.' Is God really concerned with oxen? Or isn't He really saying it for us? Yes, this is written for us, because he who plows ought to plow in hope, and he who threshes should do so in hope of sharing the crop. *If we have sown spiritual things for you, is it too much if we reap material benefits from you?* If others have this right to receive benefits from you, don't we even more? ...Don't you know that those who perform the temple services eat the food from the temple, and those who serve at the altar share in the offerings of the altar? In the same way, the Lord has commanded that *those who preach the gospel should earn their living by the gospel.*

—1 Corinthians 9:3,7-12,13-14, emphasis added

It is clear from Scripture that receiving financial recompense for spiritual work is not only permitted, it is endorsed as a right. Those who preach the gospel have the right to earn their living by the gospel, plain and simple. These same principles also apply to those who create discipleship resources that explain and teach the Word of God. They have a biblically-sanctioned right to leverage their exclusive rights afforded to them by copyright law in order to acquire for themselves financial reward for their work in creating discipleship resources. There is no Biblical mandate that suggests they should release a discipleship resource under an open license, or that they are in the wrong if they do not. They may choose to do so voluntarily, but there is no Scriptural directive to do so.

Preserving the Integrity of the Word

A second common motivation for not releasing discipleship resources under open licenses has to do with concern for the integrity of the discipleship resource. The concern is that releasing a discipleship resource under an open license that permits translation and re-use of the work by anyone, for any purpose, without needing to specifically ask permission first may be granting a license for the perversion of the original work and propagation of bad doctrine. It conjures up images of cult leaders working feverishly to translate a Christian book into another language in a corrupt and twisted manner that perverts the Gospel and results in the author's name being associated with a heretical resource.

This would clearly be an undesirable development, and there *is* a risk that this kind of thing could happen to discipleship resources. But it is crucial to understand that this risk is introduced *at the point the content is available in a digital format*, not when it is released under an open license. The assumption that content available in a digital format is somehow immune to abuse because it is under copyright does not reflect reality. Bad things happen to copyright-restricted content all the time. This is one of the unavoidable realities of life in the digital era.

This risk is introduced at the point the content is available in a digital format.

A well-known Christian organization ran into this problem with a book that had been written by the prominent leader of the organization. They discovered that, without their authorization, someone in the Middle East had translated the book into Arabic. But, to their horror, they found that the translation was of very poor quality, perverted the author's intent in numerous places, and even introduced verses from the Qu'ran into the text—something the author would never have done.

So their concern that open-licensed discipleship resources might invite such problems was understandable. It also missed a fundamental point: their book that had been corrupted by someone else *was under copyright*. Copyright law did not prevent a bad thing from happening to it, nor could it. They were trusting that copyright law would hinder the "bad guys" from doing bad things, but it did not.

There is another crucial observation in all of this. This organization only found out about the unauthorized translation of their book into Arabic because someone told them about it. Which raises some questions. How long did it take for them to find out about it? How long had the translation of the book been in circulation before they discovered it? What if this was not the only translation of the book into Arabic? What if this was not the only translation of the book into any other language? How long will it be before they discover those translations? What if the book has already been translated into a hundred other languages and they have not yet discovered it? Content owners may *think* that all is well, and their discipleship resource is safe because it is under copyright. But just because they are unaware of any nefarious use of it, does not mean it has not already happened, in dozens of languages, all over the world.

These questions underline a key point: copyright law was invented in, and thus reflects, the "paper" era, not the digital era. In the "paper" era, the cost associated with reprinting and redistributing someone else's book was so significant that only established printers (later, publishers) could do it on a large scale. Thus, it limited the potential number of competitors to only the publishing houses able to undertake it. These publishers were well-known, with clear communication channels and centralized infrastructure. Copyright law in this context made it relatively easy to draw the legal lines between the publishing companies and the content owned by each.

With the advent of the digital age, however, the rules changed. Now, anyone can publish. Mass distribution of a resource is easy to do and costs virtually nothing. (Just ask the Hollywood producers whose movies are pirated in every country of the world, over online file-sharing networks and in pirated DVDs.) In the ministry realm, the same holds true. Anyone can get access to any digital resource online and translate it—today—without ever asking permission. They can easily email PDFs of the translated content to others, or even host them on their own website, in their own language. They can even create poor-quality translations of the Bible and distribute them all over the Internet.[16]

The point is this: bad things happen to the Word of God and other discipleship resources all the time. Copyright restrictions on a discipleship resource may be a deterrent that prevents publishers and other established entities from reproducing and mass-distributing a work (e.g. a book, an evangelistic video, etc.). Copyright law gives the copyright holder the opportunity to take someone to court who violates their rights. But copyright restrictions do not prevent bad things from happening to good content. "Bad guys" will continue to do bad things with good content regardless of whether or not it is under copyright. There is simply no way to patrol what every person in every language of the world is doing with your good content in an effort to prevent bad things from happening to it.

Copyright law is a false hope for preventing the misuse of good content. Copyrights do tend to restrict the use of content, but the people who are limited by copyright law are often the "good guys"—the law-abiding body of Christ willing and able to work to-

---

16   An example of this is the LOLcat Bible translation, a translation of the entire Bible in the mythical language of cats:

Boreded Ceiling Cat makinkgz Urf n stuffs

Oh hai. In teh beginnin Ceiling Cat maded teh skiez An da Urfs, but he did not eated dem. Da Urfs no had shapez An haded dark face, An Ceiling Cat rode invisible bike over teh waterz. At start, no has lyte. An Ceiling Cat sayz, i can haz lite? An lite wuz.

An Ceiling Cat sawed teh lite, to seez stuffs, An splitted teh lite from dark but taht wuz ok cuz kittehs can see in teh dark An not tripz over nethin. An Ceiling Cat sayed light Day An dark no Day. It were FURST!!!1

—Genesis 1:1-5 (LOLCat Bible Translation Contributors, "Genesis 1," n.d., http://lolcatbible.com/index.php?title=Genesis_1).

gether to translate and use the discipleship resources to complete the task of world missions.

Copyright Law and World Missions

The mission of the Church is to make disciples of all people groups. We have already established that making disciples includes equipping the disciples with the Word of God and additional discipleship resources that teach them the Word of God in depth. For these resources to be useful and understood with clarity, they must be translated into the disciple's language and adapted for accurate communication in their culture.

We have seen that the traditional approach to translation of discipleship resources involves a "give them a fish" model and is extremely costly and time-consuming. Given the amount of time it takes to translate discipleship resources into a few hundred languages, it is unrealistic to expect that this approach to translation is a model capable of equipping believers in the nearly 7,000 living languages in the world today in a timely manner. The proposed solution is for the global church to openly collaborate in the creation and translation of discipleship resources in every language of the world. We have seen that the global church is on the rise and is ready to join in, using the technology that is becoming increasingly common in even the farthest corners of the globe.

This brings us to the issue of copyright restrictions on discipleship resources. Copyright law, as we have seen, is designed specifically to *limit* the distribution and reuse of a work by granting exclusive rights to the owner that prevent others from copying and redistributing the work without the owner's permission. The function of copyright law is not to facilitate getting the work to every person possible. Instead, it tends to make the work artificially "scarce," thus increasing the content owner's economic benefit from it.

It should come as no surprise, then, that this classic model for creating, translating, and distributing discipleship resources has only been able to make a relatively small number of resources available in a relatively small number of languages. Up until recently, ministry organizations have necessarily needed to use an expensive model (private production) designed to maximize revenue from the content (through contrived scarcity) as a means to disseminate discipleship resources. Using this classic model to reach every language in the world with adequate discipleship resources is inefficient, because that is not the purpose for which the model was created.

The classic, "all rights reserved" model for ministry creates a challenge for the global church. It maintains a complicated legal framework that is nearly impossible for much of the global church to overcome. Because of this, the global church is hindered from translating and redistributing the discipleship resources they need for spiritual maturity. The vast majority of discipleship resources are in a tiny handful of some of the world's most common languages, especially English. These resources could be of tremendous use to the global church if they were translated into the thousands of languages they speak.

> Only a handful of larger languages are served, and the rest of the global church drags on in their spiritual famine.

But most of these resources are unavailable to them, out of their reach. This is the "walled garden" of discipleship resources, and much, if not most, of the global church is outside the wall. Hundreds of millions of believers, speaking thousands of languages are prevented from translating and using the resources, although they desperately need them. These believers continue to wait for discipleship resources to be translated into their languages, but the length and expense of traditional translation projects are prohibitive. Only a handful of larger languages are served, and the rest of the global church drags on in their spiritual famine.

We Cannot Have It Both Ways

What can Christian mission organizations learn from a global summit on sustainable development? At first glance, it would seem the two have little in common. The outcome of a recent summit, however, illustrates a principle for world missions that is both clear and relevant for ministry in the 21st century. The principle is: *in the realm of Intellectual Property, we cannot have it both ways.*

Rio+20 (formally, the United Nations Conference on Sustainable Development), was held in 2012 in the Brazilian coastal city of Rio de Janeiro. The purpose of the conference was to attempt to reconcile the economic and environmental goals of the global community. Traditional means of achieving a country's economic goals (like growing its economy and developing needed infrastructure) can tend to have an adverse effect on the environment. Accomplishing both the economic and environmental goals requires modern technology. And this is where the tension arises.

Much of the technology needed to enable sustainable economic development has already been invented—by some of the most developed countries. The technology needed by poorer developing countries is the Intellectual Property of the wealthiest countries, and that Intellectual Property is very valuable. Developing countries lack the capital and research base to invent viable technologies for themselves—only those in the developed world have the ability to do so. It comes down to this: those in the developing world need the technology owned by those in the developed world, because *they do not have the means to create or acquire it for themselves in other ways.*

This story is relevant to world missions because it so clearly illustrates how, at the conceptual level, the Christian world faces a similar conundrum. The discipleship resources that hundreds of millions of believers around the world could use to foster their spiritual development have already been created—by believers from some of the most affluent countries. The resources (Intellectual Property) are usually under copyright, with "all rights reserved" for the content owner. These restrictions prevent the global church from translating, adapting, redistributing, and using the content as needed for their spiritual growth. The global church needs discipleship resources that are owned by other believers, because they do not have the means to create or acquire the resources for themselves in other ways. We can either continue to leverage the restrictions afforded by copyright law and limit what others can do with our discipleship resources, or we can work together as a global church to widely distribute discipleship resources in every language, for effective discipleship in every people group. We cannot have it both ways.

It comes down to this question: Will the "haves" give up some of the exclusive rights to their Intellectual Property for the good of the "have-nots?" Interestingly, for the attendees of the Rio+20 summit, the answer to that question was made abundantly clear. The developing countries attending the summit were hoping the summit would facilitate the transfer of the technology needed for the sustainable development of their economies, thus achieving both the overarching economic and environmental objectives.

Before the conference even began, however, the president of the Intellectual Property Owners Association (IPO)[17] made a statement to the effect that a transfer of technology like the kind hoped for by developing countries would not be an option, as it would negatively impact the bottom line of the owners of the technology in developed countries. That is, their choice was to leverage the significant economic value of the Intellectual Property contained in the technology needed by the developing world, rather than meet the

---

17   The Intellectual Property Owners Association is a U.S. trade association for owners of patents, trademarks, copyrights and trade secrets.

needs of the developing world at any cost. One commentator put it this way:

> The IPO has no interest in helping developing countries transition to a more sustainable economy if it means sacrificing valuable IPR. And the IPO's chilly message set the tone for what many pundits and participants considered a disappointing Rio+20 conference yielding few substantive results.[18]

To be sure, the inventors of these technologies have every right to enjoy the exclusive rights afforded to them as owners of their own Intellectual Property. They are under no obligation to release it free of charge so that anyone else can use the Intellectual Property without restrictions. But it is impossible, as the saying goes, to "have one's cake and eat it, too." Choosing one outcome (maximum financial recompense) necessarily rejects the other outcome (sustainable development for every country at the lowest possible cost). Unless those with the means to create what is needed are willing to sacrificially share of their own Intellectual Property, the developing world is shut out from that which would meet their needs.

In the realm of world missions, sustainable economic development is not the focus. Equipping the global church in every people group and language with discipleship resources to foster their spiritual growth is (or should be) a primary focus. Those who own the rights to discipleship resources—translations of the Bible and resources built on them—are in the same position as the owners of "green" technology in the developed world. People groups in the developing world need what they own and cannot spontaneously generate it for themselves. They often do not have the same opportunities

---

18   Rory Crump, "Intellectual property rights: the quiet killer of Rio+20," jul 2012, http://www.patexia.com/feed/intellectual-property-rights-the-quiet-killer-of-rio-20-20120702

for education and theological development in their own countries that could give rise to such resources.

Merely giving them "free of charge" (but still "all rights reserved") discipleship resources also does not solve the problem. In the realm of world missions, effectiveness of discipleship resources is all about one thing: derivatives. Distribution of digital content is easy. Getting permission to make derivatives can often be as unlikely as winning the lottery.

Without the freedom to make content effective and build on it in their own language (i.e. create derivatives), "free of charge" discipleship resources are of limited good to the vast majority of the global church. What they need is the legal freedom to translate, adapt, build on, revise, redistribute, and use the resources as though they were their own, without restriction. Until they are given permission, the "all rights reserved" of existing discipleship resources legally prevents them from doing any of this.

Free + Freed

You have seen it on websites all over the Internet: Free! Download this free ebook! Watch the free video! Free is great and a necessary first step for equipping the global church. But merely giving some discipleship resources in English away free of charge is not a global missions strategy. Only a small handful of believers outside of non-English-speaking countries can even understand them. They are about as effective for the majority of the global church as a Bible translation in Arabic would be to the average reader of English.

Making discipleship resources available free of charge is a good notion, but it does not provide what the global church actually needs: legal *freedom* to translate, adapt, redistribute, and use the resources effectively in their own languages and cultures. What the global church needs is discipleship resources that are both *free* (of charge) + (legally) *freed*.

This is where things start to get sticky. There are only two ways for the global church to get the legal freedom they need to translate a discipleship resource for effective use in their own language: either the resource is released proactively under an open-license so that they can legally translate and use it immediately, or they need to ask permission of the copyright holder first. Some of the most potentially effective discipleship resources are of significant value to the entities that own the copyrights on them. Consequently, the idea of releasing such resources under open licenses that gives everyone free and legally unrestricted access to them is often not immediately appealing. So the global church is left with one option: ask for permission. But this is not as straightforward as it might seem.

Ask, But You Are Unlikely to Receive

I recently had a conversation with a woman who works in the publishing department of a large mission organization. She mentioned that she had received a phone call that morning from a contact in a very large Christian publishing house. She told me:

> I couldn't figure out what he was talking about. He said he was calling about a request we had made to use one of their resources in one of our publications. But I did not remember ever having contacted them. So I finished the phone call, then went and checked the records. Sure enough, I *had* contacted them—nine months before. We had wanted to use a small part of one of their publications on a page in a calendar we were making and this was the first I had heard back from them. We had finished the calendar months before—without their content in it, because we had not heard back from them.[19]

---

19 Name withheld, personal communication.

Nine months. That long of a delay is not uncommon for matters of intellectual property in a world missions context. When requesting permission to use a resource that is of significant value the wait time may even be longer. But consider the situation in this story. Both parties were in the United States, maybe even in the same timezone, having a shared culture, being native speakers of the same language, in direct phone contact, possibly on a first-name basis, with immediate email contact and possibly video chat at a moment's notice. They also probably both had legal counsel with whom they could confer at any time. And it took *nine months* for the request to be answered.

Realistically, how long do you think it will take for a Christian from a village in the Sudan or northern India or anywhere else in the world to get a response, if at all? The person making the request would be on the other side of the world from the copyright holder, they might not speak the same language, their cultures are vastly different, they may not have phone contact, they probably would not know each other's names, email might not be an option, much less video chat. It is unlikely that they would have legal counsel to help them through the process, and acquiring such counsel could be extremely expensive. Not only that, the number of steps that need to be taken just to get access to use a discipleship resource is staggering. For permission to be granted, each of the following questions (at a minimum, there may be more depending on the context) needs to be answered with a "yes":

1. Can I identify the copyright holder?
2. Do I know how to contact them?
3. Can I communicate in their language?
4. Am I able to contact the copyright holder?
5. Do I have the Intellectual Property knowledge to request permission?

If all these steps can be accomplished, then the request needs to be written and sent to the copyright holder. At this point, there is an extreme time lapse of months or years before proceeding.

6. Do I get a response?
7. Did they understand my request?
8. Do I understand their contract?
9. Can I comply with the contract?
10. Can I afford the terms of the contract?
11. Can the resource be used without translation (which would require making a derivative work)?
12. Can the resource be used without adaptation (also a derivative work)?
13. Can I provide an independent back-translation?
14. Can I track the translation, with forms for every participant?
15. Can I comply with the publisher's contract requirements?
16. Do I know who owns the translation?
17. Can I supply the properly completed copyright assignments for the derivative works?
18. Can I provide the finished product to the author?[20]

If all these answers are "yes", then the resource can be legally used. But there is one more catch: what if I discover that I need to use the resource in ways that exceed the original permissions of the contract? Sometime during the translation process, I may have encountered new needs that require new permissions. I may have asked for permission to translate and print the finished translation of the discipleship resource, but what if I now realize I need permission to embed the translation into a mobile phone application, or turn it into a video? If additional permissions are needed, the

---

20 For a detailed flowchart of the steps in the process, see Tim Jore "Why unrestricted discipleship resources are the future of the global church," feb 2011, http://distantshoresmedia.org/blog/why-unrestricted-discipleship-resources-are-future-global-church

process begins again from step 5, "Do I have the Intellectual Property knowledge to request permission?"

Now consider the complexity of the global context: nearly 7,000 languages in the world (all of which need many translated discipleship resources), multiple legal jurisdictions around the world (with different terms and restrictions), and hundreds of millions of believers (most of whom do not speak English) who might need permissions to use the discipleship resources (in dozens of different ways and contexts). Any process for attempting to manage the copyright of a given resource and the individual terms of use for each request in thousands of languages would rapidly turn into a bureaucratic nightmare. To put it into perspective, if a contract for use of one discipleship resource in one language was only one page long, then requesting the use of only one discipleship resource in every language of the world would require nearly *fourteen reams* of paper!

Untangling the complexity would require more financial resources than could be expected to be recovered by the sale of the translated discipleship resources in other languages. The whole process would likely grind to a halt and collapse in on itself. Clearly, expecting the global church to navigate the legal waters of proactively contacting the copyright holder of a discipleship resource and requesting permission to use their discipleship resource is unrealistic. The process is massively complicated, costly, time-consuming, and unsustainable. This is especially the case if we are serious about meeting the need for adequate discipleship resources in every language of the world.

So it is no wonder that the global church is at an impasse. They cannot be expected to start from scratch and recreate the discipleship resources they need in each language. But the discipleship resources they could use as a starting point for translation and creation of new resources are off-limits to them, existing in a handful of languages that many, often most, of the global church does not speak. These believers are ready to help with the translation of these resources into their own languages, but they are legally prevented from doing so. Requesting permission to use the resources is not an option for the vast majority of the global church.

The only option available to the global church outside the walled garden is to wait and hope that the resources are proactively released by the copyright holders under open licenses that permit them to legally translate, adapt, redistribute, and use the resources for their spiritual growth. The burden for equipping the global church with discipleship resources rests on those who *have* discipleship resources and their willingness to release their content from copyright restrictions under an open license that permits the global church to use it without restriction. Instead of "giving them a fish" of a single translated discipleship resource, this is "teaching them to fish" and giving them the fishing rod, line, hook, and bait so they *can* fish.

Along these lines, there is another thing to consider. All discipleship resources are, by definition, built on the Word of God. They explain and apply the Word in the cultural context of the speakers of the language in which it is translated. Because of this foundational nature of the Word of God, there is an urgent need for open-licensed translations of the Bible in every language.

This presents a problem, because Bible translations tend to be among the most legally restricted discipleship resources, creating a single point of failure for the spiritual growth of the global church. When the Word of God is restricted, all the discipleship resources on which it is built are restricted as well.

CHAPTER 7

THE WORD OF GOD, RESTRICTED

The Bible is essential for spiritual growth and is the foundation on which every other discipleship resource is built. When the only translations of the Bible in the language of a people group are not available under open licenses, it can hinder the spiritual growth of that people group because it establishes a "single point of failure" for every discipleship resource in that language built on it. This, in turn, can hinder how freely and effectively the Word of God can be used and built on by others to create discipleship resources for fostering the spiritual maturity of people who speak that language. In addition, not even the speakers of that language can legally revise Bible translations that are under copyright without permission from the copyright owners. Apart from ongoing revision, language change will result in the Bible translation itself eventually ceasing to be useful to the speakers of the language.

~ ~ ~

A missionary working with an oral people group called the Tingat[1] realized that the people he was serving had a problem. The Bible had been translated into their language, but it was doing them very little good. Since most of the people were oral communicators and did not read, the printed Word of God was as useless to them as if it had never been translated.

"But," the missionary thought, "If they could *hear* the translation as an audio Bible, it would be very effective for them. Literacy would no longer be a prerequisite to discipleship and spiritual growth." So he started work with one of the pastors in the people group who was able to read the language. The plan was to record the pastor reading the Bible in his own language, then distribute the audio recordings as MP3 files via the Internet and by sharing them from mobile phone to mobile phone. The pastor was overjoyed at the thought of being able to "bridge the gap" between the printed Word of God and the people who could not read it.

But just before starting the recording sessions, the missionary thought of something. His idea of recording the Bible as audio files and giving them away was an ideal solution to the problem, but would doing so without permission from the copyright holder be legal? He was aware that copyright law in the 21st century is a serious matter and he wanted to live in submission to the ruling authorities. So he decided to pursue things through the correct, legal channels. Rather than make the recordings and hope to "get forgiveness" after the fact, he took the honorable route and attempted to get in touch with the organization that owned the copyright to the translation of the Bible in that language.

This, it turned out, was much easier said than done. It took him seven months of sending emails all over the globe to find out who even owned the copyright on the translation of the Bible and who, in the massive bureaucracy of the organization that owned the copyright, had the authority to grant him permission. Finally, after

---

1   Not their actual name.

numerous rounds of emails, the missionary learned that he needed to talk to the organization's office in the country where he served.

So the next morning, he hopped on the bus and went down to their offices. He walked in, greeted them, and explained the reason for his visit.

"Brothers," he said, "I am a missionary working with the Tingat people. As you know, you own the rights to the translation of the Bible in Tingat and I am here to ask permission to use the translation for ministry. I would like to record the Bible and give the audio recordings away for free over the Internet and on the mobile phones of the Tingat people. I am sure there will be no problem, since we share a common goal of making the Word of God available to the Tingat people, but I wanted to ask permission just the same."

"That is a fine idea!" they replied. "Here is what you need to do: write up a memorandum of understanding that clearly explains what our percentage of the royalties will be, then get back to us."

"I don't think I have explained myself clearly," the missionary said. "There won't be any royalties because we are going to do the work for free and give the audio files away for free to all the people. Won't it be great? There will be no obstacle preventing the Tingat people from hearing the Word of God in their own language!"

"Now we understand!" they exclaimed. "Here is what you need to do: write up a memorandum of understanding that clearly explains what our percentage of the royalties will be, then get back to us."

The missionary was in a dilemma. Without putting together a business model for selling access to the Word of God, he would not be able to get permission from the owners of the copyright to the Tingat translation of the Bible. But requiring payment for access to digital audio files (that cost him virtually nothing to copy and redistribute) would create an obstacle for the Tingat people, who needed unrestricted access to Word of God in their language. What was he to do?

Some would argue that he should obey God rather than man and just do it—make the recordings and distribute them for free. Others, however, see this as blatant theft, regardless of how onerous such restrictions may be. The people who work in the organization that owns the copyright to the translated Bible in Tingat have families and need to provide for them too. Stealing from them to meet someone else's needs is not an ethical solution. Both sides have valid points and there is no easy solution to this problem.

A Single Point of Failure for the Global Church

A single point of failure is a part of a system that, if it fails, will stop the entire system from working. Think of a high-performance sports car, aerodynamically shaped, with a perfectly tuned engine that puts out hundreds of horsepower. Now imagine that you have lost the key for the sports car (and, for the sake of argument, that you do not have a spare key or know how to hot-wire a car). The key is a single point of failure for the sports car, because without it, all the intricate design that makes it fast, powerful, and effective is little more than a chunk of metal, plastic, and glass in your driveway.

The spiritual growth and nourishment of the global church has a single point of failure as well: the Word of God. Without the Word of God, there is no lasting and deep spiritual growth. Without the Word of God, the Church is weak, powerless, hamstrung. One of the least-realized but most significant impediments to the advance of the Word of God has to do with limitations placed on Bible translations and enforced by copyright law.

This is not an intentional, malicious limitation. As we have already seen, it has only been in the last decade or so that a viable alternative to "all rights reserved" was created. In recent years, and at an accelerating pace, new technologies have also been invented that create unprecedented opportunities to accelerate the advance of God's Kingdom in every people group. But making the most of these opportunities depends on open-licensed Bible translations.

The story of the missionary working with the Tingat people is a true story, and one of countless others like it, in languages all over the world. Translated Scripture in thousands of languages is legally restricted by man-made rules that prevent it from being

> **Making the most of these opportunities depends on open-licensed Bible translations.**

used as needed and without hindrance for the equipping of the Church. The organizations who own the copyrights to these translations of the Bible were not established to restrict access to it, they were established to make the Word of God accessible to everyone. How, then, did things get turned around? How is it that the organizations in the best position to solve the problem are sometimes the ones inadvertently perpetuating the problem?

To find answers to these questions, we will look in an unexpected place: carpools.

Accidentally Committed to Preserving the Problem

Transportation has been a problem looking for a solution for as long as man has walked the earth. Modes and means have changed through the centuries, but the problem is still essentially the same: How do I get from one point to another efficiently and inexpensively? With the invention of the automobile, efficiency of transportation increased greatly. But for people who travel long distances frequently, it can also be a costly means of transportation.

One solution to the problem of expensive travel is the carpool. By sharing the same vehicle among several people, the cost for each person making the trip goes down significantly. But carpooling has been hindered by an information problem. How do you find out who has a car, is going where you need to go, and is willing to give you a ride for a price on which you both agree?

It used to be that this was a difficult problem to solve, because manually coordinating drivers and riders was tedious and time-consuming. So carpooling tended to work on a small scale—people from the same company and living in the same neighborhoods, for instance. In order for carpooling to work on a large scale, there did not need to be more cars and carpoolers. There needed to be better information about the cars and carpoolers already in existence.

PickupPal was invented to meet this need. The PickupPal web service helped coordinate drivers and carpoolers by sharing enough information about each to make the carpooling system work. A driver could advertise a route they drive and people looking for a ride could search for a route that would work for them. Prices were negotiated via the website and an agreed-upon ride was coordinated when there was a match that was acceptable to both parties. PickupPal used the Internet to enable the participants in the process to coordinate themselves, thus removing the inconvenience of organizing a carpool by providing better information about the cars and carpoolers already in existence. It was a fast and efficient solution to an age-old problem, so it is no surprise that many people began to use the service to coordinate rides.

But not everyone was thrilled about the service provided by PickupPal. Bus companies, in particular, were not impressed that people could now negotiate long-distance rides between cities using private parties instead of riding the bus. In May 2008, a bus company called Trentway-Wagar in Ontario did something about it. They reported PickupPal to the Ontario Highway Transport Board, claiming it provided an illegal transportation service. They cited Section 11 of the Ontario Public Vehicles Act that defined the parameters for legal carpooling, and claimed that PickupPal was in violation of them.

In the hearings that followed, it quickly became apparent that the changes and new opportunities brought on by the Internet were not yet understood by the Highway Transportation Board.

> At one point in the proceedings, Mr. Dewhirst [the founder of PickupPal] had to explain to the board that an online forum is an Internet site where people can go to discuss a particular topic. In another instance, members of the board were flabbergasted when they suggested a change be made to PickupPal and Mr. Dewhirst offered to make the update on his computer right there in the room... "The government has been blindsided by the technology, and the world has changed around them," he said.[2]

The Ontario Highway Transport Board upheld Trentway-Wagar's complaint, fined PickupPal for infractions of the Public Vehicles Act and ordered them to stop operations in Ontario. It did not matter that PickupPal provided a convenient service at a lower cost to the general public. It did not matter that they were able to leverage new technology that had not even been invented when the original laws were written. They were in violation of the law that upheld the way things had always been done and, according to those still doing things the way they had always been done, PickupPal needed to be closed down.

This story illustrates an important point. The bus companies were established to solve a specific problem: the problem of transportation. Arranging for transportation was inconvenient, and information that could establish a more convenient solution on a large scale, like carpooling, was unavailable. Bus companies were an in-

---

2   Matt Hartley, "Bus company no friend to PickupPal," nov 2008, http://www.theglobeandmail.com/news/technology/article722574.ece

novative solution to the problem, largely because other solutions were not yet technologically possible.

When the technology was invented to remove the same inconvenience and enable a new means of solving the same problem—one that bypassed the bus companies—this was seen as a threat to the existence of the companies that had been founded to solve the problem. Bus companies solved the problem of transportation in the most affordable and efficient means possible, given the technology of the time. But when new technology was invented that provided a vastly more affordable and efficient solution, the need for the bus companies as the exclusive means of solving the problem was diminished. The bus industry felt the threat acutely, and understandably so. Clay Shirky explains:

> Trentway-Wagar was arguing that because carpooling used to be inconvenient, it should always be inconvenient, and if that inconvenience disappeared, then it should be reinserted by legal fiat. Curiously, an organization that commits to helping society manage a problem also commits itself to the preservation of that same problem, as its institutional existence hinges on society's continued need for its management. Bus companies provide a critical service—public transportation—but they also commit themselves, as Trentway-Wagar did, to fending off competition from alternative ways of moving people from one place to another.[3]

It is not just bus companies that can inadvertently become committed to the preservation of the problem they exist to solve, in order to ensure their own continued existence. The world is changing rapidly and many other sectors of society—including publishing, entertainment, and education (among many others)—are undergoing massive changes, whether or not they want to.

---

3   Shirky, *Cognitive Surplus*, 41.

Once you see this pattern—a new story rearranging people's sense of the possible, with the incumbents the last to know —you see it everywhere. First, the people running the old system don't notice the change. When they do, they assume it's minor. Then that it's a niche. Then a fad. And by the time they understand that the world has actually changed, they've squandered most of the time they had to adapt.[4]

Ministries that translate the Bible and help create discipleship resources are also finding themselves in a similar situation.

Of Bus Companies and Bible Translation

Ever since the authoring of the original Biblical texts, Christians have faced a problem: how can the whole Church get access to the texts? At first, it required painstakingly writing out copies of the texts by hand. With the invention of Gutenberg's movable-type printing press, copies of the Bible (as well as other discipleship resources) could be printed rapidly at far less cost. Martin Luther, and other Reformation leaders, realized the value of this new technology. Richard Cole notes that "Luther realized the tremendous power of printers and their products; words in print became virtual missiles on the battlefield of ideas... Luther sensed that he was riding the crest of a printing boom and a wave of a relatively new technology."[5]

For five centuries, this model for creating and distributing content would persist as the most viable model for making the Word of God available to the global church. The technology of the printing press improved the efficiency and cost-effectiveness of distributing content, but that content still existed as "paper" (printed books). Be-

---

4   Clay Shirky, "Napster, Udacity, and the Academy," nov 2012, http://www.shirky.com/weblog/2012/11/napster-udacity-and-the-academy/.

5   Cole, Richard G. "Reformation Printers: Unsung Heroes." *Sixteenth Century Journal* 15, no. 3 (1984): 328-329. doi:10.2307/2540767.

cause of this, the process of providing access to the Bible was still unavoidably characterized by a high degree of inconvenience. It required translating the Bible into the desired language, then printing and binding the translation as a book, then providing physical access to the book. Providing access traditionally included filling out order forms, shipping the books, paying duties, getting through customs, acquiring and stocking warehouses with the books, stocking book stores with them, and selling copies to customers.

Bible translation organizations and other related ministries, like publishers and Bible societies, were specifically invented to manage this inconvenience. These organizations served as intermediaries— the only channels through which the Word of God was available. Their purpose was to provide optimal access to the Word of God at the lowest cost. In this way, everyone (in theory, at least) could get access to the Bible in their own language as efficiently and cost-effectively as possible.

This goal of efficiency and cost-effectiveness was constrained by the current technology of the time. Many of these organizations were founded many years ago, before the advent of digital technology, mobile phones and the Internet. Consequently, the content creation and distribution models on which these organizations were built reflect the technology of Gutenberg's era.

With the rise of the digital era, the inconvenience of creating and delivering physical, printed Bibles can be avoided. The Gutenberg-era model for creation and distribution of Bible translations is no longer the only means of solving the problem. In the digital era, delivery of digital copies of the same Bibles over the Internet to mobile phones anywhere in the world is nearly instantaneous, virtually free, and can be done by anyone. The need for a dedicated organization whose specific purpose is to function as a "middleman" is diminished, because the inconvenience that was unavoidable in the "paper" era no longer exists in the digital era.

Now that digital technology greatly diminishes the inconvenience, the entities who own the translations and managed the inconvenience on behalf of the global church in the previous era are faced with a choice. Either they welcome the new technologies and opportunities of the digital era, or they maintain their historical exclusivity and control of the content through legal means.

This can be a difficult choice to make, as both of the options have significant implications. Further muddying the waters is the fact that copyright law makes the second option (leveraging copyright for exclusivity) the default choice. "All rights reserved" happens automatically when the translation is created, and the restrictions persist for decades. Unless a copyright holder intentionally chooses to embrace the technology-fueled opportunities of the digital era by releasing their Bible translation under an open license, the second option prevails by default: the content is restricted and cannot be used in ways that take full advantage of the opportunities in the digital world.

Is it possible that, in the digital world, maintaining exclusive control over translations of the Bible (by leveraging copyright law) perpetuate the problem instead of resolving it? Owners of Bible translations in these contexts may find themselves in the position of being the gatekeeper (preventing access and use), instead of the facilitator (maximizing access and use). Because of the laws of men that govern such things, the owners of Bible translations could inadvertently hinder the Gospel, by virtue of the fact that they maintain the default "all rights reserved" of copyright law.

Do not misunderstand—this is not an indictment of copyright holders or an accusation of malicious intent on anyone's part. The point is not that there is a conscious, concerted effort to restrict access to the Word of God by leveraging copyrights. The point is that the explosion of new opportunities afforded by digital technology and the Internet caught everyone by surprise. Copyright law, however, has changed little in the last three centuries (except, as some would argue, to become more restrictive and enduring). This combination of restrictive laws governing copyright and the immense advances in digital technology has turned the tables on the whole paradigm for solving the problem of providing access to the Word of God. Through no fault of their own, owners of Bible translations may find themselves the single point of failure that can enable or pre-vent unrestricted use of translations of the Bible. And the default is already set for them to "prevent unrestricted use."

This is what happened in the story at the start of this chapter about the missionary wanting to make an audio recording of the Bible for use by the Tingat people group. Using off-the-shelf, inexpensive technology, he could easily have created an audio Bible from the translation of the Bible in that language. The audio files could then have been distributed for free over the Internet and from mobile phone to mobile phone by anyone, without hindrance.

But because of the absence of permission from the owner of the Bible in that language (whether by a specific license or an "open" license), he was legally prevented from doing so. The organization that had been created to manage the inconvenience of access to printed Bibles used their legal power over that Bible translation to ensure the continued *inconvenience* of access to the Word of God. If people could get free access to the Bible through digital means from other sources (and then share those digital files with others without going through their organization first), it would terminate the organization's role as the exclusive channel through which the Word of God was available. And that, they were unwilling to allow.

The epilogue to the story of PickupPal and the Trentway-Wagar bus company is relevant here as well. The legal hearing regarding Pick-upPal generated a lot of attention. Gas prices were high at the time, the economy was in a downturn, and environmental concern was on the rise. The public took the side of PickupPal and got the mes-sage out using everything from online petitions to T-shirts. And the message was heard.

Within weeks of Trentway-Wagar's victory that shut down Pickup-Pal's operations in Ontario, the Public Vehicles Act was amended by the Ontario legislature to make PickupPal legal again. This was the worst-case scenario for Trentway-Wagar. Not only was PickupPal now a legal means of travel, but the bus company had made a very negative impression on the general public. They were seen as the "bad guys" who were against the advance of technology and improved means of travel.

Contrary to what Trentway-Wagar may have feared, however, PickupPal's new-found legality did not cause them to go out of business. Even though carpooling between cities was now legal, the bus company did not cease to exist. It turns out that there is still a role for bus companies, even in a society where technology has made carpooling far more efficient and effective. Bus companies still fill an important role in solving the problem of transportation, even though bus travel is no longer the exclusive solution to the problem. Society has re-negotiated the role of the bus company in society, but the role has not been abolished.

In the same way, there will continue to be a need for organizations who provide access to the translated Word of God in the digital era —even when translations of the Word of God are released under open licenses so that every obstacle preventing their access and use is removed. That role will look different than it did in the "paper" era, when there was no other way to solve the inconvenience of access to the Word of God. But the need for Bible translation organizations, Bible publishers, and Bible societies will continue to exist.

One of the most ironic principles governing the digital era is this:

The one who gives away the most, first, wins.

This is especially true for organizations who hold the copyrights to crucial discipleship resources like translations of the Word of God. Now that digital technology removes the inconvenience that existed in the "paper" era, a good course of action available to those who hold the copyrights to the translated Word of God is to go boldly into the digital age and lead the way into a future of unrestricted freedom for anyone to use the Word of God, without hindrance. Contrary to what they might fear, not only will this fulfill their mandate, but doing so may also be the best way of establishing their role and continuing importance in the digital future of the global church.

More Than a "Free Download"

A common response to the need for increased access to the Word of God for people all over the world is to provide free access to it. Free downloads of digital Bibles are helpful and a good step in the right direction. But they do not solve the ultimate problem of equipping the global church from every people group and in every language with adequate discipleship resources for spiritual growth and maturity. Here is why.

The Bible is the foundation and source of every other discipleship resource. Merely providing free access to a translated Bible does not provide the necessary legal freedom for others to incorporate the Bible text into other discipleship resources, translate them, and redistribute them by any means, without restriction. In many common versions of the Bible in English, for example, permission is granted for only limited use of the Bible text. To illustrate, these are the terms of use for the New International Version of the Bible in English:

> The NIV text may be quoted in any form (written, visual, electronic or audio), up to and inclusive of five hundred (500) verses without express written permission of the publisher, providing the verses do not amount to a complete book of the Bible nor do the verses quoted account for

twenty-five percent (25%) or more of the total text of the work in which they are quoted.[6]

The terms of use for other translations are similar. Some are more permissive, allowing use of up to 1,000 verses. But some are even more restrictive, permitting only 250 verses of the complete text.

The table below lists current (at the time of writing) license restrictions on some common versions of the Bible in modern English. Note that "Max. Verses" refers to the maximum number of verses that may be used, "% of Total" refers to the maximum percentage of the text in the resource that may be Biblical text, and "Complete Book?" refers to whether or not a complete book of the Bible may be used in the resource.[7]

Version	Max. Verses	% of Total	Complete Book?
AMP[8]	500	<25%	No
ESV[9]	1,000	<50%	No
HCSB[10]	250	<20%	No
NASB[11]	1,000	<50%	No
NET[12]	not specified	<50%	No
NIV[13]	500	<25%	No

6   "Terms of Use for Biblica Online Scripture and All Services," accessed September 21, 2012, http://www.biblica.com/biblica-about-us/terms-of-use/

7   The information in this table is intended for reference only. Use of any copyright-restricted Bible translation should be made in accordance with the terms of the license available from the copyright holder.

8   "Permission to Quote Copyright & Trademark Information," accessed October 01, 2012, http://www.lockman.org/tlf/copyright.php. Proper citation required.

9   "Permissions," accessed October 01, 2012, http://www.esv.org/tools/licensing/. Proper citation required, if used for commentary or reference work must have written permission. Use of text in audio subject to more restrictive terms.

10   *Holman Christian Standard Bible* (Holman Bible Publishers, n.d.). Proper citation required.

11   "Permission to Quote Copyright & Trademark Information.". Proper citation required.

Version	Max. Verses	% of Total	Complete Book?
NKJV[14]	250	<50%	No

Table 1: Terms of Use of Selected English Bibles

Under these terms of use, if a person wants to write a book on the sovereignty of God, or create a leadership training curriculum, they are free to use up to a specific number of verses (e.g. 500) of the translated Bible without permission, but not if the total amount of verse text used in the book exceeds a set percentage (e.g. 25%) of the book. Nor can their work include a complete book of the Bible.

To exceed these permissions, the creator of the discipleship resource must enter into a formal agreement with the copyright holder of that translation of the Word of God. The terms of the agreement are negotiated, but the copyright holder holds all the cards. The author of the discipleship resource has no recourse if the terms of the agreement are not agreeable.

---

12   "Trademark and Copyright Information," mar 2010, http://bible.org/copyright. Can give away print versions (non-commercial), no non-print distribution without written permission. Non-Commercial Publication: verses (not Notes) can be quoted in any form without permission provided proper attribution. Restriction on number of verses has apparently been withdrawn but is unspecified in the license statement.

13   "Terms of Use for Biblica Online Scripture and All Services.". Proper citation required, must not be sold, not altered, online version for personal use only, commentaries/commercial/reference books using NIV must obtain permission.

14   David Milling, "How do I get permission to quote from one of your Bible translations (NKJV, NCV, ICB, The Voice, The Expanded Bible)?," jan 2012, http://help.thomasnelson.com/index.php?/Knowledgebase/Article/View/40/8/how-do-i-get-permission-to-quote-from-one-of-your-bible-translations-nkjv-ncv-icb-the-voice-the-expanded-bible. No modification, proper citation required.

Building on a Restricted Foundation

Ignoring, for a moment, the irony of having too much Scripture in a discipleship resource, consider the implications of such situations. In most languages that have Scripture translated, there is only one version of the Bible and it is owned by one copyright holder. The problem with having a single gatekeeper that determines who can do what with the Word of God is that anyone who wants to create discipleship resources in that language is completely dependent on the good graces of the entity who owns the copyright on it.

Without broad and irrevocable legal freedoms in place that permit unrestricted use of the translation of the Bible in that language, the creation and distribution of discipleship resources that promote the spiritual growth of the people who speak that language can be held hostage by a single entity with the law on their side. This is not a scenario conducive to the unrestricted and rapid spiritual growth of a people group.

For instance, what happens if someone wants to create a children's Bible that culls key stories from the translation of the Bible and simplifies the language used in them? This is a derivative work of the original translation, and derivative works are a right reserved exclusively for the copyright holder. In order for this resource to be created, there must be a license that permits it. What if, for whatever reason, the copyright holder of the Bible translation says "no" to the request for use of the Bible? What if they set conditions on the creation of the derivative work that conflict with the purposes and motivations of the person creating the derivative work? This is what happened with the missionary to the Tingat people at the beginning of this chapter. He was unable to create a free and unrestricted audio version of the Bible because the copyright holder wanted him to provide them with a revenue stream from it.

A license is necessary if someone wants to create *any* discipleship resources that incorporates significant amounts of the Biblical text, like a commentary, or a study Bible, or an interlinear Bible, or an audio Bible, or Bible story videos, or a concordance, and so on. The creation of works like these is only legally permissible if the gatekeeper who holds the copyright on the Word of God permits it. In a perfect world, this would not be a problem. But we do not live in a perfect world and this kind of scenario—which is the norm all over the world—creates all sorts of problems.

Recall the number of steps involved in getting permission to use a copyrighted resource like a translation of the Bible. The long, tedious legal process of getting permission from the gatekeeper hinders how readily and effectively the Word of God can be used. It also assumes that the gatekeeper will grant permission to use the Bible. But what if they do not? What if they are of a different denominational persuasion or have a particular theological bias and see it as their God-given duty to prevent the "heresy" espoused by the other denomination from being disseminated through the discipleship resource they are creating? Given the intensity of disagreements like these, are they likely to grant legal permission to those of a conflicting viewpoint? What if they have a strong motivation for financial recompense from the derivative works created using "their" translation of the Word of God? Even if such motivations are not inherently immoral, they can easily become an obstacle that prevents the creation of discipleship resources for the spiritual growth of a people group.

What if the owner of the Bible translation grants permission but in such a way that they put themselves in a position to control the distribution and existence of the discipleship resource in the future? This is not a hypothetical situation. It happened to a Bible scholar recently who wanted to create a commentary of the entire New Testament. This commentary helped explain the difficult passages in the New Testament, but, being a commentary on the Bible text, needed to include many Bible verses in it.

He contacted the copyright holder of the translation he wanted to use and requested permission to use their Bible translation in his commentary. They granted him permission, but it was not perpetual. He was only granted a time-limited license that permitted him to use the Bible translation in his commentary for a few years. His commentary had a shelf life, and after the expiration date, he would need to reapply for permission to continue publishing his commentary. If the owner of the Bible translation did not renew his license to use their Bible, his continued distribution of the discipleship resource he created for the growth of the global church *would be illegal.*

Not only that, if the author of the commentary wants to release it under an open license to maximize legal redistribution of it, he cannot do so. He has an exclusive agreement between himself and the owner of the Bible translation. He is free to release his own content under an open license, but his own content is inextricably intertwined with the translation of the Bible, because it is a commentary.

The problems continue. What if the author wants to continue to make the commentary freely available, but the holder of the copyright on the Bible starts to demand royalties? Because his discipleship resource is built on their Bible translation, they have the legal power to restrict access to and reuse of the content that he created.

The Urgent Need for Open-Licensed Bible Translations

Situations like this one illustrate why the lack of open-licensed translations of the Bible may be the single greatest obstacle restricting the spiritual growth of the global church. The default "all rights reserved" restrictions on the Word of God prevent the free and unrestricted use, re-use, and legal building upon the translation of the Word of God. This creates a real hindrance to the spiritual growth of the global church.

Missionaries and visitors to the developing world can testify to the fact that many (some would say most) seminaries and Bible colleges in developing nations have inadequate discipleship resources in their language. There is a reason for this. There is a reason that the global church persists in a spiritual famine of historic proportions. The restrictions that limit the usefulness of the Word of God in the digital age are a significant part of the problem.

The current context of "all rights reserved" on the Word of God is a situation that is unsustainable for a global church that is poised for explosive growth and in dire need of discipleship resources in thousands of languages. There must be both free access to the translated Word of God and the legal freedom to use it without restriction or prerequisite authorization by an entity that functions as a gatekeeper. The global church must be pre-cleared to use the Word of God in their own language for anything, without restriction, and without the direct legal oversight of any human organization. They are, and will continue to be, accountable to God for what they do with His Word.

There is also an urgent need for an open-licensed version of the Bible in English that is comprehensible by second-language speakers of English. The vast majority of discipleship resources that would be tremendously helpful to the global church are written in English. A growing number of people who own the copyrights on these discipleship resources are ready to release them under an open license. But they are unable to do so because there does not (yet) exist an open-licensed English Bible that they can use in place of the copyright-restricted text.[15]

---

15   There have been a number of attempts recently to create a version of the Bible that is released under an open license. To date, none of these attempts provide the complete Bible, in second-language-speaker-friendly English, with a reputable "chain of title" and translation team behind it. While some translations are said to be "open", the fact that the licenses under which they are released contain restrictions renders their alleged openness an illusion. As we will see in chapter 9, either a license is "open" (no restrictions or need for permission) or it is not.

When a Bible Translation Expires

There is another reason that translations of the Bible in other languages must be released under open licenses, if the global church is to be allowed to grow spiritually and without hindrance. It is a serious but subtle problem: Bible translations expire. A finished translation of the Bible in a given language is not finished for all time. It has an expiration date, but not one having to do with copyright restrictions. This expiration date has to do with how languages change, but translations of the Bible do not. As time progresses, Bible translations need to be revised or they fall out of usefulness to the speakers of that language.

A few weeks into the Uturuva Bible translation project in Papua New Guinea, we made a startling discovery. We had started the translation project from scratch, even creating an alphabet and writing system for the language. It was exciting to think that the speakers of the Uturuva language were finally going to be able to understand the Word of God in their own language, for the first time in all of history! Except, as we found out, that was not quite the case. Imagine our shock when we discovered that the translation of the New Testament in that language had been completed and published only twenty years before.

How discouraging! Here we had gone to all this work to start a brand new translation project—in a language that already had a complete New Testament. I asked the Papua New Guineans on the translation team about the existing translation and they told me they had known about it. "But," they told me, "we cannot understand it."

We found a copy of the New Testament and I asked them to read it. They gave it their best effort, but could only haltingly make out some of the words. "It's like it is not our language," they said.

What had happened? How could it be that a translation of the New Testament, that was of the highest quality when it was published, could—in twenty short years—became unusable to the people who speak that language? There may be many factors contributing to the problem, but one of the most significant factors has to do with what we addressed previously regarding language change.

Frozen Bible Translations

The implications of language change for the translation of the Bible and other discipleship resources are enormous. Recall that more than half of the languages in the world have fewer than 10,000 speakers and are comprised of primarily oral communicators. Although many of these languages will experience language change at a relatively rapid pace, translation of discipleship resources into these smaller languages is often treated as a "one time" event. The goal is usually a finished "product" that, it might be assumed, will be effective forever.

But this is not what actually happens. Even after the publication of a translation of the Bible or a discipleship resource in a language, the language itself continues to change over time. Eventually, the language will have changed so significantly that the translated discipleship resource is no longer useful to the speakers of the language. The Bible translation in their language has become separated from the modern form of the language—a historic relic of a previous form of the language that is no longer in use by anyone.

This problem is further complicated by the fact that many of the languages in the world are spoken by oral people groups. Merely giving such people groups a printed, text-based discipleship resource does not immediately slow down the rate of change.

Researchers studying oral people groups have found that for a people group to transition from being primarily oral communicators (0% literate) to having a literacy rate of just 30% often takes over a century. During that period of time, a printed Bible or other discipleship resource does them very little good, since the majority cannot read it. Making audio recordings of the Bible is a helpful bridge, but their language is still likely to change significantly over time. Unless the translation (and recording) is updated periodically, it is at risk of eventually passing completely out of use, because its usefulness at a linguistic level diminishes over time.

This was a significant part of the problem we ran into with the Uturuva translation team. The translation of the Bible into their language had been completed twenty years previously. Twenty years is the approximate length of a generation in many parts of the world where these smaller languages are spoken. So it is no surprise that the translation of the Bible into the Uturuva language—spoken by a primarily oral people group—needed to be revised within two decades after it was published. In order for their translation to continue to be effective, it needed to be revised after only one generation. This is significant, especially in light of the fact that many translations of the Bible in many languages around the world are already 3-4 generations old. It is highly likely that many of them already need significant revision before they will continue to be useful to the speakers of those languages.

Needed: An Updated Revision

By way of summary, we have seen that, while languages are dynamic and change over time, a discipleship resource that is translated into a given language does not change. It is static and impervious to the forces that affect the language into which it was translated. This means that, over time, the clarity with which the translated discipleship resource communicates Biblical truth for the people who speak that language decreases. Given enough time, the language can change right out from under it, rendering the resource as useless to that people group as the Bible verses in the Anglo-Saxon Proto-English Manuscripts are to speakers of modern English today.

In order for a discipleship resource to continue to be effective for a people group, it needs to be revised periodically. The revision process updates a translation so that it reflects the changes that have occurred in the language since the publication of the discipleship resource. The revision may substitute modern forms of words for their historical counterparts in the original translation. Grammar structures may also be updated to reflect modern sentence structures. By periodically updating the language used in a translation of a discipleship resource, the resource will continue to be optimally effective for those who speak the current form of that language, instead of locking the resource into a historical form of the language that gradually fades out of use.

Needed: A Corrected Revision

In addition to updating the language used in a discipleship resource, the revision process provides an opportunity to correct mistakes found in the previous versions. No matter how hard a translator tries, the first version of a translation is rarely perfect. This is especially true for Bible translations in minority languages that do not have a well-established writing system and literate tradition. The Bible is a linguistically complex text, and the potential for inadvertently including errors in the first version of a translation is very high.

Christians from another people group in Papua New Guinea found this out the hard way. They had waited years for a translation of the Bible in their own language, but instead of great rejoicing when it was finished, there was intense disappointment. For some reason, the translation of the Bible in their language had unfortunately used the "k" sound in many words where a "g" sound should have been used instead. They could not read the translation out loud in church the way it was written because the errors made it sound like baby talk. "It is hard," they said, "to read the Word of God in church when everyone is laughing so hard they can not even hear you."

The discovery of problems in a published translation of the Bible is not a new phenomenon. In 1631, a printing of the King James Version Bible left out the word "not" from Exodus 20:14 and turned the seventh commandment into something altogether different than what was intended: "Thou shalt commit adultery." Some years later, another printing of the Bible was discovered to have numerous errors, including in 1 Corinthians 6:9, which read: "Know ye not that the unrighteous shall inherit the kingdom of God?"

Translation procedures and printing technology continue to improve, but the fact remains that translations of the Bible are often found to have problems that need to be corrected. The problems can include anything from simple spelling errors and grammatical mistakes to syncretistic doctrine introduced by translating the name for Jesus as the name of a false god. It is unrealistic to expect translators to get everything in a translation 100% correct in the first version. Instead, there needs to be a means of rapidly revising translations that are found to have errors.

This is not always as easy as it sounds. The revision process can be difficult, but compared to the task of *getting permission* to legally revise a translation, the actual revision process can be downright easy.

Who Gets to Revise It?

Many, if not most, Bible translations are the legal property of some entity. Regardless of whether or not the organization that did the translation formally filed for a copyright, copyright laws in most countries make "all rights reserved" the default for any creative work, even a translation of the Bible or discipleship resources. So if an expatriate Bible translation team learned a language and created a translation of the Bible into it, the translation of the Bible automatically becomes the copyrighted possession of their organization without the need to register the copyright. It attaches to the translation at the point of creation.

Before continuing, we need to note two things about this scenario: First, it assumes the translation team is either translating from the Public Domain original texts (which is highly unlikely) or has permission from the publisher of the source translation (whether in English or the original languages) to create a translation of their work. Second, this is a generalization of what commonly occurs in many translation projects, although each project is different and the determination of who owns the copyright on a translation can be more complicated.[16]

A revision of a Bible translation is a derivative work of the original. The creation of derivative works is one of the rights that is reserved by copyright law for the legal owner of the content. This means that until they are given permission, the people who speak that language have no legal right to revise the translation, regardless of the fact that it is in their own language and they may be the only speakers of that language. The translation of the Bible in their language may be full of errors that need immediate correction, but they themselves are not legally permitted to revise the translation of the Bible in their own language. In such cases, the translation is often the copyrighted possession of a mission organization, Bible society, or publishing company. Until the organization that owns the rights to it does the revision for them or releases it under a li-

---

16   For instance, if a translation team worked together with native speakers of the language to create the translation, the work may have been done in such a way that the ex-patriate translation team's organization jointly owns the copyright of the translation with the members of the team who are native speakers of the language. In such cases, the native speakers of the language may not even know that they (or their heirs) are equal owners of the translation, with certain rights and privileges due them. One of their rights, in such cases, includes equal financial compensation for any sales of the finished translation. Such is the nature of copyright law.

cense permitting others to do so, no one else has the legal permission to revise it.

In contexts like these, speakers of the language can do little but wait for the organization to do a revision. Thankfully, revisions of translations are sometimes undertaken. For large languages or for languages where the original translation team is still intact and able to do a revision, the translation may be updated and improved. But for many languages, this simply does not happen. Bible translation organizations do not have the personnel to take on the thousands of new translation projects that are needed, while also revising the translations that have already been published and now need to be updated.

Most translation organizations often only have one or two people who are able to speak the languages into which they have translated the Bible. When these people are no longer able to do a revision, the organization that holds the copyright on that translation no longer has anyone who could even do a revision in that language if they wanted to. In these situations, the translation of the Bible is the legal property of an organization that cannot maintain it through time. Gradually, its effectiveness in the language—which continues to change over time—decreases, to the point that it is effectively useless. The speakers of the language, who may already be willing and able to complete a revision, are legally prevented, in these situations, from revising the translation of God's Word in their own language.

A Step in the Right Direction

Bible translations that were completed after the rise of computers are often available in digital formats, making them much easier to publish, convert into formats that are useful on mobile phones, and revise as needed. But many translations of the Bible in hundreds of languages all over the world only exist in the "paper" world—printed text on paper. These translations are more likely to need revision than newer translations, because of the greater amount of time that has passed since they were published and the subsequently increased likelihood that the language into which the translation was made has changed during that time. But because these translations do not exist in digital formats, revising these translations is much more time-consuming and labor intensive. The texts first need to be scanned and converted to digital formats before they can be revised.

Some of the organizations that own the rights to these texts have begun the process of digitizing the texts. This lays the foundation for the process of revising the translations to correct mistakes and update the language to reflect the way it is spoken today. But if this process is to be completed and the effectiveness of these translations of the Bible is to be maintained, merely digitizing the texts and making them available online and in formats optimized for use on mobile phones is not enough.

In order to make these translations effective now and into the future, the texts themselves must be released under a license that permits the speakers of these languages to legally join in the task of revising the translations. Once the translations are released under an open license, Bible translation organizations, churches, and believers in these languages will be legally able to openly collaborate in the revision process. The openly collaborative model is a sustainable and efficient approach for achieving and maintaining the optimal quality of Bible translations in thousands of languages over time.

"Who's Going to Sue Us?"

Copyright restrictions on translations of the Bible and other discipleship resources create significant obstacles and hindrances to the spiritual growth of the global church. Ministries encounter the obstacles as they attempt to get legal permission to use copyright-restricted discipleship resources. Believers in the languages run into the same obstacles when they seek to use, build upon, and redistribute discipleship resources in their own language for the spiritual growth of believers in their own people group. All over the world, the absence of a core of legally unrestricted discipleship resources in every language hinders the advance of the Kingdom of God.

When faced with these obstacles, the temptation can be to ignore the legal restrictions and use the discipleship resources as needed, regardless of violating the copyright of another entity. In some parts of the world, it is standard practice to illegally copy and redistribute copyright-restricted digital resources, sharing them by email or websites. Entire file-sharing networks are dedicated to the free redistribution of copyright-restricted discipleship resources and Bible software programs that would otherwise cost each user hundreds of dollars.

From the point of view of believers who desperately need discipleship resources in their own language, these practices are understandable. One would be hard-pressed to argue that these kinds of legal hindrances on the spread of Biblical truth are a good thing

> All over the world, the absence of a core of legally unrestricted discipleship resources in every language hinders the advance of the Kingdom of God.

for the growth of the global church. After all, it costs a person nothing to share with a friend a copy of what they got for free, thus providing access to a discipleship resource that would not otherwise be available to them.

In the case of ministry organizations, the temptation can be great because they may be in a position to violate copyright restrictions and face little chance of legal prosecution for it. In order to move the ministry forward, they may be tempted to ignore the laws that hinder them in order to get more discipleship resources to more people. All too often, "managing the risk" of getting caught and prosecuted replaces doing what is right at any cost. Expedience does not make an action ethical, even if it is supposedly "for the Kingdom." We serve the Sovereign God who rules over everything —even man-made legal systems. It is imperative, then, that we live uprightly and maintain the highest standards of ethics and integrity, even when it is frustrating and limiting.

There *is* a way through the legal complexities of life in the digital age, but the way through is not built on a violation of copyright law.

CHAPTER 8

COPYRIGHT & THE 8TH COMMANDMENT

The eighth commandment is not complicated: "Do not steal." In the "paper" world, this was unambiguous, because physical objects are intrinsically "rival"—they cannot exist in more than one place at the same time. In the digital world, however, content can effectively exist in any number of places at the same time. This ability to share content in a "non-rival" way opens up new opportunities for the advance of God's Kingdom, but it conflicts with the "all rights reserved" of copyright law. We must not adjust our ethical standards based on convenience or the likelihood of getting caught, but strive for integrity and uphold the law even when it hurts. That said, it is crucial that adequate discipleship resources be made available under open licenses in order to provide an honest and legal means of meeting the urgent spiritual need of the global church from every people group.[1]

~ ~ ~

The invention of the airplane was a pivotal moment in the history of mankind. It forever changed the way we travel, by making it possible to move people and cargo long distances at much greater speeds than was previously possible. The airplane was an amazing invention that made possible things that had previously been impossible, but not everyone was thrilled with the side effects it introduced.

In 1945, Thomas and Tinie Causby experienced an unexpected side effect brought about by the airplane, and they were not impressed. The Causbys were chicken farmers in North Carolina and low-flying military aircraft were killing their chickens (apparently because the chickens became terrified and flew into the barn walls). So the Causbys filed a lawsuit against the government for trespassing on their land.

At first glance, this case would seem to be baseless. The airplanes never touched their land; they were flying over it. So the charge of trespassing would seem to be unsupported and the case likely to be thrown out. But there was more to it than that.

When the laws governing American property rights were written, there was no concept of air travel. The law held that property lines did not merely run in two dimensions, on the surface of the earth. A property owner did not just own the surface of his land, but all the land below it, to the center of the earth, and all the space above it, to "an indefinite extent, upwards."[2] So when the Wright Brothers invented a new technology—the self-powered airplane—they

---

1   Much of this chapter, including the title, is based on an original work by Bruce Erickson, "Intellectual Property and the Eighth Commandment," jul 2012, http://distantshoresmedia.org/blog/intellectual-property-and-eighth-commandment. It is made available under a Creative Commons Attribution-ShareAlike License.

inadvertently created the potential for conflict with these age-old laws governing property rights.

The Causbys' case depended on this law. If they owned not just the surface of the land, but the air above it as well, then they could sue the American government for flying its planes over their land, and they would have a good chance of winning. But the U.S. Supreme Court did not see it that way. Lawrence Lessig, in *Free Culture* writes:

> The Supreme Court agreed to hear the Causbys' case. Congress had declared the airways public, but if one's property really extended to the heavens, then Congress's declaration could well have been an unconstitutional "taking" of property without compensation. The Court acknowledged that "it is ancient doctrine that common law ownership of the land extended to the periphery of the universe." But Justice Douglas had no patience for ancient doctrine. In a single paragraph, hundreds of years of property law were erased. As he wrote for the Court,
>
> > [The] doctrine has no place in the modern world. The air is a public highway, as Congress has declared. Were that not true, every transcontinental flight would subject the operator to countless trespass suits. Common sense revolts at the idea. To recognize such private claims to the airspace would clog these highways, seriously interfere with their control and development in the public interest, and transfer into private ownership that to which only the public has a just claim.[3]

In this situation, the established law was on the side of the property holders. They had every legal right to claim the ownership of

---

2   St George Tucker, *Blackstone's Commentaries* (Rothman Reprints, 1969), 18, quoted in Lessig, *Free Culture*, 1.

3   Ibid, 2; "UNITED STATES v. CAUSBY, 328 U.S. 256," may 1946, http://caselaw.lp.findlaw.com/scripts/getcase.pl?court=us&vol=328&in-vol=256

the space above their land, and they did. But the law on which their argument depended had been written in a time and context where it was not possible to comprehend the kind of changes that would come about with the advent of new technology like the airplane. This new technology provided enormous and unprecedented benefits to society as a whole—rapid travel by air. But it conflicted with existing laws governing property rights.

The court realized that although the law stated a property owner had the rights to the space above their land, allowing an individual property owner to arrest the development of society by impeding the public's use of airplanes for travel was a revolting idea to common sense. The court overturned the established law and limited the rights of individual property holders. They did this, not because they cared nothing for individual property, but because they cared more that the advance of society in general not be impeded by overly aggressive restrictions governing individual property. Individual property rights were a good thing, but the ability for society to enjoy the benefits of unimpeded air travel was a greater good.

When Common Sense Does Not Revolt

The laws that were written to govern physical property did not make room for the possibility of great advances brought about by new technology that enabled air travel. In a similar way, the laws governing intellectual property were also written during a time when the monumental change that would be brought about by the invention of digital technology was impossible to imagine. The original laws governing copyright, specifically, were written in the pre-digital era and so, not surprisingly, reflect a pre-digital era mindset. But in stark contrast to the laws regarding private property, the laws regarding copyright have become more restrictive over the years, not less.

20/20 Downside

Whenever a new technology is invented, the established players in that industry tend to only see how the new technology could negatively impact their bottom line. The threats posed by a new technology are seen with extraordinary clarity, while the opportunities presented by the same technology remain unseen. James Boyle in *The Public Domain* refers to this tendency as "20/20 Downside."

The invention of the videocassette recorder illustrates this. The VCR created an immediate and massive concern to movie studios because it enabled people to record television and make copies of movies that they could then share with others. This, the studios feared, could not possibly be a good thing for their business. So they did what is usually done in such situations and took one of the key players in the development of the technology to court.

In 1982, the prosecution argued in *Sony Corporation of America v. Universal City Studios, Inc.*, that Sony's technology was only useful for infringing the copyrights of those who created the content. With evocative language and shrill warnings, the prosecution warned that videocassette recorders would critically cut into their revenue stream (because no one would go to the movie theaters anymore) and bring all manner of harm. It should therefore be declared illegal. During the legal proceedings some of the arguments from the prosecution bordered on hysteria. Jack Valenti, the head of the Motion Pictures Association of America (MPAA) stated the following:

> [The defendant] has said that the VCR is the greatest friend that the American film producer ever had. I say to you that the VCR is to the American film producer and the American public as the Boston strangler is to the woman home alone.[4]

---

4   "Home Recording of Copyrighted Works" (Law Building, Moot Courtroom, UCLA School of Law, Los Angeles, Calif., apr 1982), http://cryptome.org/hrcw-hear.htm

Despite all the rhetoric and dire warnings, the court ruled against the movie industry, and declared that the public cannot be denied the lawful uses of a technology just because some (or even many) may use the technology to infringe on others' copyrights. If the movie industry was correct, this ruling should have been the beginning of the end for them. What actually happened was that the videocassette rental market soon generated more than 50 percent of the movie industry's revenue.[5] If they had won their case against Sony, the same videocassette technology that generated this revenue would not even have been allowed to exist.

When personal videocassette technology was invented, all the movie industries saw was the potential negative side of the technology. They could see the downside clearly, but the upside of the new technology—new revenue streams and increased consumption of movies—was invisible to them. Even after they were defeated in court and videocassette technology became a new and significant revenue stream for them, media industries continued to oppose new technology.

In September 1998, Diamond Multimedia introduced one of the first personal MP3 players, called the "Diamond Rio." Anyone could transfer MP3 files from their computer to the portable player and take the music with them anywhere. The general populace was thrilled. The Recording Industry Association of America (RIAA), not so much.

The RIAA filed a lawsuit the next month against Diamond Multimedia, to "protect the creative content of the music industry." The RIAA alleged that the Rio "encourages consumers to infringe the rights of artists by trafficking in unlicensed music recordings on

---

5   Tina Balio, "Museum of Broadcast Communications, 'Betamax Case,'" 1997, http://www.museum.tv/archives/etv/B/htmlB/betamaxcase/beta-maxcase.htm, quoted in James Boyle, *The Public Domain: Enclosing the Commons of the Mind* (Yale University Press, 2008), http://www.thepublicdo-main.org/, 64.

the Internet."[6] But the court ruled against the RIAA, finding that personal MP3 players were not inherently unlawful, even though they could be used in unlawful ways.

Ironically, in the few months between the filing of the original lawsuit and the final ruling in the case, the new music download industry was already flourishing, and analysts were predicting it would be a 1.4 billion dollar industry within three years.[7] Today, the media download industry—that largely depends on portable media players—is a significant source of revenue for the music industry. As with the MPAA before it, the RIAA was unable to see the potential upsides to the new technology when it was first introduced, and they sued to get it declared illegal. As the lawsuit to make the videocassette illegal failed, so did the lawsuit to make the portable media player illegal. But the media industries were only a couple years away from a significant legal victory that would have a major impact on digital technology and filesharing over the Internet.

---

6   Robert A. Starrett, "RIAA loses bid for injunction to stop sale of Diamond Multimedia RIO MP3 Player; appeal pending," jan 1999, http://findarticles.com/p/articles/mi_m0FXG/is_1_12/ai_53578852/

7   Elizabeth Clampet, "Court OKs Diamond Rio MP3 Player," jun 1999, http://www.internetnews.com/bus-news/article.php/139091

Things Get More Restrictive

In 1999, Shawn Fanning was an 18-year old college freshman with an idea for a computer program that would make it possible for anyone to share files (especially audio files in the MP3 format) with anyone else, using the Internet. His software, called Napster, launched the first generation of "peer-to-peer" file sharing. Instead of putting an MP3 on a web server for download (a relatively complicated task beyond the capability of many computer users), the Napster software enabled users to connect directly to each others' computers over the Internet and copy MP3s rapidly and easily, from one computer to another. The general populace was thrilled, but the recording industry was decidedly not.

In 2001, in *A&M Records, Inc. v. Napster, Inc.*, several members of the RIAA sued Napster. They alleged that Napster engaged in both "contributory and vicarious" copyright infringement. They claimed that the primary intent of the Napster software was for illegal redistribution of copyrighted content and so should be shut down. This was, essentially, the same claim that was brought against Sony and VCR technology twenty years before. In those cases, the U.S. Supreme Court ruled that people could not be denied the legal use of a technology, just because some used it for illegal purposes.

But this time, the Ninth Circuit Court of Appeals ruled against the technology and in favor of the industry, making Napster illegal. Interestingly, a crucial part of their ruling had to do with establishing the "commercial" nature of filesharing. Users of the Napster software did not make any money by sharing files freely with each other. But the court determined a use was "commercial" if you got for nothing something for which you would otherwise have to pay.

On the surface, this seems to make sense, but, as Boyle notes, it creates its own problems.

To put it differently, one central goal of copyright is to limit the monopoly given to the copyright owner so that he or she cannot force citizens to pay for every single type of use. The design of the law itself is supposed to facilitate that. When "getting something for free" comes to equal "commercial" in the analysis of fair use, things are dangerously out of balance. Think back to [Thomas] Jefferson's analogy ["He who receives ideas from me, receives instruction himself without lessening mine, as he who lights his candle at mine receives light without darkening me."] If I light my candle at yours, am I getting fire for free, when otherwise I would have had to pay for matches? Does that make it a "commercial" act?[8]

Four years after the Napster case, another peer-to-peer filesharing program, called Grokster, was taken to court. Grokster, unlike Napster before it, did not maintain a central directory of all the files available for download from other computers. But in *MGM Studios, Inc. v. Grokster, Ltd.*, the U.S. Supreme Court found Grokster liable because they had "intended" to induce copyright violation. This decision rested on three factors: Grokster was trying "to satisfy a known demand for copyright infringement," they did not provide any means of filtering and removing copyright-infringing content on their network, and Grokster made more money from their advertising-supported software when more people were using it, although Grokster knew they were using the software to pirate copyrighted content.

A Legal Conundrum

Common sense has not revolted at the notion of greater copyright restrictions in the digital era. Internet and mobile technology opens up new opportunities for ministry in ways that could not

8   Boyle, *The Public Domain: Enclosing the Commons of the Mind*, 76.

have been fathomed just a few decades ago. But the laws governing copyright have not become less restrictive and have become more enduring.

As a result, countless missionaries, church leaders, publishers, teachers—Christians all over the world, run into obstacles on a daily basis that have to do with legal restrictions on discipleship resources. The magnitude of this need is difficult to describe without appearing to overstate the case: nearly 2 billion Christians, in thousands of people groups, speaking nearly 7,000 languages, and all but a handful of these languages are critically under-resourced. Countless discipleship resources exist in a few major languages, but they are legally "off limits" to speakers of most other languages, because of the man-made laws governing Intellectual Property.

Imagine the frustration they encounter on a daily basis. The resource is there, available in digital format on the Internet, and it could easily be translated, adapted, and redistributed for effective ministry. But they are legally prevented from doing so.

It is as frustrating for them as it would be for the pilot of an airplane if the common sense of the Supreme Court had not revolted against the notion of property rights extending infinitely above a person's land. Think of a pilot with a life-giving supply of food, water, and medicine that is urgently needed in order to save the lives of victims of a natural disaster. He is ready, willing, and able to fly his plane to those victims and deliver what they need for life.

But what if the law of the land had not been overturned by the Supreme Court, and air travel was restricted by the property rights of the land owners? Because of the legal rights of the owners of the land thousands of feet below, he is not allowed to fly unhindered through their airspace to deliver the supplies. First, he must jump through a number of legal hoops and be granted a license to fly over their land. What if he has contacted the land owners for permission and has not heard back? What if some landowners are attempting to establish an exclusive license agreement with him so as to gain as much revenue from his flights as possible? Maybe some have simply rejected his request for permission to fly over their land and there is no alternate route. Meanwhile, people are dying without the supplies—supplies that already exist, are in his plane, and could be easily delivered. Except the law says he cannot.

What should the God-fearing, law-abiding pilot do? Obey the law and let the people who need help die? Or should he disobey the law and save the lives of the people? Common sense revolts at the idea that one should ever be put in a position where they have to choose.

Yet, this is exactly the choice faced by believers all over the world, every day. Their need, while every bit as real and severe as the need experienced by victims of a natural disaster, is spiritual and eternal in nature. The obstacle they encounter is also due to legal restrictions governing the use of property. But in their case, the legal restrictions they are facing have tightened, not loosened, and their plight is getting worse, not better. They often find themselves between a rock and a hard place—either they break the law to get the discipleship resources they need, or they do not get them.

The problem is complex; the solution is not. Before proposing a solution, we will consider why the transition from the "paper" world to the digital world has significantly increased the complexity of the problem itself.

It Wasn't Always This Complicated

In the physical world, things pertaining to intellectual property rights have historically been less complicated. This is because the means of accessing someone else's intellectual property depended on physical objects (e.g paper and ink, in the case of books). Physical objects are costly and relatively difficult to produce and distribute (and, by extension, to reproduce and redistribute).

When we buy a physical book, we do not actually buy the book it-self (the content). We buy the paper, glue and ink that comprises the means of *accessing* the content. So though we refer to it as own-ership, saying things like, "That is my book," we do not actually mean that we are the author or that we own any of the rights to the book. We mean that we own the physical object that provides a means of consuming the content.

Owning a shovel and owning a book (or a magazine, a record, a cas-sette tape, etc.) are similar. They are both physical objects to which ownership rights attach. But they are remarkably different in that the shovel is only physical property, while the book is physical property that contains content (text and images) that is the intel-lectual property of someone else.[9]

This is all well and good in the physical world because both the shovel and the book are subject to the laws of physics. A physical object cannot simultaneously exist in more than one place. They are both "rival" goods, meaning that if you have a book (or a shovel), I cannot also have it at the same time. It follows, then, that if you have a book and I want it, a transfer of ownership must take place before I can have it. There are only two ways for me to legally acquire your book: either you sell it to me, or you give it to me. (You might also loan it to me, but that is a temporary arrangement and does not affect the ownership of the book.)

Unless you sell or give the book to me, I am unable to have it with-out resorting to more dubious means of getting it: either stealing it from you or copying it. The complexity and risk of stealing a physi-cal object (e.g. breaking into someone's house to steal a book) makes physical theft a relatively rare occurrence. The complexity

---

9   A shovel might also contain the intellectual property of someone else if, for example, some part of the design has a patent on it or displays a cor-porate trademark. Furthermore, one could argue that tools like a shovel in the physical world are analogous to software in the digital world. Given our focus on content and copyright restrictions, we will not address other forms of intellectual property in this argument.

and cost of reproducing and redistributing copies of a physical book are also very high, creating "friction" in the process. This friction is so great that mass reproduction and redistribution of physical objects like books is a relatively rare occurrence that is outside the means and expertise of most people. So, for the most part, things in the "paper" (physical) world are easy to understand and predictable.

There is no ambiguity in the eighth commandment. It is pretty clear that when God says "Do not steal" (Exodus 20:15) that He means, in fact, that we are not to take what does not belong to us. Theft in this context is easily understood as "the act of stealing; specifically: the felonious taking and removing of personal property with intent to deprive the rightful owner of it."[10]

"Do not steal" applies equally to a shovel and a book, regardless of the fact that the physical book contains the copyrighted content of someone else, while the physical shovel is just a shovel. In the physical world, one does not need to contemplate the difference between stealing a shovel and stealing the intellectual property of someone else by illegally copying and redistributing thousands of copies of their book for free without their permission. Most of us do not have the means or opportunity to do so anyway. So functionally, we can treat a shovel and a book in much the same way.[11]

But the simplicity of the "paper" world does not carry over into the digital world.

---

10   "Theft," n.d., http://www.merriam-webster.com/dictionary/theft

11   Although we do not address it here, the rapid growth of 3D printing technology is starting to lower the cost of creating (and recreating) some objects in the physical world. It is not without cause that some consider the 3D printing revolution to be the start of a new, technologically-driven industrial era.

The Tangled Web of the Digital World

With the rise and widespread use of digital technology and the Internet, the neat, understandable, and straightforward legal system governing intellectual property in the physical world got thrown into disarray. At a foundational level, a significant difference between the digital world and "paper" world, is that in the digital world, content (including discipleship resources) can be transmitted like ideas, instead of objects. This can be illustrated easily.

Think of a huge elephant with red paint dripping off. Can you picture it? This idea was transmitted to you almost instantaneously and at no cost to either the initiator or recipient. You can now, for reasons known only to you, easily transmit this same idea to any number of other people in your sphere of influence, at no cost to you or them. If this sounds remarkably similar to the act of emailing a picture to a friend or sharing a music file between two mobile phones, that's because it is. Transmitting ideas in the real world and transmitting content in the digital world are functionally identical.

In the digital world, books and record albums that used to only be accessible through physical, atoms-based objects, can be accessed through digital files, comprised of "bits" (like eBooks and MP3s). This makes access to the content contained in those files much more convenient. It does so in two ways: by removing the "friction" that exists in the physical world, and by making it possible for content to be shared in a non-rival way.

As we saw above, there is an intrinsic cost and complexity in mass reproduction and redistribution of physical objects. This inconvenience tends to enforce compliance with the law in the world of "paper", but the inconvenience disappears in the digital world. Everyone who owns a computer, laptop, or mobile phone has an inexpensive digital copy machine that can make any number of exact copies of any digital content and send it to anyone, anywhere, instantly, all at virtually zero cost to themselves. In the digital world, anyone with a computer can easily become a content distributor—doing so no longer requires centralized corporations with massive infrastructure and huge budgets.

Not only has digital technology removed the friction in the process of reproducing and redistributing content, but sharing of content in digital formats can now be done in a "non-rival" way. In the physical world, if I give you my book, I cannot also have it at the same time. But in the digital world, if I give you my eBook, I *can* have it at the same time, because giving you a copy does just that—provides you with a copy, without depriving me of my own. In fact, I can give any number of copies of the book to any number of people and it does not in any way affect my access to the content myself.

This is stating the obvious, but it has significant implications. Effectively, this means that digital content is not subject to the same constraints that govern content in the physical world. The same digital file (or an exact clone of the file) *can* exist in more than one place at the same time. And this reality is what introduces some ambiguity into things that used to be simple.

How Not to Solve the Problem

At a recent meeting of ministry leaders, the topic of discussion was how to provide discipleship resources to speakers of other languages, at the lowest cost. One of them produced a USB flash drive and, with a wink, invited the others to copy the resources on it and use them for ministry. The resources were in a major world language and would be of tremendous usefulness to people working in the parts of the world where that language is spoken. But one look at the terms of use governing those discipleship resources showed that it was not licensed for others to redistribute or use without

Copyright & the 8th Commandment   219

permission. The means and opportunity of meeting the need triumphed over ethics.

Anyone who uses computers and digital technology in ministry has probably felt this tension. There is a ministry need that must be met. Maybe there is an urgent need for use of an evangelistic video, or to record and distribute an audio version of translated Scriptures, or to install Bible translation software without having a license key, or countless other ministry needs. The tools and resources are available, but the law stands in the way. We may strongly disagree with the restrictions in place. Our common sense may revolt at the idea that copyright law—especially with regard to discipleship resources—should be so restrictive in the digital age.

The temptation in these contexts can be to adopt a slipshod approach to ethics that relegates the morality of a given action to convenience, and the likelihood of getting caught. When we find ourselves in a position where we may be able to cut corners or infringe on the legal rights of others without getting caught, it is easy to elevate "meeting the need" above obedience to the law. We look both ways and determine that no one is going to sue us for it, and so we break the law.

The transition from the "paper" world to the digital world was a massive shift, but the the definition of "theft" in the digital world has already been established by the legal systems of the countries in the world. It may not be what we want to hear, but the law is very clear on the matter. God's law says you are not to steal. Man's law says what you create, you own, and what you own is "all rights reserved," plain and simple. Unauthorized distribution or use of someone else's content is, therefore, theft.

This can be very frustrating for people in ministry who have no other means to meet the spiritual needs of the people they serve. Paul's admonition to the Christians in Rome, who were also in a frustrating context (to put it mildly), is an encouragement to those facing this tension:

> Everyone must submit to the governing authorities, for
> there is no authority except from God, and those that exist
> are instituted by God. So then, the one who resists the au-
> thority is opposing God's command, and those who oppose
> it will bring judgment on themselves... For government is
> God's servant for your good.
>
> —Romans 13:1-4

There is no authority except from God, and government is God's servant *for our good*. When faced with a government whose decrees were often contrary to the advance of the Gospel, Paul reminds the Romans that God is sovereign. God was sovereign over the Roman government of Paul's day, and He rules over governments that make increasingly restrictive rules regarding intellectual property rights. His purposes may be hidden from us, but they never fail. God may move in a mysterious way, but the heart of the king is still in God's hand, and He turns it wherever He wills (Proverbs 21:1).

The government writes the laws, and the government is God's servant. So as those who bear the Name of the Sovereign God and exist to be His witnesses, we would do well to conduct ourselves in a manner "worthy of the Gospel" (Philippians 1:27) and conduct ourselves "honorably among the Gentiles" (1 Peter 2:12). Even in matters of intellectual property.

Unity, not Division

There is precedent in Scripture for Christians to disregard the "rules of man" in order to obey God. In response to the Jewish leaders' demands that they stop preaching in the name of Jesus, Peter and John answered them, "Whether it's right in the sight of God for us to listen to you rather than to God, you decide; for we are unable to stop speaking about what we have seen and heard" (Acts 4:19-20).

Attempting to apply this principle to the arena of discipleship resources and copyright law is unwise, for the simple reason that the contexts are not identical. In the case of the disciples' preaching, the "law" imposed on them provided them with no recourse but to break it, because they absolutely *had* to preach the name of Jesus. There was no way for them to obey both God and man. This is not the same context we are addressing here. If the laws of man prohibited the creation of discipleship resources at all, the case could be made that this principle applies.

Even if this principle *did* apply in the context of discipleship resources and copyright law, a missiological strategy based on it would be unlikely to provide an effective, sustainable means of meeting the need for adequate discipleship resources in every people group, for obvious reasons. It not only violates the God-given right of those who own the content, but it would likely pit Christian against Christian in legal battles, in a way that would bring discredit to the name of Christ (1 Corinthians 6:6-7). This is exactly the wrong way to resolve the problem. Instead, it is better to appeal to those who own the discipleship resources needed by the global church for generosity in the licenses that govern some of those resources. In this way, the need of the global church can be met, while also enabling the entire global church to experience greater unity, rather than division and conflict.

Toward a Legal, Ethical Solution

The technology that the global church needs in order to provide adequate discipleship resources in every language of the world, for the spiritual maturity of believers in every language, already exists. But we cannot take full advantage of these (and future) technologies in the legally restrictive and potentially dangerous context of the ministry world today. Taking full advantage of digital technology's unprecedented opportunities for the advance of the Gospel conflicts with the default rights preserved for content owners by copyright law. But the solution is not to break the law and hope we do not get in trouble for it.

That said, upholding the rights of content owners and emphasizing the importance of living in submission to God and to the man-made laws that govern matters of intellectual property does not imply that all is as it should be. The restrictiveness of copyright law combined with the urgent need for discipleship resources in thousands of languages leaves the global church with little recourse but to resort to piracy in order to grow spiritually. This should not be.

The law of the land gives content owners the right to hold on to the exclusive rights to their own content and to leverage it in whatever way they wish for maximum financial reward from it. They can do so throughout their entire life and the lives of their heirs for many decades after they die. But just because it is a government-sanctioned right and the default approach does not make it the best strategy for making disciples of all people groups.

If we are serious about completing the commission that Christ has given us, we may need to rethink our concept of ownership. We may also need to release some of our best discipleship resources under open licenses for the glory of God and the eternal good of His global church. So while we uphold the law governing the intellectual property rights of the content creators, we also appeal for greater openness and legal freedom of the discipleship resources that are created.

Some will rightfully point out that the freedom to make one's living from creating and selling discipleship resources is not just a legal right, but a Biblical one as well. This is true, as we have already seen in passages like 1 Corinthians 9. In that chapter, Paul clearly states that those who sow spiritual things have the right to receive physical benefits from their labor, and those who proclaim the gospel should get their living by the gospel. There is much to say about this right, and we will look at it in greater detail in the remaining chapters. But the key is this: while Paul does uphold this as a right, the conclusion of his argument in this exact context is easily overlooked:

> Nevertheless, *we have not made use of this right*, but *we endure anything rather than put an obstacle in the way of the gospel of Christ*... I have made no use of any of these rights, nor am I writing these things to secure any such provision... What then is my reward? That in my preaching I may present the gospel free of charge, so as not to make full use of my right in the gospel.
>
> —1 Corinthians 9:12,15,18, ESV, emphasis added

Paul models for us an attitude toward ministry that chooses to endure anything for the advance of the Gospel, rather than leverage a God-given right, when doing so puts an obstacle in the way of the Gospel. It is this attitude, when adopted by content owners, that will meet the need for adequate discipleship resources for the global church from every people group. This is the kind of humble, generous, sacrificial attitude that is able to go the distance and reach the "least of these."

Releasing restrictions on discipleship resources is not a trivial matter. Removing the legal obstacles that hinder the growth of the global church requires humility and a willingness to endure the loss of what would otherwise have been gain. But it is also not without reward. Paul states that there is inherent reward in presenting the gospel free of charge and without making full use of our rights in the gospel.

As the global church moves toward the creation of a core of legally unrestricted discipleship resources in every language, there is a great need for clarity, consistency, and legal accuracy in the terms of the licenses that govern these resources. It is important that we avoid licenses that are incomprehensible, as well as those that seem easy to understand but are not legally sound. We also need to avoid the complexity and headache of incompatible licenses. Some licenses sound like a good idea but should be avoided because they are based on a deficient understanding of how the Internet and digital technology works, making them self-defeating and unsustainable.

What we need is a license that permits everything that needs to be permitted for the growth of the global church and advance of the Gospel, while also protecting what needs to be protected. This license needs to permit the legal and unrestricted translation, adaptation, repurposing, redistribution, and use of discipleship resources. But it needs to do so in a way that minimizes exploitation and preserves the openness of the content, even through multiple generations of translations and adaptations.

What we need is a license that does not conflict with new advances in digital technology, but facilitates the free sharing of content all over the world, by whatever new means is invented in the future.

What we need is a license for freedom.

~ ~ ~

Conclusion of Part 3: *The global church is only able to freely translate, adapt, build on, revise, redistribute and use adequate discipleship resources without hindrance when those resources are released from the copyright restrictions that prevent them from doing so.*

PART 4

ENDING THE FAMINE

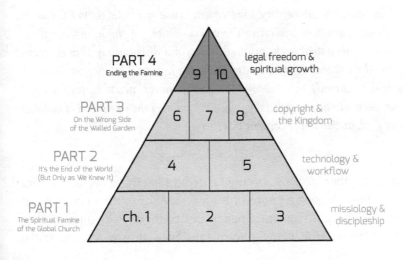

PART 4
Ending the Famine

PART 3
On the Wrong Side
of the Walled Garden

PART 2
It's the End of the World
(But Only as We Knew It)

PART 1
The Spiritual Famine
of the Global Church

9 | 10
legal freedom &
spiritual growth

6 | 7 | 8
copyright &
the Kingdom

4 | 5
technology &
workflow

ch. 1 | 2 | 3
missiology &
discipleship

CHAPTER 9

A LICENSE FOR FREEDOM

Licenses governing the use of discipleship resources tend to be restrictive, focusing on everything that people are not allowed to do with the content. These licenses do not enable the global church to legally work together in the translation, adaptation, distribution, and use of discipleship resources in any language. By contrast, the Creative Commons Attribution-Share-Alike License grants anyone the freedom to use and build upon the content without restriction, subject to the two conditions of the license: crediting the original content to the original owner, and distributing what is created from the original content under the same license. This license is ideally suited to provide the freedom the global church needs to legally equip themselves to grow spiritually, while minimizing the likelihood of commercial exploitation of the content by others.

~ ~ ~

On November 18, 2006, Jeremy Keith did something decidedly unremarkable. He took a photo of his friend, Andy, with a cheap point-and-shoot digital camera. Then he posted it on Flickr, a photo sharing website. Like many photos on Flickr, it was an amateurish photo, slightly blurry and washed-out. Apart from the fact that the picture had been taken in NASA's Vehicle Assembly Building, and part of the building's internal structure was visible in the background behind Andy, the picture was completely forgettable.[1]

Over a year later, Jeremy received an email inquiry about his photograph.

> "Is the photo *Andy in the VAB* your image on Flickr? If so can you please contact me with regard to possibly allowing us to use a part of this image in a feature film."

A little later, a second email arrived with a few more details about the request. But, being in the final stages of packing for a trip, Jeremy did not reply immediately and soon forgot about the emails. A few days later, he received a call on his mobile phone.

> "Hi. I sent you two emails about using a picture of yours..."

He started to explain how the photo was licensed and how it could be used.

> "Well," the voice on the line said, "the thing is, getting your name in the credits usually costs at least $1,500. That is why we need you to sign the license release form I sent."

What kind of movie was this, anyway? Jeremy asked where they were going to use his photo.

> "It is for a movie that is currently in production called *Iron Man*, starring Robert Downey, Jr."

His photo, in *Iron Man*? That was something that didn't happen every day. The woman faxed him the paperwork which he signed and sent back. A few weeks later, *Iron Man* was released and there, right around the three minute mark, was the background from the pic-

---

1   This story recounted in Jeremy Keith, "Iron Man and me," dec 2008, http://adactio.com/journal/1530/

ture taken on his point-and-shoot camera, with the main characters imposed over it in the foreground.

How does a blurry, washed-out photo of no apparent value wind up in a film that grossed over half a billion dollars worldwide? The answer has to do with one small thing that Jeremy did with his photo that changed its future forever: he released it under a Creative Commons license that permitted it to be reused for any purpose, without restriction. Even as a scene in a feature film from a major movie studio.

The Way We've Always Done It

Copyright attaches to creative works automatically and reserves all rights for the creator of the content. When a content creator grants permission for others to use their content, they do so by means of a license.[2] A license is a legal document that specifies the freedoms granted to others, and the conditions for those freedoms. Licenses often are comprised of multiple pages of "legalese" explicitly stating exactly what you are not allowed to do with the content. For example, consider these points taken from a typical license on a website that provides media content to consumers via the website and a software application (note that the license text is briefly explained in italics below and a more complete version of the license is available in appendix A, "A Classic License"):

- "...no rights... in or to the Content are granted to you."

  Meaning: You do not have permission to translate, adapt, build on, redistribute, or use the content, except as specifically granted in the license.

---

2   Verbal agreements may be binding, but they can be difficult to prove. Written licenses are preferable as they provide a record of the terms and conditions of the agreement.

■ "The copying... redistribution... adaptation... creating of derivative works [including translations]... is strictly prohibited..."

*Meaning: You are specifically not granted permission to trans-
late, adapt, build on, or redistribute the content. A total of 18 specific activities are absolutely forbidden in the Terms of Use for
this license.*

■ "Subject to your strict compliance with these Terms of Use,
The Owner grants you a limited... revocable... license..."

*Meaning: If you comply with every aspect of the conditions stated
above, you are granted a license providing minimal freedom to
consume the content, but that license can be revoked at any time
at the sole discretion of the owner of the content.*

■ "...[you are granted a license] to:
1. download and use The Owner's software... and
2. listen to and view media streamed from the Website;"

*Meaning: All this license permits you to do is use the software,
and consume the media online.*

■ "Provided that you [do not do 25 specific things]..."

*Meaning: The two things you are permitted to do with the con-
tent are sandwiched between long lists of everything you are expressly forbidden from doing.*

As you can see, licenses generally attempt to close all the loopholes
and maintain complete and absolute control over the content. Licenses tend to grant the user only the absolute minimum permission necessary to consume the content, usually nothing more beyond that. These licenses are not licenses for freedom, nor are they
designed to be. They are licenses to preserve the content owner's
copyright-enforced "all rights reserved."

Licenses like these worked well in the analog world of "paper", because disseminating content usually required using a third party, like a publisher or record label. The content creator would transfer to them some or all of the rights to the content they created, and the publisher or record label would market and distribute it on their behalf, keeping a significant portion of the revenue in the process.

> These licenses do not enable the global church to legally work together in the translation, adaptation, distribution, and use of discipleship resources in any language.

In the digital era, however, anyone can create and distribute content using the Internet, and traditional licenses are often too restrictive for their purposes. A new artist may want to release their music from some restrictions so that their music can be legally redistributed and heard by more people, leading to new venues to perform their music. An author may want their work to be freely available in many publications, increasing their exposure and the potential for other writing opportunities.

Writing a traditional license to provide these freedoms is a complicated undertaking. It usually requires the services of an Intellectual Property attorney, which can be expensive to secure. All of this adds up to a climate that is restrictive, costly, frustrating, and even antithetical to the very design of the Internet and computer technology.

There is another way

Eric Eldred was a computer programmer-turned-publisher who specialized in printing and making books available which were in the Public Domain. In 1998, the United States Congress passed the Sonny Bono Copyright Term Extension Act, which added 20 more years to the duration of copyright. Eldred had been preparing to print books that were about to enter into the Public Domain under the terms of the existing copyright law, but the lengthening of copyright would prevent him from doing so for another 20 years.

He went to court—and eventually the Supreme Court—to challenge the constitutionality of the act. Lawrence Lessig, a professor at Harvard Law School, was his lawyer, and they were joined by others, including computer scientists and law professors. Together, they founded the Creative Commons in 2001. Their purpose was to provide tools that enable content owners to share aspects of their copyrighted works with the public. Explaining the purpose of the organization, Lessig described it like this:

> It was intended as a grass-roots movement of creators, otherwise known as copyright owners, who would look at this default of "all rights reserved" and say "I don't need all rights," the most they (sic) need is some rights.[3]

Eldred's case generated a lot of attention, but he was eventually defeated. An hour after their defeat in the Supreme Court, the Creative Commons was given a grant of one million dollars to launch the movement. In 2002, they released the first version of the Creative Commons licenses, enabling content creators to release some of the restrictions on their copyrighted works, for reuse by others. These licenses enable content owners to change the default "all rights reserved" on their content to "some rights reserved." As James Boyle notes about the Creative Commons:

> It can be seen as re-creating, by private choice and automated licenses, the world of creativity before law had per-

---

3   Lawrence Lessig, "Early Creative Commons history, my version," aug 2008, http://www.lessig.org/blog/2008/08/early_creative_commons_history.html

meated to the finest, most atomic level of science and culture.[4]

Since 2001, Creative Commons has grown rapidly in numerous
countries. It has become the de facto means of releasing content
from copyright restrictions. By 2009, an estimated 350 million
works were released under Creative Commons licenses, including
major content repositories like Wikipedia.

But Is It Safe?

The idea of pre-clearing anyone in the world to use one's content
can seem alarming. It could seem that this is an unsafe means of increasing the usefulness of the content, because it could be inviting
abuse. The concern of others doing bad things with good content
may be a legitimate concern. As we have already seen, content
holders cross that bridge when their content goes from analog to
digital, not when they release it under an open license. Copyright
restrictions do not prevent bad things from happening to digital
content. They provide a legal platform to enforce the content
owner's rights.

In the digital world, there *is* a danger that your content will be mis-
used or that others will take advantage of it. But there is a greater
danger than that. The real danger is that, in the increasing flood of
new content available on the Internet for free, so many people will
never even know your work exists that it will be as irrelevant as if
it had never been created.

One way to increase the effectiveness of the content is to release it
from some copyright restrictions so that it can be legally used in
more places by more people for more purposes. Doing so increases
the exposure of the content and the "mindshare" of the content
creator. This is what happened with the photograph taken by

---

4   Boyle, *The Public Domain: Enclosing the Commons of the Mind*, 218.

Jeremy Keith that wound up being used in the *Iron Man* movie. Because the photographer released it under a Creative Commons license, it was available for use in ways that far exceeded the expectations of the copyright holder.

Advantages of Creative Commons Licenses

Content creators often want to grant others permission to use their content in a specified way. They correctly do so by means of a license. Unfortunately, content creators sometimes assume that writing their own licenses is a good idea. Few content creators have the legal training in copyright law that would give them sufficient understanding of licensing to author an effective license. Because of this, writing a "homemade" license often results in a license that is ambiguous, changes frequently over time, may not say what the author thinks it says, and may not be enforceable in other legal jurisdictions around the world.

Creative Commons licenses address all these shortcomings and provide many other advantages.

Royalty-free – All Creative Commons licenses are free for anyone to use without paying license fees or royalties to Creative Commons. There are no applications or registrations—a content creator can simply apply the license to their work and make the work available to the public.

Clear – Every Creative Commons license includes a human-readable summary of the license. In a few clear paragraphs, the license summary explains exactly what the legal code (the actual license) does, in terms that do not require a degree in copyright law to understand.

Accurate – The legal code for each license is written by Intellectual Property Rights attorneys and people who understand how digital technology and the Internet work. The licenses are legally defensible and have been upheld in numerous cases in various parts of the world.

Internet-optimized – In addition to providing a human-readable summary of each license, Creative Commons provides a licensing tool that creates a "machine-readable" version of the license as well, for use on the Internet. This metadata affixes to the content itself or to a web page that contains the content, and enables search engines to catalog the content according to the type of Creative Commons license.[5]

International – Creative Commons works with affiliates in various parts of the world to port the legal code of the licenses into different legal jurisdictions. This ensures that what the license says and means in one language and legal jurisdiction is enforceable in other languages and legal jurisdictions as well.[6]

Stable – Licenses that are written by well-intended people who are untrained in copyright law are often unstable, revocable, and easily changed. This makes it difficult for people to use the content legally, and with the confidence that the terms of use will not be changed at a later date, making their previously legal use of the content illegal. By contrast, Creative Commons licenses are irrevocable and stable. When content is released by a copyright holder under a Creative Commons license, it cannot be "unreleased" later —it has been locked open. This requires careful thought before licensing, but has the immense advantage of creating a context that is reliable and unchanging. People using content according to the terms of a Creative Commons license need not worry that the li-

---

5   This technology is useful in many applications, such as when searching for images. Various search engines, including Google and Flickr, provide filters that enable the searcher to limit the search results to images released under Creative Commons licenses and with specific permissions made available by the copyright holder.

6   At the time of writing, the licenses have been ported into 50 legal jurisdictions. Note that not only are the licenses translated into other languages, but the legal code itself is adjusted as necessary to account for the differing legal nuances in different jurisdictions.

cense will be unilaterally changed out from under them at some point in the future.[7]

Compatible – The freedoms granted to users by Creative Commons licenses make it very clear what content is legally compatible for use with other content. This greatly increases the usefulness of the content, making it possible to legally (and easily) remix and reuse content from various sources, according to the terms of the Creative Commons licenses used by the copyright holders.

Freedom, Conditionally

There are a number of Creative Commons Licenses, each having its own strengths.[8] Not every Creative Commons license is equally useful for the purpose of equipping the global church with discipleship resources. Some Creative Commons licenses are so open that unintentional problems can be encountered later on when using them. Many of the licenses are too restrictive, failing to grant the global church the legal freedom they need to translate and make discipleship resources effective in their own languages.

The Creative Commons licenses work by combining certain conditions under which a work is made available. These are the conditions used (in different combinations) in the licenses:

---

7   The licenses themselves are improved and upgraded by Creative Commons over time, but the changes that are made to the licenses are designed to make them backwards compatible with previous versions of the same license. See "About The Licenses," accessed September 26, 2012, http://creativecommons.org/licenses/

8   There are six main licenses: Attribution (CC BY), Attribution-ShareAlike (CC BY-SA), Attribution-NoDerivs (CC BY-ND), Attribution-NonCommercial (CC BY-NC), Attribution-NonCommercial-ShareAlike (CC BY-NC-SA), and Attribution-NonCommercial-NoDerivs (CC BY-NC-ND). Creative Commons also provides tools that work in the "all rights granted" space of the public domain. Their CC0 tool allows licensors to waive all rights and place a work in the public domain. Ibid

- **Attribution** (BY) – Requires crediting the original work to the original creator (or the owner of the work, if they are not the same).

- **ShareAlike** (SA) – Only permits redistribution of a derivative work created from the original (like a translation or adaptation) when it is made available under the same license.

- **NoDerivs** (ND) – Forbids the creation of derivative works, including translations. The work must only be passed along unchanged and in whole.

- **NonCommercial** (NC) – Forbids any use of the content in ways that are considered "commercial".

The conditions of "NoDerivs" (preventing the creation of derivative works) and "NonCommercial" (preventing commercial use of a work) are deceptively attractive. They would seem to prevent the abuse of the content by others and the commercial exploitation of the work. But licenses with these conditions do not grant the global church the freedom they need to effectively use the content.

The Problem With "No Derivatives"

Any license that includes the condition that prevents derivative works ("NoDerivs") prevents, by definition, the translation of the content into any other language, since a translation is considered a derivative work. It prevents the adaptation of the content for effective use in a different culture. It also prevents revision of the content at a later point in time to maintain the accuracy and usefulness of the translation as the spoken language changes and needed corrections to the original version of the content are discovered.

The Problem With "Non-Commercial Use Only"

Licenses containing a "non-commercial use only" condition (labeled as "NonCommercial" in Creative Commons licenses) are fairly common and appear to be a good choice for "free-of-charge" discipleship resources. In reality, they significantly limit how far and effectively a resource can be used. In the context of equipping the global church to equip themselves for spiritual growth, licenses containing a "non-commercial use only" condition perpetuate significant obstacles for the global church.

The theological and practical considerations of this topic are addressed in detail in appendix B, "The Non-Commercial Use Only" Problem. (Note: in the next chapter we will consider sustainable models for the creation of "open" discipleship resources that do not have a "non-commercial use only" condition.) This is the "thumbnail sketch" of the argument:

- **Too Restrictive** – The "non-commercial use only condition" restricts the global church from using any means necessary—even commercial models—to provide that resource to every people group in their own language. Making content available as in physical formats (like books, CDs, etc.) costs money and requires a business model— which is forbidden by this condition—if it is to be sustainable. In addition, the content itself cannot be redistributed using commercial models like ad-supported radio, websites, or mobile applications.

- **Prevents Good Things** – The "non-commercial use only condition" prevents for-profit companies from using commercial models to improve and redistribute the content, because they cannot recover their investment. In the secular world, content that is not encumbered by a "non-commercial use only" condition is frequently improved upon by for-profit companies. Because of the terms of the license (i.e. "ShareAlike"), these improvements also benefit everyone else who uses the content.

- **Makes the Global Church Work for Nothing** – The economic context of many in the global church makes it imperative that they be given the same freedom of making their living from the translation and distribution of discipleship resources that we enjoy. The "non-commercial use only" condition forbids it.

■ **Ambiguous** – Some licenses that contain a "non-commercial use only" clause qualify it by allowing a person to "only cover expenses". This begs the question: what does it mean to "only cover expenses"? Who decides what qualifies as "covering expenses" and what crosses over into commercial use? Given the complexities of countries, economics, and currencies (among other factors) that affect the answer, there is no way for the global church to know in advance if their use of content governed by this condition is ethical.

■ **Unnecessary** – The "non-commercial use only" condition is used in an effort to prevent the commercial exploitation of content by others. This condition is not needed to prevent unchecked commercial exploitation of digital content. The "open" nature of the licenses prevent the creation of a monopoly, and a license with a "ShareAlike" condition requires sharing back to the community whatever is created from the original work. These factors tend to greatly limit the possibility of commercial exploitation, while encouraging the possibility of commercial partnership. (This is addressed in greater detail later in this chapter.)

There is one license that is ideally suited for discipleship resources in the digital age. The Creative Commons Attribution-ShareAlike License—which does not have a "non-commercial use only" condition—is an excellent license that grants all the freedoms needed by the global church, while also ensuring that no one gets "locked out" of the works over time.

The Creative Commons Attribution-ShareAlike License

The sample of a traditional license we saw earlier in this chapter was characterized by clear statements of everything you are not allowed to do with the content, as it is the exclusive property of the content owner. Standing in sharp contrast to the restrictiveness of a traditional license, the Creative Commons Attribution-ShareAlike is all about what you *can* do with the content. Here is a basic overview of the license (see appendix C, "The Attribution-ShareAlike License" for the complete license, including the human-readable summary and legal code):

You are free:

- *to Share* — to copy, distribute, and transmit the work
- *to Remix* — to translate, adapt, build on, redistribute, and use the content
- to make commercial use of the work

Under the following conditions:

- *Attribution* — "Give credit where credit is due." You must attribute the original work in the manner specified by the owner of that work (but not in any way that suggests that they endorse you or your use of the work).

- *Share Alike* — If you translate, adapt, or build on the original work, you may distribute what you create only under the same or similar license to this one.

A traditional license, like the one referenced earlier in this chapter, exists to provide consumers with the right to merely access the content for consumption. It specifically does not give them any rights to the content itself—permission to use the content remains the exclusive right of the copyright holder. The license gives you permission to access the content on their website or use their software, but it does not give you the right to translate, adapt, build on, redistribute, or make publicly available the content itself.

The Attribution-ShareAlike License, by contrast, provides not only free access to the content, but grants legal freedom to actually use the content itself. In fact, the freedom granted is so far-reaching that a person can use the content in much the same way as if it were their own (though not *exclusively* their own). They are legally pre-cleared to use it in any way they need, including translating, adapting, and redistributing the content.

While this sounds like a good thing for the people using the content, this degree of freedom can raise some concerns for the owners of the original content. Apart from the concern of commercial exploitation (addressed below), one of the most common concerns about "open-licensing" a discipleship resource has to do with preserving the identity of the original content creator and the authoritativeness of the original content.[9] It could seem that, if anyone can do anything with the content, such a permissive license might invite abuse and confusion.

The Attribution-ShareAlike License is specifically designed to address this concern. The significance of the "Attribution" and "ShareAlike" conditions are considered briefly here and in detail in appendix D, "Analyzing 'Attribution' and 'ShareAlike'".

"Attribution" Points the World to You

The "Attribution" condition requires that any use of the content, like a translation or adaptation, clearly attribute the *original* work to the original creator. It clearly states:

---

9   In the digital world, especially, identifying the authoritative source of a work is important. Given the ease of copying, modifying, and redistributing content in the digital world (whether legally or illegally), it is important for anyone who encounters a derivative work to be able to identify and locate the original, authoritative work.

- the name of the original work
- the name of the original work's creator
- the website where the original work can be found
- the license under which the original work is made available.

The attribution statement is important because it provides a direct link back to the original work. It is important to understand, however, that *a statement of attribution is not a statement of endorsement*. It merely shows the consumer of the work where to find the original.

In the digital world, *you cannot control what happens to your content*, but you can control what is on your own website. When there is a statement of attribution on any derivative work—good or bad—the user is provided with a direct connection to the website of the owner of the original work. For resources available online, this link increases the "search engine optimization" of the original website. It also gives the owner of the original

Any derivative work is legally required to include a statement of attribution.

work the opportunity to exhibit the original work, against which the derivatives are compared. The owner of the original work can also list which derivative works (like translations) of the original are "authorized", or make other works available.

Note: The "Attribution" condition in the Attribution-ShareAlike License is important because it provides a direct connection between the consumer and the original content. In the event, however, that specific uses become a disadvantage, the copyright holder has the legal right to remove their name from the derivative work.

"ShareAlike" Locks the Content Open

The "ShareAlike" condition provides one crucial element to the license. It prevents the "locking down" of any derivative works, keeping them open for use by others while also limiting the potential for commercial exploitation of the content.

Without the "ShareAlike" condition, a translation of a discipleship resource would automatically become the "all rights reserved" possession of the translator. Because of the way copyright law works, the owner of the original work would need to request a license to use the translation of their own work from the translator. The "ShareAlike" condition prevents this situation by stipulating that any translations (or other derivative works) of the original content can only be made available under the same license.

The "ShareAlike" condition also prevents someone from taking the content, improving it in some way, but then redistributing their improved version of the content under a restrictive license. It requires that the freedoms granted in the original work be granted in all generations of derivative works on into the future. In this way, what was intended to be free and unrestricted, remains free and unrestricted.

How "Attribution-ShareAlike" Minimizes Commercial Exploitation

The Creative Commons Attribution-ShareAlike License is designed specifically to allow commercial use of content, but in such a way that commercial exploitation is virtually impossible. The net result is a license that does not cripple the global church, permits commercial partnership to improve the content, but prevents monopolization and price inflation. Here's how it works. (Note: this is explained briefly here and in detail in appendix B, "The Non-Commercial Use Only" Problem.)

There are three factors that contribute to the unique strengths of this license:

- **Market Economics** – In order for there to be maximum commercial value of a work, there needs to be a state-enforced monopoly that permits only one entity to sell (or otherwise monetize) the work. By releasing a free-of-charge work under an Attribution-ShareAlike License, this monopoly is destroyed. It is difficult for a third party to sell a digital resource that is freely available online, and if anyone can legally sell and redistribute a physical resource (like a book), the price will tend to remain very low—especially for popular resources.

- **The "Attribution" Condition** – The legally-mandated inclusion of a statement attributing the original work to another may tend to minimize the likelihood of a third party wanting to market and redistribute another entity's discipleship resource. But even if they do, this may actually be a better thing for the owner of the content, because the third party is marketing and promoting the discipleship resource (with a link to the owner's website) to the entire customer base. This increased mindshare for the owner of the original work is extremely valuable, and opens up many other opportunities for them that might not otherwise have existed.

- **The "ShareAlike" Condition** – Any attempt to reformat and distribute content released under an Attribution-ShareAlike License is legally required to be free of encryption or Digital Rights Management that would otherwise restrict the original freedoms given by the owner of the content. This means that even if someone packaged the content and attempted to sell it, anyone else could legally redistribute it for free from their own website. The content is locked open, forever, in all future versions and formats. Without an exclusive lock on the content, it is nearly impossible to leverage the content for commercial exploitation.

Identity and Authority in a Digital World

In the "paper" world of copyright-restricted content, protecting the distribution chain of the content was an effective strategy for preserving the identity and authoritativeness of the content creator. If you tightly controlled the distribution and maintained exclusive rights to it, you could prevent (or at least minimize) bad things happening to your content, which could reflect poorly on you. By locking everything down, you could ensure that what was in your printed book was only what you wanted to be in your printed book, nothing more, nothing less. Because it was so costly and complicated to create and distribute a book, content tended to remain static and unchanging. So if you controlled the distribution of the (mostly) static content, your identity was relatively safe.

But that only worked in the "paper" world. In the digital world, the notion that you can control the distribution chain—when every Internet-connected computing device in the world can be part of the distribution chain—does not reflect reality. In the digital world, content rarely stays static, being both trivially easy to change and transmit. You may still be able to maintain control of the *legal* distribution chain, but only by fighting against the very advantages of the Internet and digital technology. The traditional "lockdown" mindset toward content distribution finds itself threatened by every advance in technology that makes file-sharing easier, faster, cheaper, more efficient, and more anonymous.

Attempting to limit distribution also puts the content owner directly against their number one ally: the consumer. You want the consumer on your side, singing your praises. But in this context, the assumption is that the consumer is the "bad guy" who might try to use digital technology to give away free copies of your stuff.

So the default stance tends to leverage the implicit threat of legal action, and to make use of Digital Rights Management techniques to encrypt and lock down the content to prevent distribution.

In this context of attempting to preserve one's identity and author-itativeness, the world suddenly went from "offline, analog, under control" to "online, digital, out of control." Given this massive shift, the idea of releasing content under an open license that legally per-mits others to create new content from it may seem ridiculous. Wouldn't this be a recipe for disaster, by making it legal for anyone to do anything with "my stuff" and then distribute it anywhere in the world without my permission? This would seem to be a disaster for preserving one's identity and authoritativeness, and this is also *not* what a Creative Commons license does.

Releasing a work under a Creative Commons Attribution-Share-Alike License does not give away the ownership of the work.[10] It merely licenses the work in a manner that permits the global church to legally redistribute "my" work, and to make their own translations (or other derivatives) of it available in the nearly 7,000 languages of the world, without restriction (but subject to the two conditions of the license). I still own "my stuff" but have given the entire global church legal freedom to use it effectively and without hindrance for their own spiritual growth. Releasing discipleship re-sources under an Attribution-ShareAlike License is not a recipe for disaster. It may actually be the most missiologically strategic move a content creator could make.

Almost, Not Quite

Some owners of discipleship resources do realize the urgent spiri-tual need of the global church. Many want to help the global church by providing greater legal freedom in the licenses govern-

---

10   Ownership of a creative work is only relinquished when a work is in the Public Domain, where no rights are reserved.

ing the use of their discipleship resources. There is often a hesitancy, however, to go "all in" and release discipleship resources under an open license like the Attribution-ShareAlike License.

This hesitancy may exist for different reasons, but two things are the same in every situation. First, there is no obligation—ethically or legally—to release discipleship resources under an open license. The law and the Bible both state that owners of Intellectual Property are free to dispose of their property (or not) as they choose. The second point to consider in these contexts is this: either a discipleship resource is released under an open license, or it is not. There is no middle ground.

Some owners of discipleship resources have attempted to create an arbitrary division at the license level that separates the world into different jurisdictions, often along economic or linguistic lines. This can sound like an attractive solution. It would seem to prevent commercial exploitation in lucrative markets (like the West, or in larger languages) while still permitting the rest of the global church to benefit freely from the work. In reality, however, these "pseudo-open" licenses often create more problems than they solve.

Without addressing the significant theological and missiological implications of explicitly defining such divisions in a license, let us consider the implications from a practical perspective. Consider, for example, a license that only permits people in developing nations to freely translate, adapt, build on and redistribute a discipleship resource (while everyone in a developed country must first go through the proper channels to request a specific license).

Right away, we run into the problem of defining a "developing nation". Unless the owner of the discipleship resource provides a comprehensive list of countries that qualify, what definition should be used? Furthermore, when is a country no longer "developing" but "developed"? When a country crosses that line, are the Christians using the discipleship resource now infringing on the rights of its owner? Are the translations and adaptations of the content that Christians in that country freely and legally made for their own spiritual nourishment (while the pseudo-open license applied) now illegal? Are they now required to pay royalties for each use? What if their work has been in widespread use for many years and they are unable to afford the royalties?

The same kinds of problems and ambiguity arise from license restrictions that depend on the size of a language. A pseudo-open license might grant broad freedoms for translation and use of the content only in languages having fewer than, say, ten million speakers. But again, we encounter the problem of accurately drawing the line dividing the two groups. Few people outside of the academic world know or care how many people speak their language. Not only that, enumerating the number of speakers of a given language is notoriously complicated, especially as the number changes over time. What is the authoritative resource that should be consulted to resolve the ambiguity? What happens when a language grows in size and crosses the "ten million speakers" line? Are the translators of the discipleship resource now in violation of the license, even though their work was legal when their language had fewer than ten million speakers? Are Christians who received the resource for free now going to be required to pay royalties after the fact?

This is only a small sample of the kinds of problems encountered when attempting to gain the benefits of releasing a discipleship resource under an open license, while also maintaining certain restrictions. The two are mutually exclusive. Clarifying and enforcing the restrictions requires that someone be in the position of referee, authorizing or disallowing use of the content. Such licenses are, by definition, not open licenses. The unavoidable reality is that either a discipleship resource is completely open or it is not—one cannot have it both ways. Almost open is still closed.

Discipleship Resources Want to Be "Open"

Imagine a world in which every single Christian could freely share in the sum of all Biblical knowledge. Think how the world would be a better place if every believer in the world had unrestricted access to adequate discipleship resources, in their own language. Think how God would be glorified by the sacrificial giving of His Church to meet the spiritual needs of others.

This kind of vision of being able to share freely in knowledge is not new. It is the driving vision behind secular organizations like the Wikimedia Foundation, whose vision is this:

> Imagine a world in which every single human being can freely share in the sum of all knowledge. That's our commitment.
>
> —Wikimedia Foundation Vision Statement[11]

The secular world has tapped into the vision of unrestricted access to collaboratively created information and content in a big way. But the Church is, in some ways, still reflecting the same 6th century mentality of copyright restrictions that launched the Battle of Cúl Dreimhne over copying someone else's Bible.

What if the global church were to adopt a vision that was as generous, gracious, and loving as the God we serve—a vision of everyone, everywhere with free access to adequate Christian discipleship resources in their own language. The good news is, this vision is already starting to come to pass. Christians all over the world are starting to work together, across denominational and organizational lines, for this purpose. A core of open-licensed, unrestricted

---

11 "Vision," n.d., http://wikimediafoundation.org/wiki/Vision

discipleship resources is starting to be created to meet the massive need of the global church.

This pool of unrestricted discipleship resources is the Christian Commons.

CHAPTER 10

THE CHRISTIAN COMMONS

The Christian Commons is a core of discipleship resources released by their respective owners under open licenses. These licenses permit the unrestricted translation, adaptation, distribution, and use of the content by anyone, without needing to obtain permission beforehand or pay royalties. The concept of a Christian Commons is not new—it is profoundly Biblical, being rooted in Old Testament principles and lived out in the New Testament church. The Christian Commons provides the necessary content and legal freedom for believers from every people group to openly collaborate in the completion of the Great Commission. Because the content is open-licensed, speakers of any language—even those with the smallest numbers of speakers—can legally translate and use the content without hindrance.

~ ~ ~

"You have ten minutes to solve the problem. Begin!"

The tension in the room was palpable as each team started working through the word problem they had been given. A few minutes before, the faculty at our college had divided up the students from all the student leadership teams and given each group a sheet of paper with a problem to solve. Now, with the clock ticking down, we were in a race to be the first team to successfully solve the problem.

As the time continued to count down, a nagging sense that something was not right began to creep in. We read and reread the problem we had been given, but no matter how hard we tried, we could not solve it. It was as though we did not have all the pieces to the puzzle... So we started again and reread the problem once more.

Thankfully, it appeared that all the other groups were encountering the same problem. Quizzical looks and animated conversations suggested that our competitors were also struggling. Which, given our frustration and confusion, was good news—if we couldn't solve the problem, at least they couldn't either.

There was something else going on that was strange and a little distracting. The faculty who were moderating the competition kept walking around the room, between the various groups of frustrated competitors asking, over and over again, "How big is your team?" At first, we tried to ignore them, but it became increasingly difficult to do so. "How big is your team?" The clock ticked down to three minutes left. "How big is your team?"

Suddenly, it dawned on us. Our suspicions were right! We did *not* have all the information we needed to solve the problem we had been given. It was a complicated problem, but we had assumed that the solution could be correctly deduced from the content of the story problem we had each been given. We thought all that was needed was for our little team to try harder. This seemed logical—how else could you run a competition to see which team was fastest? Now we were starting to wonder if the other teams had different information than we did. Maybe they had something that would help us solve our problem, and maybe we had information that would help them...

Almost as if on cue, leaders from each team took their word problem and ran to the middle of the room where we spread the papers out on the floor. Sure enough, we had each been given the same word problem, but each team had a different set of information about the problem. No one team had been given enough information to solve the problem by themselves. Solving the problem required every team to share the information they had with the others. Only by being able to freely use the sum total of all our information, could the problem be solved. Either there would be no winner, or all the teams would win together.

We had not realized that when the faculty divided us up into teams before the competition, they had not actually said we were in teams. In fact, they had never even said it was a competition. They had merely put people in different parts of the room and handed them a word problem to solve. Our natural predisposition to competition and our default tendency toward an exclusivistic tribal mentality did the rest. We assumed that this was just another competition where there would be one winner and many losers, like all the other competitions we had experienced before.

It was this predisposition toward competition that resulted in our failure. We were so narrowly focused on solving our own problem and "winning" that we were unable to take a step back and answer the game-changing question: "How big is your team?" Everyone heard the question, numerous times, as we struggled with our own little problem. But we never took the time to answer the question, until it was too late.

By the time we realized that we were only groups of people with limited information, that the actual team was comprised of all of us together, and that the competition was not against each other but against time, it was too late. We ran out of time and failed to solve the problem. We had been given what we needed to arrive at the correct answer, but because of our inability to move beyond a "competition" mindset, we failed.

Toward a Christian Commons

The exclusive rights afforded to a content owner by copyright law can tend to foster division and a mindset geared toward competition. It does not always do so, but it does make my content exclusively mine and your content exclusively yours. By default, then, what I have is locked up behind my legal wall, for use by me, and what you have is locked up behind your legal wall, for use by you.

It is when adequate "unlocked" discipleship resources do not exist that the spiritual growth of the global church is hindered. The "walling off" of the garden (the sum total of discipleship resources in a given language) tends to segment the Church. This, in turn, tends to keep the various elements of the "team" disconnected and, effectively, in competition against each other.

The solution is not a mandatory redistribution of wealth. This is unbiblical and not what is proposed here. That said, the solution *does* involve sharing with those who "have not". This should not be alarming, however, as it is a profoundly Biblical concept and the sharing that happens is only ever a completely voluntary choice on the part of those who "have".

In the remainder of this chapter we will look at the specifics of the Christian Commons, the Biblical basis for it, new models for creating it, and its end result.

What the Christian Commons Is

The Christian Commons is the sum total of every Christian discipleship resource, in every language of the world, that is released under an open license, like the Creative Commons Attribution-Share-Alike License. Every discipleship resource in the Christian Commons is made available under a license that grants to anyone the irrevocable and unrestricted legal freedom to use any means—including commercial—to redistribute the work as-is and remix (create derivatives from) the work, including the creation of translations, adaptations, and revisions. Anyone who encounters content in the Christian Commons is legally pre-cleared to use it in any way, for any purpose, immediately, and without any hindrance.

These are the specifics of the Christian Commons itself:

Content – The Christian Commons is comprised of content, specifically discipleship resources. It is the common pool of open-licensed Christian teaching, content, information, knowledge, songs, and other resources intended to bring people to salvation and spiritual maturity. It does not include other forms of Intellectual Property, physical property, or digital tools such as the source code for software.[1]

Christian – The Christian Commons is comprised only of content that reflects and teaches established Christian doctrine. The content may reflect the views of any Christian denomination in secondary or peripheral matters, but is necessarily in agreement with orthodox Christianity in matters of primary doctrine. Thus, content in the Commons may express a variety of viewpoints on the topics that have historically been viewed differently by various Christian denominations (e.g. the mode, means, and age of baptism; the nature and function of the Lord's Supper; the order of events in the end times; etc.). All content in the Christian Commons agrees on matters of foundational Christian doctrine (e.g. the sinfulness of man, the holiness of God, the deity of Christ, His atoning sacrifice for sins, salvation by God's grace through faith, etc.). Content that that does not adhere to the foundational doctrines of the Christian faith is, by definition, not part of the Christian Commons.

---

1   There is a significant need for ministry-focused technologies that are available under open licenses (i.e. "open-source software"). As proposed here, the Christian Commons does not negate this need in any way; it merely focuses on the actual content itself, rather than the tools that provide access to the content.

Pre-cleared & unrestricted – In order for content to be included in the Christian Commons, the copyright holder must release it under a license that grants anyone unrestricted and irrevocable permission to create derivatives (including translations and revisions) from the content, redistribute, and use it. These freedoms are granted proactively, without the need for anyone to specifically ask permission first. Content in the Christian Commons is not encumbered by "non-commercial use only" or "no derivatives" restrictions. An ideal license for content in the Christian Commons is the Creative Commons Attribution-ShareAlike License, for all the reasons listed in chapter 9.[2]

Decentralized – There is no central repository or governing authority that determines what is in the Commons and what is not. The Christian Commons is decentralized and "fluid" in this regard. Repositories and collections of resources in the Christian Commons will facilitate access to existing content, but there is no single arbiter of what content is in the Christian Commons and what is not.[3]

Instantaneous – A discipleship resource that is released by the copyright holder under an open license that grants the permissions listed above is automatically part of the Christian Commons. There is no formal induction process beyond the release of the content by the owner. The resource may be obscure and not easily found by others, but at the point that it is released under an open license, it is in the Commons.

---

2   The popular "Attribution-NonCommercial" (CC BY-NC), "Attribution-NoDerivs" (CC BY-ND), "Attribution-NonCommercial-NoDerivs" (CC BY-NC-ND), and "Attribution-NonCommercial-ShareAlike" (CC BY-NC-SA) do not provide the global church the freedom they need to translate, adapt, revise, and build on discipleship resources.

3   Given the intrinsically decentralized nature of the global church, attempting to create an official repository presided over by gatekeepers who determine what is and is not "in" the Christian Commons is counterintuitive. A centralized structure such as this would be ineffective, hopelessly bureacratic, and antithetical to the very nature of the Christian Commons.

Voluntary – All content that is in the Christian Commons is there by the voluntary choice of the copyright holder. There is no mandate or compulsion for any copyright holder to release any or all of their content into the Christian Commons. If they own it, they are free to do with it as they choose. The only exception is for content created from other works that are released under a license that includes a condition requiring any derivatives to be released under the same license (like the Attribution-ShareAlike License). Such works are required to be "shared alike" using the same license under which they were released.

Multimedia – Content in the Christian Commons is comprised of multimedia resources as well as text. Christian audio and video resources are of immense importance for the equipping of the global church, the majority of which is primarily oral in their means of communication.

Multilingual – The Christian Commons is comprised of content in any language. Although most discipleship resources currently exist in only a handful of languages, the translation of discipleship resources in the Christian Commons will hopefully extend to every language of the world.

What the Christian Commons Is Not

Not a redistribution of wealth – The Christian Commons is not a mandatory taking from those who have to those who do not. Instead, it is based purely on the generosity of those who have discipleship resources and voluntarily choose to release them under an open license for the unrestricted good of the global church.

Not a revolution – The Christian Commons is not a revolution that attempts to overthrow the traditional paradigm for creation and distribution of discipleship resources. It peacefully co-exists with traditional models for equipping the global church. The "open" ethos of the Christian Commons merely provides another approach to meeting the same need, doing so in a way that leverages modern technology to accelerate the process, rather than depending on legal restrictions that conflict with the advantages made possible by technology.

Not an organization – The Christian Commons is not an organization, hierarchical structure, association, or coalition. It has no governing authority, no membership and no formal means of joining. It is merely a body of unrestricted Christian content pro-actively made available under an open license for the good of the global church.

Not the Public Domain – The Christian Commons is not the same thing as discipleship resources in the Public Domain. Discipleship resources in the Public Domain have no copyright restrictions at all, so these resources are in the Christian Commons. But not all content in the Christian Commons is in the Public Domain. Most of the content in the Christian Commons that is useful to the global church is still under copyright and has a copyright holder. The content itself has voluntarily been made available under a license that grants others the freedom to translate, adapt, build on, revise, and redistribute without restrictions. The release of the content under the open license that puts it into the Christian Commons does not, however, nullify the copyright-holder's ownership of the content. The content is still owned by the copyright holder, and the license under which the content is released depends on copyright law for its enforcement.

Not copyright assignment – Some attempts at providing "open" solutions for Christian content use an approach that involves assigning the copyright of content to a neutral third party that oversees it. The Christian Commons has nothing to do with this model. Content in the Christian Commons is still owned by the original copyright holders (except in the case of content in the Public Domain), though the freedoms granted to others for the unrestricted use of the content are broad.

Not license management – Some attempts to facilitate the legal use of discipleship content (especially worship songs) provide a means of mediating between the content owner and those wanting to use it. Content in the Christian Commons is not managed by a mediating entity because the content itself has been pre-cleared for anyone to use it freely, without requiring permission or management and oversight by a third party.

Not for the half-hearted – There is a very clear line between "open" content and "closed" content. Those who legally own discipleship resources often find themselves in a position where they really want to release restrictions on their content to bless the global church. But there can often be a strong motivation to also try to maintain some restrictions on the content at the same time, such as trying to prevent bad things from happening to it or attempting to ensure that no one takes commercial advantage of it. One cannot have it both ways. Either content is unrestricted and released into the Christian Commons under an open license, or it is not. Once content is released into the Christian Commons under an open license like the Attribution-ShareAlike License, there is no going back. The license is irrevocable and the content is locked open, forever.

The Biblical Basis for the Christian Commons

The world has changed rapidly in the last two decades. The creation of a Christian Commons is a means of aligning Great Commission strategies with Scripture, as well as with the technological resources God has given the global church in the 21st century.

The Original Christian Commons

In the early church, some believers had plenty while others were in lack. In order to meet the physical needs of those who lacked, the ones who had plenty voluntarily gave up their exclusive ownership of *some* of what they had, for the good of the entire church.

> Now all the believers were together and had everything in common. So they sold their possessions and property and distributed the proceeds to all, as anyone had a need.
>
> —Acts 2:44-45

They realized that what they owned was not really theirs, but had been given to them by God to meet the needs of others. They had a greater goal than merely their own well-being and comfort. So they voluntarily (not under compulsion) chose to give up some of their individual and exclusive ownership of some of their possessions and property, without repayment. They chose to have these things in common.

To be sure that the significance of this is not missed, Luke mentions the same thing two chapters later:

> Now the full number of those who believed were of one heart and soul, and no one said that any of the things that belonged to him was his own, but they had everything in common.
>
> —Acts 4:32, ESV

But this time, we are told what the outcome was of their selfless and sacrificial choice to have everything in common:

> There was not a needy person among them...
>
> —Acts 4:34, ESV

Those in the church who could not meet their own needs had their needs met by those who had plenty. The church was not divided along organizational or denominational lines. They were united ("of one heart and soul") and their unity led directly to generous sharing—without restrictions—of what they owned.[4]

Note again: no one was required to do this. Giving up property for use by others was not a mandate—it was a voluntary choice on the part of the owners of the property. No one was required to give anything up, or less of a Christian if they do not. Not only that, if they *did* decide to give something up, they were not required to give *everything* up. Peter made this perfectly clear when speaking to Ananias about the land he had sold:

> "Wasn't it yours while you possessed it? And after it was sold, wasn't it at your disposal?"

> —Acts 5:4

With Peter, we strongly affirm the right to private property! We also affirm that contributing to the Christian Commons is neither a mandate nor an "all or nothing" proposition. Releasing one work into the Christian Commons does not assume or require releasing everything one owns into it. One might choose to give everything, or one might choose to give some things, or one might choose to not be part of it. All options are equally valid and Biblically-supported.

The need and the solution of the Church in the 1st century is essentially the same in the 21st century: some people are in need, while others have an abundance and can voluntarily meet that need if

---

4   Some argue that this model was a temporary arrangement, only used because the early church thought Christ was coming back in that generation. Interestingly, there does not appear to be evidence in the text itself to support this assumption. It may not have been the only model used by the early church, but a straightforward reading of the text would seem to suggest that this *is* a model put forward as a highly effective means of meeting the needs of the church.

they so choose. In the first century, the need was for tangible property. This need still exists today, and meeting it is a good thing, although it does not replace the great thing of "making disciples of all nations." In the realm of discipleship, the need faced by believers is for intellectual property ("discipleship resources"), rather than physical property.

The Christian Commons, as proposed here, is an implementation of the Biblical principle of voluntarily holding some discipleship resources "in common" in the arena of Intellectual Property, for the express purpose of meeting the spiritual needs of the entire global church. Those who own the copyrights on discipleship resources can help meet the needs of others in the global church who are lacking by voluntarily releasing the content under an open license. By putting a discipleship resource into the Christian Commons, anyone in the global church is given the legal freedom to use it for spiritual growth without any restrictions.

The Privilege of Sharing in Ministry

One of the greatest privileges for every Christian (not just clergy) is being directly involved in ministry. Jesus Christ "personally gave some to be apostles, some prophets, some evangelists, some pastors and teachers, *for the training of the saints in the work of ministry*, to build up the body of Christ..." (Ephesians 4:11).

Sharing in ministry is costly and difficult. But those who have experienced it can testify that sharing in ministry is a rich privilege. In the first century, the churches of Macedonia were among the least likely to want to give generously to meet the needs of others, but they begged insistently to be involved in sharing in the ministry:

> We want you to know, brothers, about the grace of God granted to the churches of Macedonia: During a severe testing by affliction, their abundance of joy and their deep poverty overflowed into the wealth of their generosity. I

testify that, on their own, according to their ability and beyond their ability, they begged us insistently for *the privilege
of sharing in the ministry to the saints...*[5]

—2 Corinthians 8:1-4, emphasis added

It is a tremendous privilege to give sacrificially to meet the needs of
the global church—both their physical and their spiritual needs.

Providing for Those with No Rights

God cares for those who cannot care for themselves. Throughout
Scripture we see a recurring pattern of God being the defender of
the helpless. God says of Himself that He "watches over the sojourners [and] upholds the widow and the fatherless" (Psalm 146:9).

When God gave the law to Israel, He specifically instructed those
who "have" to make provision for those who "have not".

When you reap your harvest in your field and forget a sheaf
in the field, *you shall not go back to get it*. It shall be for the sojourner, the fatherless, and the widow, that the Lord your
God may bless you in all the work of your hands. When you
beat your olive trees, *you shall not go over them again*. It shall
be for the sojourner, the fatherless, and the widow. When
you gather the grapes of your vineyard, *you shall not strip it
afterward*. It shall be for the sojourner, the fatherless, and
the widow.

—Deuteronomy 24:19-21, ESV

---

5   Later in the same chapter, Paul states that the purpose of generosity is
not to create a burden for those who "have" but instead that there may be
equality: "It is not that there may be relief for others and hardship for
you, but *it is a question of equality*— at the present time your surplus is
available for their need, so their abundance may also become available for
our need, *so there may be equality*. As it has been written: "The person who
gathered much did not have too much, and the person who gathered little
did not have too little" (2 Corinthians 8:13-15, emphasis added).

There are two things to note about this principle that are immediately applicable here. The first is that in Israel at that time, the sojourners, the fatherless, and the widows had limited rights and were easily exploited. The law ("you shall not steal") was on the side of those who had land and could feed themselves legally. In this passage, God instructs those who own property to not make full use of their rights, so as to provide for those who have nothing.

What if we adopted this principle for the building of the Christian Commons? Instead of "going back to pick up every last sheaf", "going over our olive trees a second time", and "stripping our vineyards", we could live by this principle in the realm of discipleship resources. Rather than lock up *everything* we own under "all rights reserved", we could proactively release some of our resources under open-licenses and into the Christian Commons. In so doing, we would help provide for the global church—many of whom have no legal rights to acquire discipleship resources in any other way.

The second point to note about this passage is the clear statement of God's blessing for those who live by this principle: "that the Lord your God may bless you in all the work of your hands." God cares deeply for the well-being of His Church, especially those who cannot provide for themselves. When we provide for the (spiritually) hungry, God blesses the work of our hands.

Avoiding Partiality

In Luke 10, Jesus told a story about a Samaritan who willingly incurred a financial burden to meet the need of someone who could not meet their own needs. James picks up this theme of "loving your neighbor as yourself" in the context of not showing partiality between "neighbors" based on their socioeconomic status.

> My brothers, *do not show favoritism* as you hold on to the faith in our glorious Lord Jesus Christ. For example, a man comes into your meeting wearing a gold ring and dressed in fine

clothes, and a poor man dressed in dirty clothes also comes in. If you look with favor on the man wearing the fine clothes and say, "Sit here in a good place," and yet you say to the poor man, "Stand over there," or, "Sit here on the floor by my footstool," haven't you discriminated among yourselves and become judges with evil thoughts?...

Indeed, if you keep the royal law prescribed in the Scripture, Love your neighbor as yourself, you are doing well. *But if you show favoritism*, you commit sin and are convicted by the law as transgressors.

—James 2:1-9, emphasis added

The legal climate governing the world of Intellectual Property Rights is, by default, partial to those who have money. The process of negotiating rights, writing up legal agreements, and paying attorney fees can require a significant amount of capital. Such agreements are often only established when there is potential for financial profit for the parties involved. In the context of world missions, this collides with the linguistic and economic reality of the global church.

The global church needs discipleship resources translated into the thousands of languages they speak, but they are often not financially well off. Most of the languages in the world have fewer than 10,000 speakers. This means the base of potential consumers of a discipleship resource in languages like these is so small that it will often not be a viable undertaking for organizations using traditional funding models. These languages will also generate small "numbers" and meager analytics for a "free of charge" (but copyright-restricted) resource. Often for these reasons, the classic model for creating, translating, and distributing discipleship resources tends to be less favorably inclined for the small and the "have-nots."

A few verses later, and in the same context, James continues:

What good is it, my brothers, if someone says he has faith but does not have works? Can his faith save him?

If a brother or sister is without clothes and lacks daily food and one of you says to them, "Go in peace, keep warm, and eat well," but you don't give them what the body needs, what good is it? In the same way faith, if it doesn't have works, is dead by itself.

—James 2:14-17

In a spiritual sense (and often a physical sense as well), this is the exact context of the global church in most languages of the world. They have nothing to eat spiritually, while speakers of a handful of languages (especially English) have an unending feast of discipleship resources. Picture a famished beggar on the street, while a table is spread before him in a sumptuous feast—a feast with "Do Not Cross" lines around it that legally prevent him from meeting his desperate need for food. This is not anyone's intent! No one purposefully raised the barriers to prevent others from joining the feast. The way copyright law works, however, means that those who own the content are the only ones who can tear down the barriers, by releasing the legal restrictions that the law grants to them alone.

> Copyright law means that those who own the content are the only ones who can tear down the barriers, by releasing the legal restrictions that the law grants to them alone.

It is good to pray in faith that God would meet the spiritual needs of the global church. It is better to pray in faith while also helping to meet their needs by giving them what they need. Effectively meeting their needs moves beyond the "give them a fish" mentality of "free of charge" access to legally-restricted content. Instead, it "teaches them to fish" and provides them with the "fishing tackle" they need—the legal freedom to translate, adapt, build on, revise, redistribute, and use existing discipleship resources in their own languages, without any restrictions.

The Gospel of Giving: God's Blessing

The Christian Commons is built on the concept of voluntarily and sacrificially giving of ourselves, without receiving payment for what we give or maintaining control over the gift, in order to meet the needs of the global church. When applied to the realm of Intellectual Property and discipleship resources, specifically, it can seem revolutionary. But it is actually neither new nor revolutionary. Even for the church in Acts, it was not a new concept. The origins of voluntary giving of an individual's wealth for the good of the whole is profoundly Biblical. It is one of the foundational principles established for God's chosen people, Israel.

The Israelites were commanded by God to be generous to their brothers and loan the poor whatever they needed. These were loans, not gifts, and they were expected to be paid back by the recipient of the loan. But there was a catch. At the end of every seven years, the Israelites were to cancel the debts that were owed to them by their fellow Israelites in the land. So, if a poor person had not paid back the loan and the 7-year cycle was up, the debt was canceled. The loan became a gift.

> At the end of every seven years you must cancel debts. This is how to cancel debt: Every creditor is to cancel what he has lent his neighbor. He is not to collect anything from his neighbor or brother, because the Lord's release of debts has been proclaimed.
>
> —Deuteronomy 15:1-2

The purpose of this mandate to loan generously and cancel debts at the end of every seven years was specifically intended to meet the needs of the poor. One of the ways by which God's people are to be different from the world in which they live is through their generosity to those less well-off.

> If there is a poor person among you, one of your brothers within any of your gates in the land the Lord your God is giving you, you must not be hardhearted or tightfisted toward your poor brother. Instead, you are to open your hand to him and freely loan him enough for whatever need he has.
>
> —Deuteronomy 15:7-8

God, however, knows how desperately wicked our hearts are. In a context like the one established among the children of Israel, the tendency would be to willingly loan to the poor in the early part of the seven year cycle (when there is a good chance of the loan being repaid), but become increasingly restrictive and possessive toward the end of the cycle (when the debt is more likely to be canceled and the loan become a gift). This is why God specifically instructed His people to not give in to their propensity for stinginess:

> Be careful that there isn't this wicked thought in your heart, 'The seventh year, the year of canceling debts, is near,' and you are stingy toward your poor brother and give him nothing. He will cry out to the Lord against you, and you will be guilty.
>
> —Deuteronomy 15:9

Instead, God instructed His people to give generously, even when there was no possibility of being repaid. God promised great blessing for those who do so:

> Give to him, and don't have a stingy heart when you give,
> and *because of this the Lord your God will bless you in all your*
> *work and in everything you do.* For there will never cease to be
> poor people in the land; that is why I am commanding you,
> "You must willingly open your hand to your afflicted and
> poor brother in your land."
>
> —Deuteronomy 15:10-11, emphasis added

The Israelites who generously gave of their own physical property to meet the physical needs of their brothers were promised by God that they would be blessed for it.

This same principle is restated in the New Testament when Paul told the Philippians that their generous gifts were "a fragrant offering, an acceptable sacrifice, pleasing to God" (Philippians 4:18). The Philippians had sacrificially given of their property and resources to meet the needs of others, and in this context, Paul assured them God's blessing would be on them to meet their own needs.

> And my God will supply all your needs according to His
> riches in glory in Christ Jesus.
>
> —Philippians 4:19

God has promised to bless and supply the needs of His children who give willingly of what they own to meet the needs of others.

The Gospel of Giving: Joy for The Giver

When the time came for the Israelites to build the temple, David called an assembly. He willingly gave hundreds of tons of his own gold and silver (the finest, best gold he had) for use in building it. Then he invited the children of Israel to voluntarily do the same, asking, "Now who will volunteer to consecrate himself to the Lord today?" (1 Chronicles 29:5b). The Israelites responded with generosity to the call to build God's temple.

> Then the leaders of the households, the leaders of the tribes
> of Israel, the commanders of thousands and of hundreds,
> and the officials in charge of the king's work gave willingly.
> For the service of God's house they gave 185 tons of gold and
> 10,000 gold coins, 375 tons of silver, 675 tons of bronze, and
> 4,000 tons of iron.
>
> —1 Chronicles 29:6-8

The voluntary donations for the temple totaled more than 46,000 tons of gold, silver, and bronze, not counting other metals and precious stones (cf. 1 Chronicles 22:14; 29:4,7). This was a tremendous offering, but what is interesting was the result.

> Then the people rejoiced *because of their leaders' willingness to
> give*, for they had given to the Lord with a whole heart. King
> David also rejoiced greatly.
>
> —1 Chronicles 29:6-9, emphasis added

The people who had the means and disposition to give generously did so willingly. They gave away a significant amount of their own material possessions and wealth, and the result was great joy. But the joy was not just for the givers. The generosity of the givers resulted in God's blessing of joy for the entire nation of Israel. They gave of the very best of their material wealth and property for the building of God's temple; a physical building. In the same way, when those who are in a position to give generously of the very best of their Intellectual Property do so, the entire global church is blessed and filled with joy. These gifts of discipleship resources are given for the building up of God's church from every nation, tribe, people and language; a spiritual building (1 Peter 2:4-5).

This same principle of "joy for the giver" is mentioned again in Hebrews, although in a context where the "gift" was exacted from them by theft.

> ...you joyfully accepted the plundering of your property,
> since you knew that you yourselves had a better possession
> and an abiding one.
>
> —Hebrews 10:34 (ESV)

How did these believers wind up having joy when they were being robbed? They were commended for joyfully accepting the loss of their property, because their focus was not on their possessions in this life. They knew they had a better, eternal possession stored up for them where moth and rust do not destroy and where thieves do not break in and steal (Matthew 6:19-20).

The Gospel of Giving: Glory and Thanksgiving to God

In Paul's second letter to the church in Corinth, he exhorted them to follow through with their good intentions of giving of their own resources to provide for the well-being of others in the church who were in need. Paul makes it clear that giving is a voluntary activity, not one that should be done grudgingly or from compulsion. Paul also reminds the Corinthians that God rewards each person according to their generosity and that one cannot outgive God.

> Remember this: The person who sows sparingly will also
> reap sparingly, and the person who sows generously will
> also reap generously. Each person should do as he has de-
> cided in his heart—not reluctantly or out of necessity, for
> God loves a cheerful giver. And God is able to make every
> grace overflow to you, so that in every way, always having
> everything you need, you may excel in every good work.
>
> —2 Corinthians 9:6-8

Generous giving to meet the needs of other believers results in three things: God's provision for the giver, thanksgiving and glory to God from the recipient, and affection for the giver from the recipient.

> Now the One who provides seed for the sower and bread for food will provide and multiply your seed and increase the harvest of your righteousness. *You will be enriched in every way for all generosity*, which *produces thanksgiving to God* through us. For the ministry of this service is not only supplying the needs of the saints, but is also *overflowing in many acts of thanksgiving to God. They will glorify God* for your obedience to the confession of the gospel of Christ, and for your generosity in sharing with them and with others through the proof provided by this service. And *they will have deep affection for you* in their prayers on your behalf because of the surpassing grace of God in you.
>
> —2 Corinthians 9:10-45, emphasis added

The gifts given by the Corinthians met a need that could not otherwise be met. Can we not also expect the same blessings that were promised to the Corinthians, when the gift that is given involves the releasing of discipleship resources into the Christian Commons, as a gift to the entire global church to meet their spiritual needs?

Building the Christian Commons

The process of creating a discipleship resource can be time-consuming and costly. It is understandable, then, why traditional licenses are usually used to provide the maximum revenue stream from the resources created, whether by sales or donations to the exclusive distributor. The growth of the Christian Commons does not depend on a costly content-creation model that is stripped of the revenue stream. There are a number of alternative models that can provide sustainable growth for the Christian Commons. Four of these models are summarized below and addressed in greater detail in appendix E, "Sustainable Models for Building the Christian Commons".

- **Collaboratively-Created Resources** – The global church collectively has tens of millions of unused hours each month.[6] Digital technology like the Internet and mobile phones make it possible to treat the aggregate "free time" of the global church as an asset that can be used in the translation and distribution of discipleship resources in thousands of languages. By adopting a model of social production, instead of private production, the cost associated with creating and translating massive amounts of content in many languages drops significantly. At the same time, the speed of production and distribution of the translated content increases significantly. The open collaboration of the global church to create and translate discipleship resources is a strategic and important means of building the Christian Commons.

- **Voluntary Early Release of Content** – As much as 95% of books written in the last one hundred years are out of print and not available in digital formats, making them difficult (if not impossible) to access.[7] Some Christian authors and publishers are finding that the commercial value of many books are significantly depleted within only a few years after publishing, even though the "all rights reserved" of their copyright lasts for seventy years after their death. Instead of waiting for the term of copyright to expire many years in the future, owners of discipleship resources could sell them for a period of time, then voluntarily release them under open licenses for the good of the global church.

---

6   This unused time is called "cognitive surplus" and its significance in the Digital Era is explained in detail in the book by the same title: Shirky, *Cognitive Surplus*

7   Boyle, *The Public Domain: Enclosing the Commons of the Mind*, 10.

- **Sponsored Works** – Foundations, seminaries, churches, and donors could fund the creation of discipleship resources that are released under open licenses from the outset. This requires understanding that many discipleship resources typically have a dual purpose: ministry tool and revenue generator, from direct sales of the resource or donations to the exclusive owner (or distributor) of the discipleship resource. This is not a problem, but the "revenue generation" purpose depends on restrictive license terms governing the resources in order to maintain the revenue stream. As sponsors realize the immense missional value of creating discipleship resources that have a single purpose of ministry, funding the creation open-licensed discipleship resources can be seen for what it is: incredibly strategic for the Kingdom, without the hindrance of also serving as a revenue generator.

- **A Gift of Intellectual Property** – Those who own the rights to discipleship resources that could be of use to the global church could give a portion of what they have (and of what they create in the future) as a gift, released under an open license into the Christian Commons.

Distributing the Christian Commons

The traditional means of distributing discipleship resources is built on a "pull" model, like a magnet. Content owners maintain exclusive control of their "all rights reserved" content and attempt to attract consumers to the content. This is not a bad way of doing things. Some resources get to millions of people using this model.

The Purpose-Driven Life was marketed and distributed in this way. It is arguably the most successful discipleship resource in recent history, in terms of number of sales. It was published in 2002 by Zondervan and by 2007 it had been translated into 56 languages, with

30 million copies sold.[8] This is an impressive set of numbers, by anyone's reckoning.

But the reality is that, even with a wildly popular book and the marketing muscle and financial resources of Zondervan, it took 5 years to get that resource translated into less than 0.8% of the world's languages. If the rate of 56 languages every 5 years is maintained, it would take more than 600 years to reach the rest of the languages with this discipleship resource. Recall, however, that more than half of the world's languages have fewer than 10,000 speakers each and so represent extremely limited market opportunities for a publishing company, compared to languages with hundreds of millions of speakers.

The "pull" model that attempts to attract all potential consumers to the distribution channel is unable to go the distance to equip disciples in every people group and every language of the world with the discipleship resources they need for spiritual maturity. The people who can be reached by it are only those who are within the "magnetic force field" of the limited distribution channels. Many in the global church are far beyond the reach of traditional distribution points and so do not get access to the content.

Nuclear Fission: A Distribution Model that Goes Farther

The point here is not to denigrate the traditional approach to distribution. Up until the dawn of the digital era, there were few, if any alternatives. But now there is a viable alternative—the "open" approach. It makes the most of the opportunities afforded by the digital age, the rise of the global church and their soon-to-be ubiquitous mobile technology. This model can not only go the distance to every language of the world, but it can do so rapidly and at significantly less expense than the traditional model.

---

8   "Rick Warren and Purpose-Driven Strife" (ABC, mar 2007), http://abc-news.go.com/Nightline/story?id=2914953&page=1

This new approach requires that content be released under open licenses so that *anyone* can legally help push the content outward to anyone, anywhere in the world. Instead of attempting to pull potential consumers of the content into a small number of legal distribution channels (the "pull" model), the content is released under open licenses that permit anyone to become a legal distribution channel (the "push" model). Anyone who has the content can legally redistribute it to all their friends who can, in turn, redistribute it to all of their friends, and so on. By inviting (and permitting) the global church to become the content distribution network for discipleship resources available in digital formats, the resource can spread extremely rapidly and at virtually zero marginal cost.

This process is similar in concept to the extremely rapid and multiplicative effect of nuclear fission. As one atom splits, it releases neutrons that cause other atoms to split which release still more neutrons that cause other atoms to split, and so on. The process accelerates extremely rapidly, releasing an immense amount of energy in a very short amount of time. This kind of exponential effect is characteristic of the "push" model for distributing content. If everyone who gets a copy of a discipleship resource one day gives copies to two people the next day, the number of discipleship resources given *exceeds the population of the world* in a little over one month.

Distribution by Any Means

If a resource is restricted by copyrights so that it exists on only one website and cannot be legally redistributed by others, that resource can be much more easily blocked by governments who maintain a "blacklist" of prohibited websites. Resources in the Christian Commons, however, are not subject to these obstacles. Discipleship resources in the Christian Commons can be legally distributed from any number of channels (including BitTorrent and the darknet). They can be hosted on *any* website, and they can also be legally distributed by any other means and technology available to the global church.

Because the purpose of these resources is exclusively ministry, there is no need to "count the numbers" and track the analytics. Consequently, resources in the Christian Commons can be legally distributed using offline, off-the-grid, under-the-radar methods without restrictions or caveats. This minimizes the risk associated with attempting to distribute content exclusively over the Internet or requiring Internet access in order to use the resources. In parts of the world where it is dangerous to be a Christian, this is an extremely important consideration.

The Spiritual Feast of the Global Church

In past centuries, the creation and distribution of discipleship resources was characterized by legal restrictions, high costs, and limitations. In many ways, there was little alternative because the only means of distributing content involved the costly creation of physical media like books, records, and cassette tapes. But in recent years, the rise of digital technology, the Internet and the mobile phone has changed the rules and opened up new opportunities for the advance of God's Kingdom in every people group.

The global church is on the rise. They are digital, mobile, networked laborers, working for the advance of God's Kingdom. The existence of a growing church, equipping themselves with the technology to not merely consume, but to create discipleship resources to support their spiritual growth, may prove to be the greatest opportunity ever for the advance of God's Kingdom to every people group and in every language. The global church is not able to take full advantage of these opportunities, however, because of the absence of unrestricted discipleship resources that they can use as though they were their own, free of charge and free of legal hindrance. This is a massive obstacle, but one that can be overcome by the voluntary choice of those who own the discipleship resources that can help meet the spiritual need of the global church.

This obstacle is already starting to erode, like a dam that starts to show more and more droplets of water before it finally bursts. All over the world, believers are starting to understand how copyright and licensing works and, more importantly, how excessive controls on discipleship resources can inadvertently hinder the global church from growing spiritually. Some are choosing to "endure anything rather than create an obstacle for the Gospel" (1 Corinthians 9:12) and are releasing their discipleship resources into the Christian Commons. Steps are being taken to end the spiritual famine of the global church, although much remains to be done.

The classic approach to accomplishing the Great Commission often involved locking people out of "our stuff." We worked in relatively small, isolated teams, with clearly-defined boundaries of who was "us" and who was "them." Throughout the history of world missions there have been a lot of closed doors, competition, and legal hindrances to ministry.

But that was then. A better, faster, cheaper, and more effective means of accomplishing the Great Commission is now possible. The future of world missions in the digital age involves open collaboration as the body of Christ, to provide unrestricted discipleship resources in every language, for every people group. It is about freedom, transparency, collaboration, and sharing.

The past may have been restricted and closed; the future of the global church is Open.

~ ~ ~

Conclusion of Part 4: *The creation of the Christian Commons, comprised of discipleship resources voluntarily released under open licenses like the Attribution-ShareAlike License, enables the global church to translate,* *adapt, build on, revise, redistribute and use discipleship resources without restriction or obstacle.*

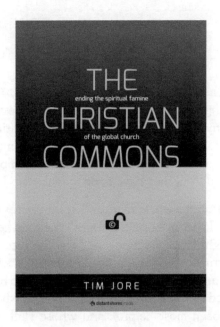

This book is available for free in digital formats at

thechristiancommons.com

Please feel free to give copies to others and join us on the website where you can discuss the content with the author and other readers.

ACKNOWLEDGEMENTS

This book is the fruit of much grace from God, "who works all things according to the counsel of his will" (Ephesians 1:11, ESV). One of the many evidences of His grace in the writing of this book has been the many people He has led to invest countless hours into every aspect of it. My thanks to them is both incomplete and inadequate, compared to all they have done to make this book possible.

First, I must thank the whole team at Distant Shores Media. I am especially grateful to Bruce Erickson for all the time he has spent discussing copyright law, missiology, and the intersection of the two. His help in writing this book has been immense, such that much of the coherency and usefulness of this book is due to his involvement in it. I also need to thank my brother, Ben Jore, whose theological insights have been most helpful, and whose skill in organization and editing has rescued readers of this book from what would otherwise have been a very painful experience.

My deepest gratitude goes to our legal team at the IPR law firm of Coats and Bennett for their help in understanding copyright law and charting a course through its sometimes-murky waters. A book like this could only be undertaken with the help of a top-notch legal team that is passionate about the Kingdom. It is a great blessing to have such a capable and visionary team working with us.

I am indebted to the entire network of Distant Shores Media supporters and volunteers. God continues to use your support and encouragement to open many doors for the Word (Colossians 4:3). Your generosity has made possible both the writing of this book and the ability to release it under an open license for free redistribution. Thank you for being willing to "endure anything rather than create an obstacle for the Gospel" (1 Corinthians 9:12). My thanks also to Jerrell Hein, Phil Haugen, Kurt Hein, Wade Mobley, Seth Stoll, Keith Williams, Timothy Warner, and the many others who have read through drafts of this book and provided very helpful feedback.

Finally, my love and gratitude to my dear wife, Angie, who has sacrificed much for the writing of this book.

APPENDIX A: A CLASSIC LICENSE

This is an excerpt from an actual license on a website that makes media content available to consumers via the website and a software application.

Except as expressly set forth in these Terms of Use or otherwise expressly granted to you in writing by The Owner, no rights (either by implication, estoppel or otherwise) in or to the Content are granted to you.

The copying, reproduction, re-arrangement, sale, leasing, renting, lending, distribution, redistribution, modification or adaptation, downloading, side loading, exchanging, creating of derivative works, uploading, posting, transmitting, communication to the public or publication by you, directly or indirectly, of the Content, including the removal or alteration of advertising, except pursuant to the express limited grant of rights hereunder, is strictly prohibited.

You agree to abide by any and all additional notices, information or restrictions in respect of the Properties contained in any part of the Website.

Subject to your strict compliance with these Terms of Use, The Owner grants you a limited, personal, non-exclusive, non-commercial, revocable, non-assignable and non-transferable license to:

1. download and use The Owner's software in accordance with its pre-defined functionality only; and
2. listen to and view media streamed from the Website;

Provided that you:

1. retain and do not alter or tamper with any trademark, copyright and other proprietary or legal notices contained in the original Content or any permitted copy you may make of the Content;
2. do not, and do not allow or aid or abet any third party (whether or not for your benefit) to, copy or adapt the object code of the Website or Services (including, without limitation, software, HTML, JavaScript, or other code); to reverse engineer, decompile, reverse assemble, modify or attempt to discover any source or object code, circumvent or attempt to circumvent or copy any copy protection mechanism or access any rights management information;
3. do not copy or seek to copy or "rip" any audio and/or audiovisual content from the Website or any part of the Service;
4. do not embed or otherwise exploit The Owner's product for commercial gain (which includes, for example and without limitation, selling advertising on your site or otherwise monetizing any ele-

ment of your site which contains The Owner's brand); and

5. do not adapt, copy, republish, communicate to the public, display, transfer, share, distribute or otherwise exploit the Content, except as under these Terms of Use.

The Owner alone shall be responsible for determining, in its discretion, whether any use of The Owner's Online brand constitutes commercial use in each case.

Appendix B: The "Non-Commercial Use Only" Problem

The "non-commercial use only" condition is included in licenses to prevent the commercial exploitation of free discipleship resources. The condition is generally effective for this purpose, but it critically hinders the global church from being able to equip themselves to grow spiritually, without restriction.

The Creative Commons Attribution-ShareAlike License (introduced in chapter 9 and included in appendix C, The Attribution-Share-Alike License) ensures that derivative works—like translations of the original content—are released under the same license. Until the implications of the "ShareAlike" condition are adequately understood, it might not seem to address the concern that other entities like publishers or media companies could make commercial use of the content. After all, the license specifically states that making commercial use of the content is permitted. So the immediate reaction by those wanting to prevent commercial exploitation of a discipleship resource is to reject such an open license and use one with a "non-commercial use only" on the license to prevent the commercial "abuse" of free resources.

There are two primary reasons that motivate content creators to include a "non-commercial use only" condition: to preserve their own revenue stream from the content or to prevent the commercial exploitation of the content by other entities (e.g. publishers). If the interest is to preserve one's own revenue stream from the resource, then a "non-commercial use only" condition makes sense.

There are, however, many in the second category—content owners who want to release their discipleship resources under licenses that permit the global church to make the most use of it, while at the same time preventing commercial exploitation by others. Many view the "non-commercial use only" condition as the best (or only) way to accomplish this. On the face of it, that would seem to be correct, and the condition does prevent commercial exploitation of the content. But while it may prevent exploitation, it also drastically and unnecessarily hinders how far the resource can go and how effectively it can be used by the global church.

There are nearly 7,000 languages in the world and adequate discipleship resources (including, but not limited to, the Bible) are needed in each one. These discipleship resources need to be translated and then revised over time to preserve their effectiveness as the language into which they are translated changes. The traditional means of providing translated discipleship resources depends on someone translating the content into other languages (doing it for them). This approach is costly, time-consuming, and has limited reach. After decades of Bible translation, fewer than 8% of the world's languages have a translated Bible and fewer still have adequate discipleship resources to teach and explain the Word (Nehemiah 8:8). In addition, many of the languages that have portions of translated Scripture already need revisions to those translations.

It could be argued that, given enough time and money, an organization or formal coalition of mission corporations could conceivably develop the technical infrastructure needed to translate and distribute adequate discipleship resources into all the languages of the world that need them, and maintain the translations over time. It is unlikely, however. What would be *very* likely in an approach like this would be significant inefficiency due to the massive bureaucracy that would be necessary to support it. Just accounting for the legal side of things would be incredibly complex. Managing the legal rights and licensing restrictions of discipleship resources in thousands languages, with hundreds of different applications, hundreds of millions of different users, dozens of different platforms, and non-conforming term lengths could severely impede the system from the outset.

A vastly preferable approach (practically, as well as missiologically) is to enable the global church to openly collaborate in the legal translation and maintenance of their own discipleship resources. But for this goal to be reached, the entire global church must be given the legal freedom to use any means necessary—even commercial funding models—to get the job done. The global church must be given the freedom to "make their living from the Word" so they can take the content to the ends of the earth. The linguistically "least of these" (which is most of the languages in the world) may not otherwise be reached. This cannot happen for discipleship resources that are released under a license that contains a "non-commercial use only" condition. Here's why.

In the developing world, the global church must be able to recover the expenses incurred in the translation and distribution of discipleship resources. Many, if not most, do not have the luxury of income from another source. Either they can translate and sell the resource at locally-accessible prices to provide for their needs (which is, by definition, commercial use) or many will have no means of making the content available at all. The presence of a "non-commercial use only" condition on discipleship resources critically hinders the global church from equipping themselves.

We will look at the problems inherent in the "non-commercial use only" condition in greater detail below. First, we will address the issue of preventing commercial exploitation of a resource released under Attribution-ShareAlike, a license that specifically does not include the "NonCommercial" condition. The global church cannot take it "the last mile" if the condition exists, but what is to prevent the abuse of the content if the "non-commercial use only" condition does not exist? There are three points to consider along these lines: market economics, the significance of the "Attribution" condition, and the significance of the "ShareAlike" condition.

Minimizing Commercial Exploitation – Market Economics

Assume for a moment that, as is almost always the case, a discipleship resource that is released under an Attribution-ShareAlike License is also available free of charge online in digital formats. The license permits anyone to redistribute the resource, for free or commercially. So what happens when anyone can legally distribute the content for any price, but the content is already available online from the content creator's website for free? A third-party distributor would be hard-pressed to generate a significant profit from a free resource available online.

But what about the creation of a physical object from the content, like the printing of a book? The Attribution-ShareAlike License is non-exclusive, so any publisher can make the book available commercially. If the resource is of any value, this will likely result in the book being available for sale from multiple publishers, causing the actual cost to consumers of the paper-and-ink versions of the book to be driven down to near the cost of printing it.

This is not without precedent. Two hundred years before the advent of modern copyright law, a monk named Martin Luther was becoming a prolific writer and starting to have a significant and far-reaching influence with his writings. In the absence of copyright law and exclusive contracts that legally tie an author to one publisher (excluding all others), one might wonder how Luther managed to make any money from his writing. As it turns out, Luther had little interest in making money from his writings, compared to his ultimate goal. Luther's goal in the writing of pamphlets and other literature was not to make money but to bring about freedom for a global church in theological captivity. And the pre-copyright context of 16th century Europe was an ideal platform to do just that.

There were a number of printers in Luther's hometown of Wittenburg, Germany, during the Reformation. In those days, there were no legal obstacles to printing, so any printer could print, reprint, and sell anything that was of interest to their customers, without restriction. Luther's pamphlets were of great interest to their customers, so whenever a new one was written, any printer who got his hands on a copy (produced by another printer) could immediately turn around and recreate it on his own press, print as many as desired, and sell them for a profit.[1]

So what was the outcome of this pre-copyright era free-for-all? We know that Luther did not go out of business—he was not writing to make money and his livelihood was provided for by his university post and benefactors. The printers of Wittenburg did not go out of business either. No one printer had an exclusive publishing deal with Luther and got fabulously wealthy while the others starved—the wealth was spread out among the printers. In fact, Wittenburg became a wealthy town because of Luther's works.[2]

---

1   Cole, Richard G. "Reformation Printers: Unsung Heroes." *Sixteenth Century Journal* 15, no. 3 (1984): 336. doi:10.2307/2540767.

2   Tom Standage, "Social media in the 16th Century: How Luther went viral," *The Economist* (dec 2011), http://www.economist.com/node/21541719#

The consumers of the printed content also benefited from the way things were during the Reformation. The absence of a copyright-enforced monopoly that artificially inflated the price to secure higher revenues meant that the price for each pamphlet stayed low, especially for best-sellers, since more printers would print them, driving the price down. It also meant that more people got access to the content at this low price, because any printer could make it available to their customer base. Included in that customer base might be printers from nearby towns who could then recreate and reprint the content, extending its reach to their customer bases as well, and so on. In this manner, the content that brought about the Reformation was made available to the greatest number of people possible, rapidly, and at the lowest cost possible.

The point to draw from this is not that copyrights are evil or should never be leveraged for increased revenue. The point is that there are two ways to distribute content: one that maximizes revenues (by tightly controlling exclusive legal rights), and one that maximizes reach (by releasing content under an open license). As we consider the needs of the global church in thousands of languages, it only makes sense to adopt a content distribution model that maximizes the reach of the content. But doing so necessarily requires releasing the content under a license that removes the restrictions that limit the content's reach.

One of the restrictions that severely limits the reach of content intended for the global church is the "non-commercial use only" condition. This "non-commercial use only" condition was not a restriction that limited the reproduction of Luther's Intellectual Property, nor could it have been at that point in history. Because commercial means of distributing the content were not prohibited, the ideas that became the Reformation were able to spread farther, faster, more effectively, and less expensively than would otherwise have been the case. The same is true today.

Minimizing Commercial Exploitation – "Attribution"

Consider the significance of the statement of attribution that is legally required by the Attribution-ShareAlike License. By releasing your content under this license, you permit anyone to use and distribute it, but only if they comply with the condition of attributing the original to you. Now consider a scenario where two publishing companies (or other content owners) are in competition with each other. Each publisher owns a version of the Bible in English and they are attempting to increase the number of sales of their version to consumers.

What would happen if one of the publishers released their version of the Bible under a Creative Commons Attribution-ShareAlike License? Now the rival publisher could legally print unlimited numbers of copies of their competitor's version of the Bible, without sharing any of the revenues with them. At first glance, this could seem like a disaster for the publisher who released their Bible under the open license. But would that really happen?

> The danger that people will pirate content or take commercial advantage of a free resource is dwarfed by the real danger—that few will ever know that the content and its creator even exist.

Look at it from the perspective of the second publisher. They can now print and distribute their own "all rights reserved" Bible as well as their competitor's Bible, without paying them a dime. Would they? Maybe, but not necessarily. They do not own the copyright on the other Bible and they are legally required to attribute the Bible to a website they do not own. Would they want to market their competitor's version of the Bible to their own customer base? It depends on many factors, including the potential for reduced sales and licensing agreements of their own copyright-restricted version of the Bible. In many (if not most) contexts, they might very well not want anything to do with publishing a "rival" version of the Bible.

For the sake of argument, let us say the second publisher decides to publish and sell their competitor's version of the Bible that is available under an Attribution-ShareAlike License. If the second publisher is able to sell a copy of the Bible to just one of their customers, it means that one more person who previously had not heard of the Bible or seen any value in it, now has heard of it and considers it to be valuable enough to purchase a copy. And in that copy is a legally-mandated statement of attribution with a link back to the copyright owner. This increases the exposure for the original publisher, as well as opening up additional opportunities for them to make more resources available (for free or for sale) to the user via their website. What has happened is that the second publisher who sold the copy of the first publisher's Bible, did the marketing for the first publisher, at no cost to the first publisher.

In the Information Era, mindshare is everything. The danger that people will pirate content or take commercial advantage of a free resource is dwarfed by the real danger—that few will ever know that the content and its creator even exist. From this vantage point, there is significant advantage for owners of content who make their work available without a "non-commercial use only" condition, so that any publishing company could distribute the work on behalf of the content owner, for free. This would significantly increase the mindshare of the content owner, by introducing them to huge audiences who might not otherwise have ever known of the content or its creator. By giving the content away freely and without a "non-commercial use only" condition, other opportunities are now open to the creator of the content that would not have been possible before.

Market economics and the "Attribution" condition are not alone. They are joined by a third factor that greatly minimizes the likelihood of commercial exploitation of a free resource: the "Share-Alike" condition.

Minimizing Commercial Exploitation – "ShareAlike"

Consider a situation where an organization is creating discipleship resources that they intend for use by the global church. They have gathered a group of theologians and are developing top-notch discipleship resources of the highest quality and of immediate usefulness to believers all over the world, available on computers and mobile phones. But the organization is facing a dilemma: they want to release the content for free to the global church, but in such a way that others will not take commercial advantage of it. They are aware that a "non-commercial use only" condition will severely limit how far the resources can go and how effectively they can be used by the global church. So they do not want to include the condition in their license.

It turns out, however, that some of the project's donors have expressed concern that they may not be able to support a project that does not make the most of commercial opportunities (e.g. licensing the content to software developers for use as modules in Bible study software). The ministry feels they cannot justify letting commercial companies make a profit from work supported by donations. They want all free Bible software to use the resources freely, but they don't want those who sell their software for hundreds of dollars to sell the content as add-ons without sharing the income. What are they to do?

This is where the "ShareAlike" condition of the Attribution-Share-Alike License comes into play. Let us assume that the ministry releases their content under this license and makes the discipleship resources freely available on their website. Any Bible software company can now legally take the content and convert it for use in their Bible study software. They can then charge whatever they want for that module of content, without sharing any of the revenues back to the organization that created the content. A disaster, right?

Probably not. Although any software company can legally convert the content for use in their software program, they are legally prevented by the Creative Commons Attribution-ShareAlike License from encrypting the content or using any form of Digital Rights Management to "lock it down" in any way. So the module that the software company makes available for purchase on their website must be an "open" module that is not tied to a particular license key or user account. This is good, but it gets better.

The Attribution-ShareAlike License requires that anything created from the original work—including a repackaging of the work into other formats (like software modules)—be released under the same license, granting to anyone else *the same freedoms* that were granted by the original creator of the content. One of the freedoms granted is the freedom to redistribute. What this means is that anyone who buys the software module containing the content created by the ministry organization can legally give away any number of copies of the software module to anyone they want. They can even make the software module available on their own website. Technically, they could even sell the software module that was created by the software company from the original content created by the ministry organization.

So it would actually be a good thing for the ministry organization that created the content if the software company used their own resources to create a module for their Bible study software from the content and sold it on their website. The ministry organization could buy a single copy of the module and make it freely available on their own website to any users of the Bible study software. Not only that, each software module sold by the software company is required to attribute the original content to the ministry organization and include a hyperlink back to their website, where users can find the free software module. It will be difficult for the makers of the Bible study software to make a profit from selling the software module when they are legally required to direct their customers to the website of the creators of the original content, where the software module is available for free.

Given the nature of the "ShareAlike" condition, the Attribution-ShareAlike License is more conducive to intentional and gracious partnership than commercial exploitation.

Reasons To Avoid "Non-Commercial Use Only"

Market economics and conditions of the Attribution-ShareAlike License tend to minimize the likelihood of commercial exploitation of content released under its terms. In the context of equipping the global church with adequate discipleship resources in every language of the world, there are specific reasons why avoiding licenses with a "non-commercial use only" condition is a good idea.

Too Restrictive

As mentioned above, a "non-commercial use only" condition hinders the global church from using any means necessary to get the content translated into the smallest languages that have fewer than 10,000 speakers. Picture the Christian in Africa who has the ability and disposition to translate discipleship resources for use by believers who speak his language. But in his economic context, he does not have the option of doing the translation work pro bono. He can either cultivate his field and sell his maize to put his kids through school and pay medical expenses, or he can translate discipleship resources into his language of fewer than 10,000 speakers.

He cannot do both. If he is not legally allowed to "make his living by the Word" and receive financial compensation for his translation work by selling it to local churches or publishers, it will not be possible for him to do the work, without funding from the copyright owner or under contract.

The need to be able to recover expenses is crucially important when the medium of delivering the content is not digital. In the digital world, the cost of pushing bits of information to a mobile phone anywhere in the world is negligible. But to convert those digital bits into a physical format like books or DVDs costs real money (and time). Discipleship resources that are encumbered by a "non-commercial use only" condition are handicapped in these contexts because they are legally prevented from being part of a commercial process that would otherwise cover the expense of translation, adaptation, and redistribution.

In order to help meet the need of the global church for discipleship resources, portable and inexpensive "print on demand" systems have been developed for use in remote regions of the world. These print systems can run completely off the grid on solar power and can turn out over 10,000 two-hundred-page books a year at a little over one dollar a book. The technology is already developed, the system works. But apart from discipleship resources released under an open license that does not include a "non-commercial use only" condition, the global church still faces an insurmountable obstacle when attempting to get those books into the hands of the people who need them.

In addition to paying the wages of the translators, these ministry printshops must be able to sell the printed books in order to pay for the cost of ink, paper, replacement parts, and the wages of the press operators. Content released with a "non-commercial use only" condition cannot be legally redistributed in this way. But content released under an Attribution-ShareAlike License can. And because of it, the content can be extended by the global church to reach much farther than even the biggest professional publishing houses can reach.

The presence of a "non-commercial use only" condition can severely restrict how content can be used, even when it is not being directly sold or part of a traditional commercial process. CBC/Radio-Canada, Canada's national public broadcaster, used to include music that was released under Creative Commons licenses. But without explanation, they stopped doing so in 2010. An animated discussion broke out on the comments section of their website as listeners demanded to know why they had completely stopped using music released under Creative Commons licenses.

Eventually, the CBC/Radio-Canada Programming Director Chris Boyce gave an explanation:

> The issue with our use of Creative Commons music is that a lot of our content is readily available on a multitude of platforms, some of which are deemed to be 'commercial' in nature (e.g. streaming with pre-roll ads, or pay for download on iTunes) and currently the vast majority of the music available under a Creative Commons license prohibits commercial use.[3]

The use of advertising to support access to otherwise free content is a common means of funding ministry. Many Christian radio stations are built on that model, as are some Christian magazines, and countless Christian websites. But the use of content in conjunction with advertising is often considered a commercial use. If you recall the sample license that was included at the beginning of chapter 9 (with the long list of what you were not allowed to do with the content), the terms of that license could not be more clear about the association of advertising with commercial use of the content:

---

3   Matthew Lasar, "Why the CBC banned Creative Commons music from its shows," oct 2010, http://arstechnica.com/media/news/2010/10/cbc-radio-fans-crabby-over-creative-commons-snub.ars

> Provided that you... do not embed or otherwise exploit The Owner's product for commercial gain (which includes, for example and without limitation, *selling advertising on your site* or otherwise monetizing any element of your site which contains The Owner's brand)...

In 2008, Creative Commons attempted to help clear up the ambiguity by commissioning a study from a professional market research firm to explore understandings of the terms "commercial use" and "non-commercial use" among Internet users when used in the context of content found online. The findings suggest that creators and users approach the question of noncommercial use similarly:

> Both creators and users generally consider uses that earn users money or involve online advertising to be commercial, while uses by organizations, by individuals, or for charitable purposes are less commercial but not decidedly non-commercial.[4]

Content that is released with a "non-commercial use only" condition is likely to be incompatible with any of the advertising-based means of distributing Christian content. This includes advertisements on websites, radio stations, publications, even in smartphone applications that integrate mobile advertisements that provide a revenue stream to the creator of the application.

Prevents Good Things

Not only does the "non-commercial use only" condition severely restrict how far content can go and where it can be used, it also prevents good things from happening to the content. Companies and organizations that are legally allowed to recover their expenses by selling what they create from the content are in a posi-

---

4   "Defining Noncommercial," n.d., http://wiki.creativecommons.org/Defining_Noncommercial

tion to make considerable improvements to the content that benefit everyone (because of the "ShareAlike" condition). The Attribution-ShareAlike License tends to encourage partnership in mutually beneficial projects that include a commercial element to them. This happened with Wikipedia and a German company called Direct Media Publishing.

In 2004, Direct Media made select portions of the German language version of Wikipedia—which is released under an Attribution-ShareAlike License[5]—available on CD, for sale. In preparation for publishing the CD, they worked together with the German Wikipedia community to improve the content in the selected articles to get the content to a publishable level. They fixed typos, adjusted the wording, and improved the clarity of the articles. Because of the "ShareAlike" condition, all the improvements made by Direct Media were shared back to the community, not kept for themselves to provide marketing leverage.

But because a "non-commercial use only" condition is not part of the license, Direct Media was legally able to sell the finished CD, which became a bestseller on the German version of Amazon's online store. Due to the "ShareAlike" condition in the license, the community benefited from Direct Media's work, and due to the absence of a "non-commercial use only" condition, Direct Media was able to make their project financially viable and beneficial to them. In fact, the CD was so successful that the next year DirectMedia released an updated DVD of over 200,000 articles, available for sale as well as a free download. One Euro from the sale of every DVD went to supporting the German Wikimedia foundation. This was a voluntary donation, as there is no requirement for it in the Attribution-ShareAlike License.

---

5   At the time, the content in Wikipedia was licensed under the GNU Free Documentation License, which is nearly identical to the Creative Commons Attribution-ShareAlike License.

This same kind of thing happens in the open-source software world. We have seen how the Linux operating system is developed by many different contributors, including over 600 commercial companies. Because the license under which the source code is released does not prevent commercial use of the software but does require that any improvements to the software be released under the same license (functionally similar to the Attribution-ShareAlike License), everyone benefits from the improvements made by anyone else. The commercial companies, many of whom are fierce competitors, all work together to improve the software that benefits them all.

Makes the Global Church Work for Nothing

Here's a question for you: Does the presence of a "non-commercial use only" condition mean that no money whatsoever can change hands in the use of this resource? We often do not even apply that same standard to ourselves when we give out free resources in large quantities. For example, consider the presenter of a seminar or Bible study group that prints out multiple pages of a resource for use by the attendees. The resource itself may be free, but there is often the expectation that an offering will be taken to help cover the expenses of the conference. Sometimes the free resource is given away with the request that everyone chip in a dollar to help cover the cost of reproducing the resource and making it available.

The global church must be allowed to have this freedom as well. If we say their translation and distribution of a discipleship resource must not include any financial transaction whatsoever, we create a distinction between "us" and "them" that is difficult to justify. They have the same costs and needs to recover their expenses, and in many economically disadvantaged parts of the world, the global church feels those costs much more acutely than we do. Unless they also are given the freedom to legally recover their expenses, we implicitly require that the global church work for nothing in the translation and distribution of discipleship resources.

The Bible is very clear that the worker is worthy of his wages. The Bible is also very clear about what God thinks of making people work for nothing. The prophet Jeremiah prophesied to Shallum, the son of Josiah, about his greed and tyranny:

> "Woe to him who builds his palace by unrighteousness,
>   his upper rooms by injustice,
> *making his own people work for nothing,*
>   *not paying them for their labor.*
> He says, 'I will build myself a great palace
>   with spacious upper rooms.'
> So he makes large windows in it,
>   panels it with cedar
>   and decorates it in red.
>
> "Does it make you a king
>   to have more and more cedar?
> Did not your father have food and drink?
>   He did what was right and just,
>   so all went well with him.
> *He defended the cause of the poor and needy,*
>   and so all went well.
> Is that not what it means to know me?"
>   declares the LORD.

—Jeremiah 22:13–16, NIV, emphasis added

In the context of a global church in desperate need of discipleship resources, the point here is not that formal contracts for translation work are not being honored. The point is that telling the global church "you can use my content for your own spiritual growth!" but not allowing them to pay themselves even minimum wage in the work of translating the resource into their languages so that it *can* be used is effectively the same thing as expecting them to work for nothing.

For this reason, some qualify the "non-commercial use only" condition so that it allows people only to recover their expenses, nothing more. This sounds good, but creates its own problems.

Ambiguous

What does it mean to "only cover your expenses" and, more importantly, who decides what qualifies as "covering expenses" and what crosses over into commercial use? Consider a DVD of free discipleship teaching videos that are released with a "you can only recover your expenses" condition. DVDs cost money to make and distribute, but what criteria determine whether the price tag for the DVD is commercial or merely covering expenses? Can I charge one dollar per DVD? Can I charge two dollars? Five? It probably depends on what it actually cost to create the DVD. Will an accounting be made to the copyright holder of every expense that went into the creation of the DVD, including the cost of the DVDs, mass replication, printing, shipping & handling, airfare to the target country, wages for the distributors, etc.? Can funds be solicited from others to distribute the free resources? Will the determination of "expenses only" or "commercial" be dependent on the economic context of different world regions? Who decides what those regions are and how the prices should fluctuate accordingly?

Including a condition that says "non-commercial use only but you can recover your expenses" can only mean one of three things:

1. It is an ambiguous request that cannot be quantified and so will not be enforced
2. It will be quantified and enforced
3. It will be arbitrarily decided by the copyright holder and enforced.

In the first case, because of the lack of set criteria to determine what is commercial use and what is not, the condition in the license amounts to little more than a statement of what the owner of the content would prefer. There is no way for potential users to know in advance if their use of the content and the amount of money they are charging for the redistribution of it complies with the license. They are left to guess at whether their use of the resource is ethical or not.

Actual enforcement of a "non-commercial use only" condition in the second and third cases requires that there be an entity overseeing each and every use of every resource in every context, monitoring the amount of money that changes hands and ensuring that the resource is not used in such a way that it crosses their own, arbitrary line of what constitutes a commercial use. The existence of an entity in a position of authority to authorize or forbid the use of a resource like this is the antithesis to freedom.

It follows then, that a license with a "non-commercial use only" condition is actually not an "open" license. Content released under open licenses do not have these kinds of concerns associated with them. Open-licensed resources are freely available for anyone to access, build on, redistribute, and use without restriction or the concern that too much money was involved in the process.

Unnecessary

The presence of the "ShareAlike" condition in the Attribution-ShareAlike License makes the presence of a "non-commercial use only" condition unnecessary for the prevention of flagrant, unchecked commercial exploitation of a discipleship resource. The license itself destroys the potential for monopoly of the resource, which is necessary for commercial exploitation to be possible. The lack of monopoly, combined with the "ShareAlike" condition that requires sharing back to the community whatever is created from the content, limits the possibility of commercial exploitation and encourages the possibility of commercial partnership.

If this were not the case and a "non-commercial use only" condition were actually necessary to prevent "going out of business (or ministry)," then why do so many of the most successful open-licensed projects not include the condition? The Linux operating system does not have it. The Open Street Map project uses an Attribution-ShareAlike License, as does Wikipedia. If a "non-commercial use only" condition were necessary to ensure their continued existence, they would have used a license that includes the condition.

These projects do not use licenses that include the condition, because the projects themselves exist for reasons that the contributors to the projects consider greater than making money from the content. Each one is intended to accomplish a purpose and meet a specific need for people all over the world. Linux provides a free computer operating system. Open Street Map provides free maps. Wikipedia provides free information. But none of these projects finds it necessary to include a "non-commercial use only" condition in order to keep the content free. They all realize that including such a condition would severely restrict the usefulness and reach of the content. They also realize that the "ShareAlike" condition is sufficient to prevent commercial exploitation without hindering the effectiveness of the project.

The Bible Is Not Silent about "Non-Commercial Use Only"

Not surprisingly, the Bible does not specifically mention "non-commercial use," nor is there a Greek or Hebrew term in the original texts for "Intellectual Property Rights." The concept of "Intellectual Property" as contrasted with "Physical Property" is a fairly recent, man-made invention. It used to be that information was as free as the air, but that is no longer the default in modern society.

The Bible has much to say, however, about property, money, generosity, and the poor. These principles apply as much to Intellectual Property as they due to physical property.

Enduring Anything

Paul explained to the Corinthians that those who sow spiritual things have the right to reap material things (payment) for their work. But he also stated that a better way was to be willing to endure anything rather than make use of this right, when doing so would put an obstacle in the way of the Gospel:

> Nevertheless, we have not made use of this right, but *we endure anything rather than put an obstacle in the way of the gospel of Christ...* I have made no use of any of these rights, nor am I writing these things to secure any such provision... What then is my reward? That in my preaching I may present the gospel free of charge, *so as not to make full use of my right in the gospel.*
>
> —1 Corinthians 9:12,15,18, ESV, emphasis added

Releasing a discipleship resource under an Attribution-ShareAlike License *will* likely result in making less money directly from that resource than could otherwise have been the case. Not only that, others might be able to make some money from it without needing to share the proceeds with you. We have already seen how flagrant exploitation of the content is unlikely, if not impossible—but that is not the point. The point is this: if releasing my content under an Attribution-ShareAlike License is necessary for the advance of the Gospel in every language and people group, am I willing to endure anything—including not making as much revenue from the resource—for the glory of God and the good of His Church?

The author of a book on spiritual maturity and freedom from sin was recently contacted by a well-known publisher requesting the rights to publish the book. Instead of signing an exclusive publishing deal, the author informed the publisher that they could publish it, but that the content of the book was being released under an open license for the good of the global church. The author put it this way:

> When I released my book under an Attribution-ShareAlike License, I felt a little bit like Moses' mother. Put your baby out there, and he will either be eaten by crocodiles or will save millions of people from slavery.[6]

This is the kind of willingness to endure anything that removes obstacles from the Gospel for the growth of the global church.

Loving the Global Church (As Yourself)

In the parable of the Good Samaritan (Luke 10:25-37), Jesus told a story of a man who was attacked by robbers, beat up, and left for dead. He was in a bad way and unable to help himself, but neither a priest nor a Levite who happened to pass by was willing to help him. A Samaritan, however, social and religious outcast though he was, had compassion on him. He dressed the man's wounds, took him to an inn and then did something amazing. He paid the innkeeper a significant amount of money to care for the man, with the promise of more money if the innkeeper incurred additional expenses in caring for the man.

The irony of the story is rich. The church leaders—the chosen ones who had the most reason to care for the man—turned a blind eye to the obvious need in front of them. They pretended like the urgent need facing them did not even exist, then passed by on the other side, presumably so they would not be hindered from continuing their "ministry."

---

6   Mary Swenson, "Key 4," jun 2012

But the outsider—the one who had no obligation to do so—helped the man who was in distress and could not help himself. Not only did he prove to be the one who was merciful, but he took upon himself the financial expense of meeting the needs of someone who could not help himself, with no thought of repayment. He illustrates the principle that Jesus frequently emphasized: "Go and learn what this means: 'I desire mercy and not sacrifice'" (Matthew 9:13).

> Never in all of history have there been so many believers in so many people groups, speaking so many languages, who urgently need theological famine relief.

The global church is in a spiritual famine of historic proportions. Those of us who own the discipleship resources they need have the opportunity to show mercy and help meet their need. Never in all of history have there been so many believers in so many people groups, speaking so many languages, who urgently need theological famine relief. They are unable to help themselves and they need mercy from those who will "love their neighbors as themselves" and willingly give up their right to financial reward in order to provide for their spiritual needs. They need discipleship resources available under licenses that do not restrict them from using any means necessary—even commercial ones—to make the content available in their own languages.

False Motives Still Build the Kingdom

One of the most common concerns that content owners have about releasing discipleship resources under open licenses that do not include a "non-commercial use only" condition is that a rival publisher could then take the content, print a million copies of it and make obscene amounts of money from it—money that never gets shared back to the original publisher. As we have already seen, this outcome is highly unlikely. But for the sake of argument, let us assume that someone does actually find a way to make loads of money from someone else's free resource and they do so, without sharing any of the revenue back to the copyright holder. What does Scripture say about it?

It might not be what we want to hear, but the response modeled by the apostle Paul in Philippians 1:18 is: Rejoice! Rejoice, because now people who might not otherwise have received a copy of the resource now have the resource. True, the original publisher didn't get paid for it. But the Kingdom of God was still advanced.

Although the context is different, the Biblical principle recorded in Paul's letter to the Philippians is clearly applicable. While in prison for proclaiming the Gospel, he said this to the church in Philippi:

> Some indeed preach Christ from envy and rivalry, but others from good will. The latter do it out of love, knowing that I am put here for the defense of the gospel. The former proclaim Christ out of selfish ambition, not sincerely but thinking to afflict me in my imprisonment.

> —Philippians 1:15-17 (ESV)

Paul's adversaries were not sincere. They were preaching Christ from "envy and rivalry," specifically and intentionally to afflict him while he was in prison. Paul, however, believed in the sovereignty of God and looked at the situation from the vantage point of God's purposes, not his own well-being. From that perspective, Paul was able to see that the only thing that mattered was the advance of God's Kingdom ("Christ is proclaimed"), even if it was being advanced by people who were motivated by envy and rivalry instead of a humble, God-given, holy ambition.

What does it matter? Just that in every way, whether out of false motives [i.e. a desire for financial gain by selling the discipleship resource of another without remuneration to them] or true [i.e. a desire to get the resource to the most people possible without any hindrance] Christ is proclaimed [i.e. the resource is made available to the global church without restriction for their spiritual maturity]. *And in this I rejoice.*

—Philippians 1:18, emphasis added

The global church *must* have the freedom to recover their expenses and make their living from the Word. There is no other way for adequate discipleship resources to be able to go the distance to every people group in the world. Our strategies for fulfilling the Great Commission must start with the foundational belief in the sovereignty of a good and loving God whose purposes in Christ never fail. Even when He brings those purposes to pass in ways that do not maximize our own revenue stream.

Giving Without Pay

There is a clear Biblical precedent that connects the building of the Kingdom of God with the relinquishing of our rights to financial compensation. The connection is made by Jesus, when he sent out his disciples.

Then He said to His disciples, "The harvest is abundant, but the workers are few. Therefore, pray to the Lord of the harvest to send out workers into His harvest." ...Summoning His 12 disciples, He gave them authority over unclean spirits, to drive them out and to heal every disease and sickness... Jesus sent out these 12 after giving them instructions: "...As you go, announce this: 'The kingdom of heaven has come near.' Heal the sick, raise the dead, cleanse those with skin diseases, drive out demons. *You have received free of charge;*

give free of charge. Don't take along gold, silver, or copper for your money-belts."

—Matthew 9:37-10:9, emphasis added

The cornerstone on which the Great Commission is built is that all authority in heaven and on earth belongs to Jesus. This includes authority over unclean spirits, sickness, and death. It also includes authority over everything pertaining to the financial matters of ministry. Jesus' instruction "you have received free of charge; give free of charge" was intended to strengthen the disciples' belief in the sovereignty of a good God who would meet their needs and provide for them.

We are, like the disciples, prone to worry about making ends meet. They worried about having enough food and drink, and about what they would wear. Jesus taught them that their only concern was to be about the advance of the Kingdom, not in providing for their own needs:

> So don't worry, saying, 'What will we eat?' or 'What will we drink?' or 'What will we wear?' For the idolaters eagerly seek all these things, and your heavenly Father knows that you need them. But seek first the kingdom of God and His righteousness, and all these things will be provided for you. Therefore don't worry about tomorrow, because tomorrow will worry about itself.
>
> —Matthew 6:31-34

Anyone willing to release their rights to what they have freely received from God, for His glory and the advance of His Kingdom, can expect that God Himself will provide for their needs.

APPENDIX C: THE ATTRIBUTION-SHAREALIKE LICENSE

This is the human-readable summary and Legal Code of the Creative Commons Attribution-ShareAlike 3.0 Unported License (CC BY-SA, http://creativecommons.org/licenses/by-sa/3.0). Footnotes are added for clarity and are not in the original license text.

Human-Readable Summary

You are free:

- *to Share* — to copy, distribute, and transmit the work
- *to Remix* — to adapt the work[1]
- to make commercial use of the work

Under the following conditions:

- *Attribution* — You must attribute the work in the manner specified by the author or licensor (but not in any way that suggests that they endorse you or your use of the work).

- *Share Alike* — If you alter, transform, or build upon this work, you may distribute the resulting work only under the same or similar license to this one.

With the understanding that:

- *Waiver* — Any of the above conditions can be waived if you get permission from the copyright holder.
- *Public Domain* — Where the work or any of its elements is in the public domain under applicable law, that status is in no way affected by the license.
- *Other Rights* — In no way are any of the following rights affected by the license:
  - Your fair dealing or fair use rights, or other applicable copyright exceptions and limitations;
  - The author's moral rights;[2]
  - Rights other persons may have either in the work itself or in how the work is used, such as publicity or privacy rights.

---

1   This includes creating translations of the work, which are considered adaptations, or derivatives, of the original.

2   This includes the right of licensors to request removal of their name from the work when used in a derivative or collective they do not like.

■ *Notice* — For any reuse or distribution, you must make clear to others the license terms of this work. The best way to do this is with a link to this web page.

Creative Commons Legal Code

CREATIVE COMMONS CORPORATION IS NOT A LAW FIRM AND DOES NOT PROVIDE LEGAL SERVICES. DISTRIBUTION OF THIS LICENSE DOES NOT CREATE AN ATTORNEY-CLIENT RELATIONSHIP. CREATIVE COMMONS PROVIDES THIS INFORMATION ON AN "AS-IS" BASIS. CREATIVE COMMONS MAKES NO WARRANTIES REGARDING THE INFOR MATION PROVIDED, AND DISCLAIMS LIABILITY FOR DAMAGES RESULTING FROM ITS USE.

License

THE WORK (AS DEFINED BELOW) IS PROVIDED UNDER THE TERMS OF THIS CREATIVE COMMONS PUBLIC LICENSE ("CCPL" OR "LICENSE"). THE WORK IS PROTECTED BY COPYRIGHT AND/OR OTHER APPLICABLE LAW. ANY USE OF THE WORK OTHER THAN AS AUTHORIZED UNDER THIS LICENSE OR COPYRIGHT LAW IS PROHIBITED.

BY EXERCISING ANY RIGHTS TO THE WORK PROVIDED HERE, YOU ACCEPT AND AGREE TO BE BOUND BY THE TERMS OF THIS LICENSE. TO THE EXTENT THIS LICENSE MAY BE CONSIDERED TO BE A CONTRACT, THE LICENSOR GRANTS YOU THE RIGHTS CONTAINED HERE IN CONSIDERATION OF YOUR ACCEPTANCE OF SUCH TERMS AND CONDITIONS.

1. Definitions

1. **"Adaptation"** means a work based upon the Work, or upon the Work and other pre-existing works, such as a translation, adaptation, derivative work, arrangement of music or other alterations of a literary or artistic work, or phono-

gram or performance and includes cinematographic adaptations or any other form in which the Work may be recast, transformed, or adapted including in any form recognizably derived from the original, except that a work that constitutes a Collection will not be considered an Adaptation for the purpose of this License. For the avoidance of doubt, where the Work is a musical work, performance or phonogram, the synchronization of the Work in timed-relation with a moving image ("synching") will be considered an Adaptation for the purpose of this License.

2. "**Collection**" means a collection of literary or artistic works, such as encyclopedias and anthologies, or performances, phonograms or broadcasts, or other works or subject matter other than works listed in Section 1(f) below, which, by reason of the selection and arrangement of their contents, constitute intellectual creations, in which the Work is included in its entirety in unmodified form along with one or more other contributions, each constituting separate and independent works in themselves, which together are assembled into a collective whole. A work that constitutes a Collection will not be considered an Adaptation (as defined below) for the purposes of this License.

3. "**Creative Commons Compatible License**" means a license that is listed at http://creativecommons.org/compatiblelicenses that has been approved by Creative Commons as being essentially equivalent to this License, including, at a minimum, because that license: (i) contains terms that have the same purpose, meaning and effect as the License Elements of this License; and, (ii) explicitly permits the relicensing of adaptations of works made available under that license under this License or a Creative Commons jurisdiction license with the same License Elements as this License.

4. **"Distribute"** means to make available to the public the original and copies of the Work or Adaptation, as appropriate, through sale or other transfer of ownership.

5. **"License Elements"** means the following high-level license attributes as selected by Licensor and indicated in the title of this License: Attribution, ShareAlike.

6. **"Licensor"** means the individual, individuals, entity or entities that offer(s) the Work under the terms of this License.

7. **"Original Author"** means, in the case of a literary or artistic work, the individual, individuals, entity or entities who created the Work or if no individual or entity can be identified, the publisher; and in addition (i) in the case of a performance the actors, singers, musicians, dancers, and other persons who act, sing, deliver, declaim, play in, interpret or otherwise perform literary or artistic works or expressions of folklore; (ii) in the case of a phonogram the producer being the person or legal entity who first fixes the sounds of a performance or other sounds; and, (iii) in the case of broadcasts, the organization that transmits the broadcast.

8. **"Work"** means the literary and/or artistic work offered under the terms of this License including without limitation any production in the literary, scientific and artistic domain, whatever may be the mode or form of its expression including digital form, such as a book, pamphlet and other writing; a lecture, address, sermon or other work of the same nature; a dramatic or dramatico-musical work; a choreographic work or entertainment in dumb show; a musical composition with or without words; a cinematographic work to which are assimilated works expressed by a process analogous to cinematography; a work of drawing, painting, architecture, sculpture, engraving or lithography; a photographic work to which are assimilated works expressed by a process analogous to photography; a work

of applied art; an illustration, map, plan, sketch or three-dimensional work relative to geography, topography, architecture or science; a performance; a broadcast; a phonogram; a compilation of data to the extent it is protected as a copyrightable work; or a work performed by a variety or circus performer to the extent it is not otherwise considered a literary or artistic work.

9. **"You"** means an individual or entity exercising rights under this License who has not previously violated the terms of this License with respect to the Work, or who has received express permission from the Licensor to exercise rights under this License despite a previous violation.

10. **"Publicly Perform"** means to perform public recitations of the Work and to communicate to the public those public recitations, by any means or process, including by wire or wireless means or public digital performances; to make available to the public Works in such a way that members of the public may access these Works from a place and at a place individually chosen by them; to perform the Work to the public by any means or process and the communication to the public of the performances of the Work, including by public digital performance; to broadcast and rebroadcast the Work by any means including signs, sounds or images.

11. **"Reproduce"** means to make copies of the Work by any means including without limitation by sound or visual recordings and the right of fixation and reproducing fixations of the Work, including storage of a protected performance or phonogram in digital form or other electronic medium.

2. Fair Dealing Rights. Nothing in this License is intended to reduce, limit, or restrict any uses free from copyright or rights arising from limitations or exceptions that are provided for in connection with the copyright protection under copyright law or other applicable laws.

3. License Grant. Subject to the terms and conditions of this License, Licensor hereby grants You a worldwide, royalty-free, non-exclusive, perpetual (for the duration of the applicable copyright) license to exercise the rights in the Work as stated below:

1. to Reproduce the Work, to incorporate the Work into one or more Collections, and to Reproduce the Work as incorporated in the Collections;

2. to create and Reproduce Adaptations provided that any such Adaptation, including any translation in any medium, takes reasonable steps to clearly label, demarcate or otherwise identify that changes were made to the original Work. For example, a translation could be marked "The original work was translated from English to Spanish," or a modification could indicate "The original work has been modified.";

3. to Distribute and Publicly Perform the Work including as incorporated in Collections; and,

4. to Distribute and Publicly Perform Adaptations.

5. For the avoidance of doubt:

    1. **Non-waivable Compulsory License Schemes.** In those jurisdictions in which the right to collect royalties through any statutory or compulsory licensing scheme cannot be waived, the Licensor reserves the exclusive right to collect such royalties for any exercise by You of the rights granted under this License;

    2. **Waivable Compulsory License Schemes.** In those jurisdictions in which the right to collect royalties through any statutory or compulsory licensing scheme can be waived, the Licensor waives the exclusive right to collect such royalties for any exercise by You of the rights granted under this License; and,

    3. **Voluntary License Schemes.** The Licensor waives the right to collect royalties, whether individually or, in the event that the Licensor is a member of a collecting society that administers voluntary licensing schemes,

> via that society, from any exercise by You of the rights granted under this License.

The above rights may be exercised in all media and formats whether now known or hereafter devised. The above rights include the right to make such modifications as are technically necessary to exercise the rights in other media and formats. Subject to Section 8(f), all rights not expressly granted by Licensor are hereby reserved.

4. Restrictions. The license granted in Section 3 above is expressly made subject to and limited by the following restrictions:

1. You may Distribute or Publicly Perform the Work only under the terms of this License. You must include a copy of, or the Uniform Resource Identifier (URI) for, this License with every copy of the Work You Distribute or Publicly Perform. You may not offer or impose any terms on the Work that restrict the terms of this License or the ability of the recipient of the Work to exercise the rights granted to that recipient under the terms of the License. You may not sublicense the Work. You must keep intact all notices that refer to this License and to the disclaimer of warranties with every copy of the Work You Distribute or Publicly Perform. When You Distribute or Publicly Perform the Work, You may not impose any effective technological measures on the Work that restrict the ability of a recipient of the Work from You to exercise the rights granted to that recipient under the terms of the License. This Section 4(a) applies to the Work as incorporated in a Collection, but this does not require the Collection apart from the Work itself to be made subject to the terms of this License. If You create a Collection, upon notice from any Licensor You must, to the extent practicable, remove from the Collection any credit as required by Section 4(c), as requested. If You create an Adaptation, upon notice from any Licensor You must, to the extent practicable, remove from the

Adaptation any credit as required by Section 4(c), as requested.

2. You may Distribute or Publicly Perform an Adaptation only under the terms of: (i) this License; (ii) a later version of this License with the same License Elements as this License; (iii) a Creative Commons jurisdiction license (either this or a later license version) that contains the same License Elements as this License (e.g., Attribution-ShareAlike 3.0 US)); (iv) a Creative Commons Compatible License. If you license the Adaptation under one of the licenses mentioned in (iv), you must comply with the terms of that license. If you license the Adaptation under the terms of any of the licenses mentioned in (i), (ii) or (iii) (the "Applicable License"), you must comply with the terms of the Applicable License generally and the following provisions: (I) You must include a copy of, or the URI for, the Applicable License with every copy of each Adaptation You Distribute or Publicly Perform; (II) You may not offer or impose any terms on the Adaptation that restrict the terms of the Applicable License or the ability of the recipient of the Adaptation to exercise the rights granted to that recipient under the terms of the Applicable License; (III) You must keep intact all notices that refer to the Applicable License and to the disclaimer of warranties with every copy of the Work as included in the Adaptation You Distribute or Publicly Perform; (IV) when You Distribute or Publicly Perform the Adaptation, You may not impose any effective technological measures on the Adaptation that restrict the ability of a recipient of the Adaptation from You to exercise the rights granted to that recipient under the terms of the Applicable License. This Section 4(b) applies to the Adaptation as incorporated in a Collection, but this does not require the Collection apart from the Adaptation itself to be made subject to the terms of the Applicable License.

3. If You Distribute, or Publicly Perform the Work or any Adaptations or Collections, You must, unless a request has been made pursuant to Section 4(a), keep intact all copyright notices for the Work and provide, reasonable to the medium or means You are utilizing: (i) the name of the Original Author (or pseudonym, if applicable) if supplied, and/or if the Original Author and/or Licensor designate another party or parties (e.g., a sponsor institute, publishing entity, journal) for attribution ("Attribution Parties") in Licensor's copyright notice, terms of service or by other reasonable means, the name of such party or parties; (ii) the title of the Work if supplied; (iii) to the extent reasonably practicable, the URI, if any, that Licensor specifies to be associated with the Work, unless such URI does not refer to the copyright notice or licensing information for the Work; and (iv) , consistent with Section 3(b), in the case of an Adaptation, a credit identifying the use of the Work in the Adaptation (e.g., "French translation of the Work by Original Author," or "Screenplay based on original Work by Original Author"). The credit required by this Section 4(c) may be implemented in any reasonable manner; provided, however, that in the case of a Adaptation or Collection, at a minimum such credit will appear, if a credit for all contributing authors of the Adaptation or Collection appears, then as part of these credits and in a manner at least as prominent as the credits for the other contributing authors. For the avoidance of doubt, You may only use the credit required by this Section for the purpose of attribution in the manner set out above and, by exercising Your rights under this License, You may not implicitly or explicitly assert or imply any connection with, sponsorship or endorsement by the Original Author, Licensor and/or Attribution Parties, as appropriate, of You or Your use of the Work, without the separate, express prior written permis-

sion of the Original Author, Licensor and/or Attribution Parties.

4. Except as otherwise agreed in writing by the Licensor or as may be otherwise permitted by applicable law, if You Reproduce, Distribute or Publicly Perform the Work either by itself or as part of any Adaptations or Collections, You must not distort, mutilate, modify or take other derogatory action in relation to the Work which would be prejudicial to the Original Author's honor or reputation. Licensor agrees that in those jurisdictions (e.g. Japan), in which any exercise of the right granted in Section 3(b) of this License (the right to make Adaptations) would be deemed to be a distortion, mutilation, modification or other derogatory action prejudicial to the Original Author's honor and reputation, the Licensor will waive or not assert, as appropriate, this Section, to the fullest extent permitted by the applicable national law, to enable You to reasonably exercise Your right under Section 3(b) of this License (right to make Adaptations) but not otherwise.

5. Representations, Warranties and Disclaimer

UNLESS OTHERWISE MUTUALLY AGREED TO BY THE PARTIES IN WRITING, LICENSOR OFFERS THE WORK AS-IS AND MAKES NO REPRESENTATIONS OR WARRANTIES OF ANY KIND CONCERNING THE WORK, EXPRESS, IMPLIED, STATUTORY OR OTHERWISE, INCLUDING, WITHOUT LIMITATION, WARRANTIES OF TITLE, MERCHANTIBILITY, FITNESS FOR A PARTICULAR PURPOSE, NONINFRINGEMENT, OR THE ABSENCE OF LATENT OR OTHER DEFECTS, ACCURACY, OR THE PRESENCE OF ABSENCE OF ERRORS, WHETHER OR NOT DISCOVERABLE. SOME JURISDICTIONS DO NOT ALLOW THE EXCLUSION OF IMPLIED WARRANTIES, SO SUCH EXCLUSION MAY NOT APPLY TO YOU.

6. Limitation on Liability.

EXCEPT TO THE EXTENT REQUIRED BY APPLICABLE LAW, IN NO EVENT WILL LICENSOR BE LIABLE TO YOU ON ANY LEGAL THEORY FOR ANY SPECIAL, INCIDENTAL, CONSE-

QUENTIAL, PUNITIVE OR EXEMPLARY DAMAGES ARISING OUT OF THIS LICENSE OR THE USE OF THE WORK, EVEN IF LICENSOR HAS BEEN ADVISED OF THE POSSIBILITY OF SUCH DAMAGES.

7. Termination

1. This License and the rights granted hereunder will terminate automatically upon any breach by You of the terms of this License. Individuals or entities who have received Adaptations or Collections from You under this License, however, will not have their licenses terminated provided such individuals or entities remain in full compliance with those licenses. Sections 1, 2, 5, 6, 7, and 8 will survive any termination of this License.

2. Subject to the above terms and conditions, the license granted here is perpetual (for the duration of the applicable copyright in the Work). Notwithstanding the above, Licensor reserves the right to release the Work under different license terms or to stop distributing the Work at any time; provided, however that any such election will not serve to withdraw this License (or any other license that has been, or is required to be, granted under the terms of this License), and this License will continue in full force and effect unless terminated as stated above.

8. Miscellaneous

1. Each time You Distribute or Publicly Perform the Work or a Collection, the Licensor offers to the recipient a license to the Work on the same terms and conditions as the license granted to You under this License.

2. Each time You Distribute or Publicly Perform an Adaptation, Licensor offers to the recipient a license to the original Work on the same terms and conditions as the license granted to You under this License.

3. If any provision of this License is invalid or unenforceable under applicable law, it shall not affect the validity or enforceability of the remainder of the terms of this License,

and without further action by the parties to this agreement, such provision shall be reformed to the minimum extent necessary to make such provision valid and enforceable.

4. No term or provision of this License shall be deemed waived and no breach consented to unless such waiver or consent shall be in writing and signed by the party to be charged with such waiver or consent.

5. This License constitutes the entire agreement between the parties with respect to the Work licensed here. There are no understandings, agreements or representations with respect to the Work not specified here. Licensor shall not be bound by any additional provisions that may appear in any communication from You. This License may not be modified without the mutual written agreement of the Licensor and You.

6. The rights granted under, and the subject matter referenced, in this License were drafted utilizing the terminology of the Berne Convention for the Protection of Literary and Artistic Works (as amended on September 28, 1979), the Rome Convention of 1961, the WIPO Copyright Treaty of 1996, the WIPO Performances and Phonograms Treaty of 1996 and the Universal Copyright Convention (as revised on July 24, 1971). These rights and subject matter take effect in the relevant jurisdiction in which the License terms are sought to be enforced according to the corresponding provisions of the implementation of those treaty provisions in the applicable national law. If the standard suite of rights granted under applicable copyright law includes additional rights not granted under this License, such additional rights are deemed to be included in the License; this License is not intended to restrict the license of any rights under applicable law.

Creative Commons Notice

Appendix D: Analyzing "Attribution" and "ShareAlike"

The Attribution-ShareAlike License is suggested as an ideal license for discipleship resources intended for use by the global church. The "Attribution" condition provides a crucial pointer to the original work for users of derivative works, ensuring the authoritativeness of the original. The "ShareAlike" condition locks the work "open", by requiring all derivative works to be made available under the same license.

Of the six primary Creative Commons Licenses, the Attribution -ShareAlike is optimally suited for discipleship resources intended for use by the global church. The two conditions of the license work together to form a license that provides the necessary legal freedom, even through multiple generations of derivative works. The two conditions of the license are considered in detail here.

"Attribution" Points the World to You

The "Attribution" condition requires that any use of the content, like a translation or adaptation, clearly attribute the *original* work to the original creator. This attribution statement should provide a hyperlink to the website of the owner of the original content (where applicable), and state the license under which the original work is available. A statement of attribution for an adaptation of a fictitious study guide for the book of Romans might say something like this:

> Based on *A Study of Romans* by John Doe (www.example.com), available under a Creative Commons Attribution-ShareAlike License (http://creativecommons.org/licenses/by-sa/3.0).

This simple statement of attribution accomplishes a number of important things. It clearly states:

- the name of the original work
- the name of the original work's creator
- the website where the original work can be found
- the license under which the original work is made available.

Any derivative work made from this fictitious example is legally required to include a similar statement of attribution. This provides an unbroken chain back to the original work.

What is the worst thing that you could imagine happening to a discipleship resource that you release under Attribution-ShareAlike? For some, it is the possibility that someone of the denomination they disagree with most might take their resource and change the doctrinal distinctives of it to reflect their own particular view of baptism, the Lord's Supper, eternal security, etc. The thought that their name might be associated (in the attribution statement) with doctrine about which they disagree is horrifying to them. For others, the concern is that the discipleship resource could be corrupted—whether malevolently or accidentally—by others and this might reflect back to them, given that their name is clearly stated in the attribution statement.

It is important to understand that *a statement of attribution is not a statement of endorsement.* An attribution of the original work to the original creator, does not in any way imply that the creator of the original work endorses (or is even aware of) this particular use of it. The statement of attribution merely states what the original work is, who the creator of the original work is, and that they released the work under a license that permits reuse of the content.

In the traditional model of the analog world, any mention by name in a work was often seen as an implicit endorsement of the work by the named entity. Not so in the digital world and the realm of the Creative Commons. In this new context, attribution is nothing more than an indicator to the consumer of the derivative work that the work is built using portions of an original work created by the original content creator who provides no official endorsement, authorization or connection to the content of the derivative work. This is why the terms of the Attribution-ShareAlike License specifically state that the attribution is not to be made in a way that suggests any endorsement of the derivative by the creator of the original content.

The second thing to note about the statement of attribution is the importance of the link to the website specified by the creator of the original work. In the digital world, *you cannot control what happens to your content.* Attempting to control or prevent the creation of derivative works is fighting a losing battle. You *can*, however, control what is on your own website. The Attribution-ShareAlike License requires that any derivative work—good or bad—contain a hyperlink, where hyperlinks are possible, to the website specified by the copyright holder of the original work on which the derivative work is based. This simple requirement changes everything.

A hyperlink is a statement attributing authoritativeness to the original content creator. It says, effectively, "I acknowledge that what I have created is not my work alone and the original on which it is based is located here." Each hyperlink back to the original is a vote in favor of the authoritativeness of the original. In terms of Internet search algorithms, this boosts the "search engine optimization" of the original website, increasing their ranking in relevant search results. All of this translates into increased exposure and mindshare for the creator of the original content. As more of their content is used in other derivative works that are then distributed by others all over the digital world, each one of those works is legally required to contain a link back to the original. This is nothing but good for the creator of the original content.

People tend to want to go to the original. The "Attribution" condition provides any consumer of the content with a clear "chain of title" back to the original work. When they click on that hyperlink to get to the original, they are taken to the website specified by the creator of the original work. The content creator now has both the authority and the opportunity to establish their own identity in the mind of the consumer, based on the original content that is available on their website, which is controlled by them and is the highest authority for their work. The original, authoritative work is thus able to exhibit its doctrinal soundness and provide the standard by which all derivatives are to be judged.

On their authoritative website, the content owner may list which translations of the content are "official" and which ones are user-generated. They may have other works available to the consumer (whether free or otherwise). They may provide a forum for discussing the content or to request help with translation of the content into other languages. They may also have an up-to-date list of known derivative works that should be avoided, alerting consumers to content that is specifically not endorsed by the creator of the original content.

For all these reasons, the requirement of "Attribution" is a crucial component of the Attribution-ShareAlike License. That said, there may be situations and contexts where a content owner does not want attribution in a derivative work. If content has been released under an Attribution-ShareAlike License and the use of the content does not violate the license, the owner of the original cannot require the creator of the derivative work to "cease and desist" their use of the content. But Creative Commons licenses provide several mechanisms that allow the copyright holder to choose not to be associated with derivative works or uses of their content with which they disagree. The Creative Commons FAQ says this on the topic:

> All CC licenses prohibit using the attribution requirement to suggest that the original author or licensor endorses or supports a particular use of a work. This "No Endorsement" provision protects reputation, and its violation constitutes a violation of the license and results in automatic termination. Second, licensors may waive the attribution requirement—choose not to be identified as the author or licensor of the work—if they wish. Third, if a work is modified or incorporated into a collection, and the original author or licensor does not like the how the work has been modified or used in the collection, Creative Commons licenses require that the person modifying the work or incorporating the work into a collection remove reference to the original author or licensor upon notice. Finally, if the selected Creative Commons license permits modifications and adaptations of the original work, then the person modifying the work must indicate that the original has been modified. This ensures that changes made to the original work—whether or not ac-

ceptable to the original author or licensor—are not attrib-
uted back to the licensor.[1]

"ShareAlike" Locks the Content Open

As important as the "Attribution" condition is, the "ShareAlike"
condition is equally important. It prevents the "locking down" of
any derivative works, keeping them open for use by others while
also limiting the potential for commercial exploitation of the content.

Another commonly used Creative Commons license is called the
"Creative Commons Attribution License (CC BY)." As you might
guess, it is identical to the "Creative Commons Attribution-Share-
Alike License (CC BY-SA)" apart from the fact that the "ShareAlike"
condition is not used. The foundational difference between the two
is that derivative works made from an Attribution license are not
required to be distributed under the same license. By contrast, derivative works made from an Attribution-ShareAlike License are.
This might not seem like a significant difference at first, but the implications become especially clear in the context of world missions
and the translation of discipleship resources by and for the global
church that speaks other languages.

Let's say the fictitious work *A Study of Romans* is released by John
Doe under a Creative Commons Attribution license, without the
"ShareAlike" condition. The work is made available online and is
soon discovered by believers in other parts of the world who are
bilingual in English. Word gets out, people get interested, and legal
translations of the work are started by believers speaking a dozen
different languages. They complete their translations and each one
duly provides a statement of attribution in the beginning of the

---

1   "Frequently Asked Questions," n.d.,
     http://wiki.creativecommons.org/Frequently_Asked_Questions

work, specifying that it is a translation from John Doe's original work. So far so good, but note carefully what has happened.

The Attribution license (without a ShareAlike condition) grants anyone legal freedom to translate the work, but when they do so, what they create automatically belongs to them, with "all rights reserved" by default. Such is the nature of copyright law. In this situation, John Doe would be legally locked out of the translations of his own book, in the same way that others were locked out of his original book before he released it under an open license. Unless the translators of the work choose to voluntarily release their translations under an open license—so that others, including John Doe, can access and use them—their translation work is their own and all rights are reserved to them.

Now imagine that a publishing company finds out about these translations and has the opportunity and means to strike a deal with the translators. The company would be able to legally buy the rights to those translations without any obligation to make them available with the same freedom that was given by John Doe when he originally released it. The Creative Commons Attribution License is an excellent license that can be extremely useful in the right contexts. But it is not ideal as a general license for use in the equipping of the global church with adequate discipleship resources in every language of the world, because it fails to maintain the openness and freedom of derivative works made from the original content.

Now imagine the exact same context, with the exception that John Doe released the fictitious *A Study of Romans* under a Creative Commons Attribution-ShareAlike License. Everything remains the same with one crucial difference: John Doe (and anyone else) are able to access and use the translations of his work with the same freedom that he made available in his original work. The Attribution-ShareAlike License includes the legal requirement that derivative works of the original content may only be distributed under the same (or functionally similar) license. In this way, what was intended to be free and open, remains free and open, forever.[2]

---

2   Another advantage of this license that stems from the ShareAlike condition is that it is ideally suited to prevent the problems of "joint ownership" of works that are created collaboratively. When each contributor to a project agrees to release their contributions under an Attribution-ShareAlike License, the completed work can be freely used according to the terms of the license without the ambiguity and legal complications of a jointly owned, "all rights reserved" work. This is one of the many reasons that openly collaborative projects like Wikipedia use the Attribution-ShareAlike License.

APPENDIX E: SUSTAINABLE MODELS FOR BUILDING THE CHRISTIAN COMMONS

Four models for the building the Christian Commons are described below. The models involve creating new discipleship resources collaboratively, voluntarily releasing works openly before the copyright term expires, sponsoring the creation of open-licensed works, and gifting discipleship resources to the global church.

Collaboratively-Created Resources

One of the primary means of building the Christian Commons is by the open collaboration of the global church. Open collaboration (based on a model of social production) is an extremely powerful, inexpensive, and efficient means of creating vast amounts of content. This content, when it is in a well-managed system like a wiki, tends to progressively improve in quality over time. We have seen that the global church is already on the rise and ready to join in the task of equipping themselves with discipleship resources. Open collaboration as a global church enables anyone, anywhere to work together to create and translate discipleship resources in any language *at the same time*. This massively parallel approach has the potential to provide discipleship resources in any language very quickly.

It is unrealistic to expect that a single organization (or any number of formal partnerships) could ever develop adequate capacity to undertake and maintain translation projects (and revisions of translations) for all the discipleship resources needed by believers in thousands of languages, all at the same time, and on into the future. A more effective means of meeting this need is for the global church to openly collaborate toward this end. By working in parallel, the body of Christ all over the world will be able to accomplish far more, at far less cost, and in far less time than would otherwise be possible.

The concept of open collaboration is related to the concept of *cognitive surplus*, the spare brainpower that is available outside of a person's vocation. In essence, cognitive surplus is both an individual's free time as well as the aggregate free time of every individual in a group. How much surplus are we talking about? In *Cognitive Surplus*, Clay Shirky suggests using a unit of measurement to help understand how much cognitive surplus is actually available: the number of hours it took to create the English-language version of Wikipedia. It contains over 3 million articles (1,600+ volumes of Encyclopedia Britannica). According to studies done by IBM researcher Martin Wattenberg, the approximate time it took to create this massive resource is one hundred million hours. That is a lot of time, but what is even more interesting is how this relates to the amount of time spent in other activities, namely watching television.

Americans watch roughly two hundred *billion* hours of TV every year. That represents about two thousand Wikipedias' projects' worth of free time annually. Even tiny subsets of this time are enormous: we spend roughly a hundred million hours every weekend just watching commercials. This is a pretty big surplus. People who ask "Where do they find the time?" about those who work on Wikipedia don't understand how tiny that entire project is, relative to the aggregate free time we all possess.[1]

If Americans alone have more than two hundred billion hours of cognitive surplus every year, how much cognitive surplus is available in the entire global church, that numbers more than one billion people (and some put the number closer to two billion)? To put this into perspective, look at it this way: if we assume the entire global church numbers one billion people and one out of every ten of these Christians worldwide gives only one hour of their time a month (one hundred million hours), their aggregate time would be enough to create an amount of content equivalent to the entire English version of Wikipedia *each month*. What we need in order to equip the global church with discipleship resources is not more people, more time, or more money. What we need is for the global church to work together in ways that make the most of the technology and the resources we already have.

When the global church openly collaborates, their aggregate knowledge and available time become a massive resource that dwarfs the immense need for discipleship resources in every language of the world. Given the highly successful track record of openly collaborative projects, there is good reason to believe that this model will be very effective in the creation of vast numbers of discipleship resources of the highest quality in every language. New discipleship resources (like Bible translations, Bible study notes, Bible encyclopedias, concordances, etc.) can be created and

---

1   Shirky, *Cognitive Surplus*, 10.

translated into any language in less time and with less expense than would otherwise be possible. Open collaboration harnesses the cognitive surplus of the global church to create massive amounts of discipleship resources, without restricting them using traditional licensing in order to generate a revenue stream from them.

Voluntary Early Release of Content

If you have ever tried to obtain a copy of an out-of-print book that was first published in the twentieth century, you may have discovered that it can be a very difficult feat to accomplish. In fact, as much as 95% of books written in the last one hundred years are out of print, making them difficult (if not impossible) to access.[2] The books are of virtually no commercial value anymore, so they are unlikely to be digitized or reprinted by the publisher. But these books are also still restricted by copyright, so they cannot be digitized and freely distributed by others either.

It is likely that the percentages are very similar for books that are specifically Christian in focus and worldview, although the exact numbers are not known. The content contained in many of these Christian books would be of significant value to the global church, but they are unlikely to be legally accessible to them anytime for many decades. Until seventy years after the death of the author—when the book passes into the Public Domain—Christian books like these cannot be digitized, translated, or freely redistributed by others. They are effectively as lost to the global church as if they had never been written.

There is an intriguing twist to this dilemma. Up until 1976, books written in the U.S. were covered by copyright restrictions that lasted for twenty-eight years, at which point the books would pass into the Public Domain. If the copyright holder wanted to extend

---

2   Boyle, *The Public Domain: Enclosing the Commons of the Mind*, 10.

the copyright on their work after the twenty-eight years ended, they had to apply for an extension. Here is where things get interesting: 85% of works that were created under these copyright terms *never had their copyright renewed* and were released into the Public Domain after twenty-eight years.[3] From this we can conclude that for nearly nine out of ten works, there was no longer commercial benefit in copyright terms that extended longer than twenty-eight years. If there had been, it is likely the copyright would have been renewed so the copyright holder could continue leveraging the restrictions afforded to them by copyright law to perpetuate the revenue stream.

Christian authors and publishers are finding the same thing. Within a few years after publishing, the full commercial benefit of some books has already been realized. Which leads to this question: what if Christian content creators (or copyright holders) voluntarily released their content into the Christian Commons *before the term of their government-granted copyright expires*, for the good of the global church? They could set an arbitrary length of time–maybe seven years (using the length of time set in Deuteronomy 15)–during which time they would sell the resource to recover their expenses, then release it into the Christian Commons. Or they might sell the resource until they receive the payment for the work done during the creation of the resource, then release it. Copyright law says the content creator can be paid for the creation of a work for their entire lifetime plus seventy years after their death (in the U.S., and with similar restrictions in most other parts of the world). But there is no reason the creator of the content cannot voluntarily shorten the length of their own exclusive use of their content, for the good of the global church.

A note on this approach is in order, however. Before publishing, authors of books are often required to sign over some (or all) of their rights to a publisher. It is the publishers, not the authors, who hold all the cards in these situations. This results in significant compli-

---

3   Ibid, 9.

cations, especially since half of Christian content is published by secular publishers who are unlikely to have any interest in spiritual or other non-economic motives for releasing copyright restrictions on what they own.[4] This suggests, then, that Christian publishing companies (and others who own the rights to discipleship resources) have a tremendous opportunity to bless the global church by releasing some of the rights to some of what they own.

Sponsored Works

Sponsoring the creation of discipleship resources is a very effective and widely-used approach to creating content. Churches pay the salary of their pastor while on sabbatical to write a book or sermon series. Seminaries pay the professor who writes a commentary or teaching curriculum. Donations are collected to fund the translation of an evangelistic video into another language. Foundations provide the capital to extend the reach of a discipleship resource into other languages. There are many variations on the same theme.

What if sponsors of discipleship resources were to decide they do not want to sponsor a work that will be restricted under a license that necessarily withholds it from Christians speaking the vast majority of languages? Instead of expecting that the people being paid to create resource will maintain the "all rights reserved" afforded to them by copyright law (to gain additional revenue from the sale or exclusive licensing of the resource), there is an alternative. The funders of the resource could provide the funding to the content creators on the condition that the resource be released under an open license and into the Christian Commons so that the entire

---

4   Ted Olsen, "HarperCollins Buys Thomas Nelson, Will Control 50% of Christian Publishing Market," oct 2011,
     http://blog.christianitytoday.com/ctliveblog/archives/2011/10/harper-collins_b.html

global church could benefit from it without restriction. By so doing, the funders maximize the missiological value of their investment.

This approach has significant merit, but potential funders need to understand that the dual nature of traditional discipleship resources can complicate things. Many discipleship resources serve a two-fold purpose: ministry tool and revenue generator, either from direct sales or donations to the exclusive owner. Because of this two-fold purpose, the sponsors of a discipleship resource (e.g. donors, foundations, etc.) often balk at supporting a project which does not make the best use of commercial opportunities. After all, if they are giving their hard-earned money to the project, it could be alarming to find that others were allowed to use the resource without being required to pay royalties back to the project.

So content creators who want to release their discipleship resources under an open license like the Attribution-ShareAlike License face a conundrum. If they do not release their content under an open license, they necessarily cut out the vast majority of the global church from joining in to legally translate the discipleship resource into the thousands of languages that need it. But if they do release the content under an open license, there may be a concern that their sponsors will withhold the funding they need, because they are not restricting the content so as to maximize revenue.

The problem with the "our sponsors might get mad if we release the resource under Attribution-ShareAlike" is often based on an incorrect assumption about how to get discipleship resources to those who need them. Ironically, this incorrect assumption actually used to be the correct assumption. It has become incorrect, only because a new model now exists that was not even an option a decade ago.

It used to be that there was only one way of getting discipleship resources to those who needed them: by using a private production model to create restricted access content that was distributed through limited channels as both a ministry tool and also a revenue generator (to fund more ministry). With the rise of the Digital Age and the advance of the Internet and mobile phones around the world, the ministry landscape has changed drastically in the last decade. We now have the ability to use an "open" approach to equip the global church—an approach that uses a social production model in the creation and translation of content. The content in the "open" model has only one purpose: ministry. Because the resources are not intended to generate income, they can be released from the traditional licensing model restrictions that limit the reach of the content. The resources can be legally distributed by any number of distributors, exclusively as a ministry tool. However, until sponsors understand that a project can only be "open" when the content it creates is legally "open-licensed," there will likely be confusion and concern about the apparent failure of the content owners to legally lock it down.

When considering the possibility of funding a project to create discipleship resources, a potential sponsor wants to be sure that the content is as effective as possible.[5] The traditional means of ensuring effectiveness was to use a strategy that locks out competitors, unless they are willing to pay a license fee. Going this route is fine, but doing so also prevents the majority of the global church from ever getting access to that resource. There is no way around it—that is the nature of the traditional model that depends on restricting access to (and use of) the content.

A Gift of Intellectual Property

The Biblical concept of giving to God a portion of what we have may be an effective model for meeting the needs of the global

---

5 A useful resource for foundations and other sponsors considering the possibility of funding content-creation projects using open licenses is Phil Malone"An Evaluation of Private Foundation Copyright Licensing Policies, Practices and Opportunities" (2009), http://cyber.law.harvard.edu/publications/2009/Open_Content_Licensing_for_Foundations

church. This is not to suggest that everyone should give away all their discipleship resources under an open license and then attempt to develop a completely new model for funding the creation of additional resources. Instead, content creators could consider giving a portion of what they have (or what they create in the future) to meet the needs of the global church, by releasing it into the Christian Commons under an open license. What would happen if just a small portion of the hundreds of new discipleship resources created each year were voluntarily released under an Attribution-ShareAlike License for the good of the global church?

If this were to happen, the global church could find themselves going from famine to feast in very little time. Translation of the content would still be needed, and translating a book is not a trivial undertaking. But compared to getting the legal right to translate the content, the translation itself is often the easy part. If those who own the content were to voluntarily give a portion of what they have by releasing it under an open license, the global church would be tremendously blessed.

Note that this gift of Intellectual Property is not referring to a gift from the revenue generated by selling the content. Nor is it referring to giving "free of charge" access to otherwise completely restricted content. It is referring to a voluntary release of the restrictions on the "firstfruits" of the content itself, putting it into the Christian Commons. In keeping with the Biblical "firstfruits" principle, these would be the best discipleship resources we have—those that would be of the greatest usefulness to the global church.

BIBLIOGRAPHY

à Kempis, Thomas. *The Imitation of Christ - In Four Books*. Translated by Right Rev. R. Challoner, D.D., V.A. McGlashan and Gill, 1873.

Ahonen, Tomi. "Latest Annual Edition of TomiAhonen Almanac 2012 Is Now Released. Lets Share Some Data from It.," *Communities Dominate Brands,* feb 2012. http://communities-dominate.blogs.com/brands/2012/02/latest-an-nual-edition-of-tomiahonen-almanac-2012-is-now-released-lets-share-some-data-from-it.html .

———. "Latest Mobile Numbers for End of Year 2012 - This Is Getting Hu-mongous.," *Communities Dominate Brands*, dec 2012. http://communi-ties-dominate.blogs.com/brands/2012/12/latest-mobile-numbers-for-end-of-year-2012-this-is-getting-humongous.html.

———. "Preview of Mobile Stats to End of Year 2010: 5.2 Billion subscribers, 350M people got their first phone this year.," *Communities Dominate Brands* nov 2010. http://communities-dominate.blogs.com/brands/2010/11/preview-of-mobile-stats-to-end-of-year-2010-52-billion-subscribers-350m-peo-ple-got-their-first-phone.html.

———. "The State of the Union blog for Mobile Industry - all the stats and facts for 2012," *Communities Dominate Brands,* feb 2012. http://commu-nities-dominate.blogs.com/brands/2012/02/the-state-of-the-union-blog-for-mobile-industry-all-the-stats-and-facts-for-2012.html.

Anderson, Chris. *Free: The Future of a Radical Price*. Hyperion, 2009.

Balio, Tina. "Museum of Broadcast Communications, 'Betamax Case,'" 1997. http://www.museum.tv/archives/etv/B/htmlB/betamaxcase/beta-maxcase.htm.

Benkler, Yochai. "Yochai Benkler on the new open-source economics." Oxford, England, jul 2005.
http://www.ted.com/talks/yochai_benkler_on_the_new_open_source_economics.html.

Boyle, James. *The Public Domain: Enclosing the Commons of the Mind.* Yale University Press, 2008. http://www.thepublicdomain.org/.

Brooks, Thomas. *Heaven on Earth,* 1667.
http://www.monergism.com/thethreshold/sdg/heavenweb.html.

Bunyan, John. *The Pilgrim's Progress.* Edited by W. R. Owens. Oxford University Press, 2003.

Challies, Tim. "Reflections on Leaving India." *Challies Dot Com,* November 16, 2012. http://www.challies.com/articles/reflections-on-leaving-india.

Clampet, Elizabeth. "Court OKs Diamond Rio MP3 Player," jun 1999.
http://www.internetnews.com/bus-news/article.php/139091.

Cole, Richard G. "Reformation Printers: Unsung Heroes." *Sixteenth Century Journal* 15, no. 3 (1984). doi:10.2307/2540767.

Condon, Bernard. "Babble Rouser," jul 2008.
http://www.forbes.com/forbes/2008/0811/072.html.

Contributors, LOLCat Bible Translation. "Genesis 1," n.d. http://lolcat-bible.com/index.php?title=Genesis_1.

Contributors, Wikipedia. "Wikipedia:Size in volumes." Wikimedia Foundation, Inc., jun 2012. http://en.wikipedia.org/w/index.php?title=Wikipedia:Size_in_volumes&oldid=462112380.

Corbet, Jonathan, Greg Kroah-Hartman, and Amanda McPherson. "Linux Kernel Development: How Fast it is Going, Who is Doing It, What They are Doing, and Who is Sponsoring It." The Linux Foundation, nov 2010. https://www.linuxfoundation.org/sites/main/files/lf_linux_kernel_development_2010.pdf.

Creson, Bob. "Hearing the Christmas story again–for the first time," n.d.
http://www.wycliffe.net/Stories/tabid/67/Default.aspx?id=2086.

Crump, Rory. "Intellectual property rights: the quiet killer of Rio+20," jul 2012. http://www.patexia.com/feed/intellectual-property-rights-the-quiet-killer-of-rio-20-20120702.

Erickson, Bruce. "Intellectual Property and the Eighth Commandment," jul 2012. http://distantshoresmedia.org/blog/intellectual-property-and-eighth-commandment.

Friedman, Thomas L. *The World Is Flat: A Brief History of the Twenty-first Century*. Farrar, Straus and Giroux, 2005.

Geere, Duncan. "The History of Creative Commons." *Wired UK*. http://www.wired.co.uk/news/archive/2011-12/13/history-of-creative-commons.

Giles, Jim. "Internet Encyclopaedias Go Head to Head." *Nature* 438: 900–901. http://www.nature.com/nature/journal/v438/n7070/full/438900a.html.

Gravelle, Gilles. "What Happens When A Crowd Translates the Bible?," dec 2011. http://blog.theseedcompany.org/bible-translation-2/what-happens-when-a-crowd-translates-the-bible/.

Grudem, Wayne. "Systematic Theology." Accessed January 14, 2013. http://www.waynegrudem.com/systematic-theology/.

Harper, William Rainey, Ernest DeWitt Burton, and Shailer Mathews. *The Biblical World*. University of Chicago Press, 1918.

Hartley, Matt. "Bus company no friend to PickupPal," nov 2008. http://www.theglobeandmail.com/news/technology/article722574.ece.

Howe, Jeff. *Crowdsourcing: Why the Power of the Crowd Is Driving the Future of Business*. Crown Business, 2008.

Jore, Timothy. "Why unrestricted discipleship resources are the future of the global church," feb 2011. http://distantshoresmedia.org/blog/why-unrestricted-discipleship-resources-are-future-global-church

Keith, Jeremy. "Iron Man and me," dec 2008. http://adactio.com/journal/1530/.

Kelly, Kevin. "The World Question Center 2008," 2008. http://www.edge.org/q2008/q08_6.html#kelly.

Lakhani, Karim R., Lars Bo Jeppesen, Peter A. Lohse, Jill A. Panetta, and Copenhagen Business School CBS. *The Value of Openness in Scientific Problem Solving*, 2007.

Lasar, Matthew. "Why the CBC banned Creative Commons music from its shows," oct 2010. http://arstechnica.com/media/news/2010/10/cbc-radio-fans-crabby-over-creative-commons-snub.ars.

Law, William. *A Practical Treatise Upon Christian Perfection*. Repr. [of the 1726 Ed.]., 1734.

Lessig, Lawrence. "Early Creative Commons history, my version," aug 2008. http://www.lessig.org/blog/2008/08/early_creative_commons_history.html.

———. *Free Culture: How Big Media Uses Technology and The Law To Lock Down Culture and Control Creativity*. The Penguin Press, 2004.

Lewis, M. Paul, ed. *Ethnologue: Languages of the World*. Dallas, TX, USA: SIL International, 2009. http://www.ethnologue.com.

Livermore, David A. *Serving with Eyes Wide Open*. Baker Books, 2006.

Malone, Phil. "An Evaluation of Private Foundation Copyright Licensing Policies, Practices and Opportunities." http://cyber.law.harvard.edu/publications/2009/Open_Content_Licensing_for_Foundations.

Mandryk, Jason. *Operation World: The Definitive Prayer Guide To Every Nation*. IVP Books, 2010.

Milling, David. "How do I get permission to quote from one of your Bible translations (NKJV, NCV, ICB, The Voice, The Expanded Bible)?," jan 2012. http://help.thomasnelson.com/index.php?/Knowledgebase/Article/View/40/8/how-do-i-get-permission-to-quote-from-one-of-your-bible-translations-nkjv-ncv-icb-the-voice-the-expanded-bible.

Moynahan, Brian. *God's Bestseller: William Tyndale, Thomas More, and the Writing of the English Bible—A Story of Martyrdom and Betrayal*. St. Martin's Press, 2003.

Olsen, Ted. "HarperCollins Buys Thomas Nelson, Will Control 50% of Christian Publishing Market," oct 2011. http://blog.christianitytoday.com/ctliveblog/archives/2011/10/harpercollins_b.html.

Olson, Bruce R. *Bruchko*. Creation House, 1989.

Piper, John. "Go and Make Disciples, Baptizing Them...," nov 1982. http://www.desiringgod.org/resource-library/sermons/go-and-make-disciples-baptizing-them.

———. "The Supremacy of God among 'All the Nations.'" *International Journal of Frontier Missions* 13. http://www.ijfm.org/PDFs_IJFM/13_1_PDFs/04_Piper.pdf.

Platt, David. *Radical: Taking Back Your Faith From the American Dream*. Multnomah Books, 2010.

Poe, Marshall. "The Hive." *The Atlantic*. http://www.theatlantic.com/magazine/archive/2006/09/the-hive/5118/.

Reed, Matthew. "Press Release: Africa Mobile Subscriptions Count to Cross 750 Million Mark in Fourth Quarter of 2012." *Informa Telecoms & Media*, 12 nov 2012. http://blogs.informatandm.com/6384/press-release-africa-mobile-subscriptions-count-to-cross-750-million-mark-in-fourth-quarter-of-2012/.

Sanders, Oswald. *Spiritual Leadership*. Second Revision. The Moody Bible Institute of Chicago, 1994.

Sheff, David. "Crank It Up," aug 2008. http://www.wired.com/wired/archive/8.08/loudcloud.html.

Shirky, Clay. *Cognitive Surplus*. New York, NY: Penguin Press, 2010.

———. "Napster, Udacity, and the Academy," nov 2012. http://www.shirky.com/weblog/2012/11/napster-udacity-and-the-academy/.

Slaton, Joyce. "A Mickey Mouse Copyright Law?," jan 1999. http://www.wired.com/politics/law/news/1999/01/17327.

Spurgeon, Charles. "Paul—his Cloak and His Books," November 29, 1863. http://www.spurgeon.org/sermons/0542.htm.

Standage, Tom. "Social media in the 16th Century: How Luther went viral." *The Economist*. http://www.economist.com/node/21541719#.

Starrett, Robert A. "RIAA loses bid for injunction to stop sale of Diamond Multimedia RIO MP3 Player; appeal pending," jan 1999. http://findarticles.com/p/articles/mi_m0FXG/is_1_12/ai_53578852/.

Surowiecki, James. *The Wisdom of Crowds*. New York: Anchor Books, 2005.

Swenson, Mary. "Key 4," jun 2012.

Tucker, St George. *Blackstone's Commentaries*. Rothman Reprints, 1969.

Wilder, Royal Gould, Delavan Leonard Pierson, James Manning Sherwood, and Arthur Tappan Pierson. *The Missionary Review of the World*. Funk & Wagnalls, 1912.

Williams, Keith. "The Little Phone That Could: Mobile-Empowered Ministry." *International Journal of Frontier Missiology* 27: 139–145. http://ijfm.org/PDFs_IJFM/27_3_PDFs/mobile_williams.pdf.

Willis, Avery, and Steve Evans. *Making Disciples of Oral Learners*. ILN, 2007.

"About The Licenses." Accessed September 26, 2012. http://creativecommons.org/licenses/.

"Analysis — Mobile Asia Congress 2011," 2011. http://www.wirelessintelligence.com/analysis/2011/11/mobile-asia-congress-2011/.

"Asia Pacific Mobile Observatory 2011," 2011. http://www.gsma.com/mobile-observatory/.

"Berne Convention for the Protection of Literary and Artistic Works." World Intellectual Property Organization, sep 1886. http://www.wipo.int/treaties/en/ip/berne/trtdocs_wo001.html.

"Boor of Chad Ethnic People Profile," n.d. http://www.joshuaproject.net/people-profile.php?peo3=10945&rog3=CD.

"China mobile phone users exceed 1 billion – Shanghai Daily," mar 2012. http://www.shanghaidaily.com/nsp/Business/2012/03/30/China%2Bmobile%2Bphone%2Busers%2Bexceed%2B1%2Bbillion/.

"Defining Noncommercial," n.d. http://wiki.creativecommons.org/Defining_Noncommercial.

"Definitions and Terms Related to the Great Commission," n.d. http://www.joshuaproject.net/definitions.php.

"Ethnologue report for language code: bvf," 2009. http://www.ethnologue.com/show_language.asp?code=bvf.

"Ethnologue report for language code: cmn," 2009. http://www.ethnologue.com/show_language.asp?code=cmn.

"Ethnologue report for language code: din," 2009. http://www.ethnologue.com/show_language.asp?code=din.

"Ethnologue report for language code: hin," 2009. http://www.ethnologue.com/show_language.asp?code=hin.

"Ethnologue report for language code: zho," 2009. http://www.ethnologue.com/show_language.asp?code=zho.

"Ethnologue: Statistical Summaries," 2009. http://www.ethnologue.com/ethno_docs/distribution.asp?by=size.

"Facts & Stats," n.d. https://www.innocentive.com/about-innocentive/facts-stats.

"Fatally Flawed - Refuting the recent study on encyclopedic accuracy by the journal Nature." Encyclopædia Britannica, Inc., mar 2006. http://corporate.britannica.com/britannica_nature_response.pdf.

"Frequently Asked Questions," n.d. http://wiki.creativecommons.org/Frequently_Asked_Questions.

"Friends of Bible Pathway Ministries." Accessed November 24, 2011. http://www.biblepathway.org/English/FriendsofBP.html.

"Gartner Highlights Key Predictions for IT Organizations and Users in 2010 and Beyond," jan 2010. http://www.gartner.com/it/page.jsp?id=1278413.

"Great Commission Statistics about Peoples, Countries and Languages," n.d. http://joshuaproject.net/great-commission-statistics.php.

"Hindi Bibles, facts, materials and people groups that speak Hindi," n.d. http://www.joshuaproject.net/languages.php?rol3=hin.

"Home Recording of Copyrighted Works." Law Building, Moot Courtroom, UCLA School of Law, Los Angeles, Calif., apr 1982. http://cryptome.org/hrcw-hear.htm.

"Information Note to the Press (Press Release No. 05/2012)." Telecom Regulatory Authority of India, jan 2012. http://www.trai.gov.in/WriteReadData/trai/upload/PressReleases/859/Press_Release_Nov-11.pdf.

"Key Global Telecom Indicators for the World Telecommunication Service Sector," nov 2011. http://www.itu.int/ITU-D/ict/statistics/at_glance/KeyTelecom.html.

"Languages Completed." The JESUS Film Project, 13 jan 2013. http://www.jesusfilm.org/film-and-media/statistics/languages-completed.

"M-Pesa transactions surpass Western Union moves across the globe - Business News" oct 2011. http://www.nation.co.ke/business/news/-/1006/1258864/-/4hyt6qz/-/index.html.

"Major Bible Translation Ministries Unite to Eradicate 'Bible Poverty'." *OutreachMagazine.com*, December 13, 2012. http://www.outreach-magazine.com/news-and-stories/5110-Major-Bible-Translation-Ministries-Unite-to-Eradicate-%E2%80%98Bible-Poverty%E2%80%99.html.

"Missiologist Confirms Great Commission Trends for Ministry." *Mission Network News*, February 1, 2012. http://mnnonline.org/article/16768.

"Mobile Web Overtakes PC Web in China." *mobiThinking*, 17 oct 2012. http://mobithinking.com/blog/mobile-web-overtake-in-china.

"Monitor: The meek shall inherit the web." *The Economist*. http://www.economist.com/node/11999307.

"Nature's Responses to Encyclopaedia Britannica," mar 2006. http://www.nature.com/nature/britannica/index.html.

"Permission to Quote Copyright & Trademark Information." Accessed October 1, 2012. http://www.lockman.org/tlf/copyright.php.

"Permissions." Accessed October 1, 2012. http://www.esv.org/tools/licensing/.

"Research Data," n.d. http://public.imb.org/globalresearch/Pages/ResearchData.aspx.

"Rick Warren and Purpose-Driven Strife." ABC, mar 2007. http://abcnews.go.com/Nightline/story?id=2914953&page=1.

"Scripture Access Statistics 2012," 2012. http://www.wycliffe.net/resources/scriptureaccessstatistics/tabid/99/Default.aspx.

"Snapshot: Developing world accounts for four in every five mobile connections." https://www.wirelessintelligence.com/print/snapshot/101021.pdf.

"TOP500 - Statistics," nov 2011. http://i.top500.org/stats.

"Terms of Use for Biblica Online Scripture and All Services." Accessed September 21, 2012. http://www.biblica.com/biblica-about-us/terms-of-use/.

"The Imitatio Christi Through Six Centuries." Accessed January 14, 2013. http://www.smu.edu/Bridwell/Collections/SpecialCollectionsandArchives/Exhibitions/ImitatioChristi.

"Theft," n.d. http://www.merriam-webster.com/dictionary/theft.

"Trademark and Copyright Information," mar 2010. http://bible.org/copyright.

"UNITED STATES v. CAUSBY, 328 U.S. 256," may 1946. http://caselaw.lp.findlaw.com/scripts/getcase.pl?court=us&vol=328&invol=256.

"Vision," n.d. http://wikimediafoundation.org/wiki/Vision.

"World Development Indicators." http://data.worldbank.org/data-catalog/world-development-indicators.

"World Internet Usage Statistics News and World Population Stats," 2011. http://www.internetworldstats.com/stats.htm.